ⓃEFF
ENTERTAINING
COOKBOOK

IN ASSOCIATION WITH GOOD HOUSEKEEPING

EBURY PRESS LONDON

First published by Ebury Press
an imprint of The Random Century Group
Random Century House
20 Vauxhall Bridge Road
London SW1V 2SA

Catalogue record for this book is available from the British Library

ISBN 0 09 177167 6

Editor: Felicity Jackson
Designer: Roger Daniels
Photographers: James Murphy, Alan Newnham
Stylists: Roisin Nield, Ian Hands
Home Economists: Allyson Birch, Meg Jansz
Recipe Testers: Deborah Greatrex, Jane Suthering
The publishers would also like to thank
Pam Brierley and Suzanne Noble

Typeset by BMD Graphics Ltd, Hemel Hempstead
Printed and bound in Italy by New Interlitho S.p.a.

CONTENTS

Cooking Charts

TEMPERATURE CONVERSION CHART

Circotherm	100°C	110°C	120°C	130°C	140°C	150°C	160°C	170°C	180°C	190°C	200°C
Conventional Electric	100°C/200°F	110°C/225°F	130°C/250°F	140°C/275°F	150°C/300°F	160°C/325°F	180°C/350°F 190°C/375°F	200°C/400°F	220°C/425°F	230°C/450°F	250°C/475°F
Conventional Gas	¼	¼	½	1	2	3	4-5	6	7	8	9

IMPORTANT NOTE:
The above conversion chart is for your guidance only. Slight variations in temperature can be expected during the cooking period.
This in no way should affect the finished product.

CIRCO-ROASTING

Type	Beef 1.4-1.8 kg (3-4 lb)	Lamb (Leg) 1.4-1.8 kg (3-4 lb)	Pork (Loin) 1.4-1.8 kg (3-4 lb)	Chicken 1.4-1.75 kg (3-3½ lb) 1.8-2.25 kg (4-5 lb)	Turkey 3.6-4.5 kg (8-10 lb)	Duck 1.75-1.8 kg (3½-4 lb)
Temperature on grill control knob	175°	175°	175°	175°	175°	175°
Cooking Time	40-60 minutes (rare). 60-75 minutes (medium).	60-85 minutes (medium).	90-110 minutes.	60-70 minutes. 80-90 minutes.	130-150 minutes.	75-90 minutes depending on size.
Shelf Positions (with railings) (without railings)	2nd 1st	2nd 1st	2nd 1st	2nd 1st	2nd 1st	2nd 1st
Instructions	Turn half way. Season as desired.	Turn half way. Season as desired.	Turn half way. Rub skin with oil and sprinkle with salt.	Brush with combination of paprika and melted butter or margarine if desired. Season. Turn half way.	Brush with oil or margarine if desired. Turn half way.	Pierce while cooking to let fat run off. Brush with water. Sprinkle with salt.

Represents the oven shelf which slides in at the 2nd or 1st positions. Place the roasting pan below.

THERMO GRILLING MEAT

Type	Lamb Chops 1 cm (½ inch) thick	Steak 1-2 cm (½-¾ inch) thick, 175-225 g (6-8 oz) weight	Pork Chops about 1-2 cm (½-¾ inch) thick	Chicken Joints	Sausages	Hamburger about 2 cm (¾ inch) thick
Circotherm Temp	180-190°	180-190°	180-190°	180-190°	180-190°	180-190°
Cooking Time Cooking Time may vary according to weight, thickness and temperature of the meat. For very rare steaks, grill in the conventional manner or thermo grill from frozen.	20-25 minutes.	**Medium rare** 12-15 minutes or until spongy to touch. **Medium** 15-25 minutes or until slightly firmer and more resistant to touch. **Well done** 25-35 minutes or until firm to touch.	30-45 minutes depending on size and weight.	30-45 minutes depending on size and weight.	Small sausages 20 minutes. Large sausages 25-30 minutes.	25-30 minutes.
Instructions	Place on wire shelf. Season with pepper and rosemary. Thicker chops will take 30-35 minutes.	Place on wire shelf. Season with pepper. Brush with butter or oil (if desired) after they begin to brown.	Place on wire shelf. Brush with fat if very lean; may be topped with pineapple and grated cheese if desired.	Place on wire shelf. Brush with melted butter and paprika or barbecue sauce.	Place on wire shelf.	Place on wire shelf. Season; may be brushed with barbecue sauce if desired.

THERMO GRILLING FISH

Type	Mackerel	Herring	Plaice	Halibut or Turbot Steaks 175 g (6 oz), 2-2.5 cm (¾-1 inch) thick	Cod Steaks	Salmon Steaks
Circotherm Temp	180°	180°	180°	180°	180°	180°
Cooking Time	Whole 18-20 minutes. Filleted 10-12 minutes.	Whole 15-20 minutes.	10-15 minutes.	15-20 minutes.	15-20 minutes.	15-20 minutes.
Instructions	Grease wire shelf. Place fish on shelf. Season, sprinkle with lemon juice and brush with oil. If whole, make 3 diagonal cuts on each side.	Prepare as for mackerel.	Fillet or skin. Brush with melted butter and season. Place on buttered foil if very thin. Dip in milk and breadcrumbs.	Dip in milk and then seasoned flour. Brush with melted butter.	Brush with melted butter, sprinkle with lemon juice. Season, then cover with sliced tomatoes and grated cheese if desired.	Brush with melted butter and sprinkle with lemon juice.

Introduction

Neff UK Ltd is delighted to provide a selection of recipes representing the finest of traditional British and foreign cuisine, developed especially for your Circotherm oven by Good Housekeeping.

The Circotherm oven offers several benefits not available in conventional gas and electric ovens. A fan at the back of the oven circulates hot air around the food, sealing in nutrients and browning it evenly. Due to the efficiency of the Circotherm system it is possible to cook foods at lower temperatures and without preheating, resulting in a saving of time and energy. Because the air is continually drawn to the back of the oven by the fan, the oven door can be opened while baking even the most delicate soufflés, without fear of them collapsing.

In addition, since the temperature throughout the oven is the same, three trays of cakes, biscuits or hors d'oeuvres can be prepared at one time – a significant time saver when entertaining.

Circotherm cooking is excellent for roasting meats and poultry. Their natural juices are sealed in by the circulating air, keeping them succulent and more nutritious. Additional fats are usually unnecessary when using the Circotherm so calorie content is kept to a minimum.

Because the circulating air is under pressure as it leaves the ducts at the back of the oven, the Circotherm system can be used to prepare foods usually cooked under a grill. Thermo grilling is the term used to describe this method. Steaks, chops, sausages and poultry can be cooked perfectly without turning, by placing them on a wire shelf above the roasting tin or grill pan. The Circotherm knob is turned to 180°-190°C to give maximum browning and crisping in the shortest possible time.

A complete meal can be planned around a thermo grilled main course; for instance, fillet steaks can be thermo grilled on one shelf, while spanokopittes and profiteroles bake on the others. With a little pre-planning the oven can be filled with sweet and savoury dishes that require no supervision and allow you to spend more time with your guests.

The conventional radiant grill is most suitable for thin cuts of meat or very rare steaks which require rapid browning, or for preparing large quantities of toast.

We are certain you will enjoy using your Neff Circotherm oven, hob and microwave for the preparation of the recipes Good Housekeeping has created and wish you happy cooking and *bon appétit*.

ALICE PORTNOY
Product Manager

Entertaining

Entertaining at home can – indeed, should – be fun. All too often, however, it can seem like a daunting prospect, particularly when large numbers of people are involved. The key to success lies in organisation. Whether you are planning a formal dinner party for eight, a casual lunch, or a tea party for friends, careful planning will make the occasion one that you, as well as your guests, will enjoy to the full.

PLANNING AHEAD

Whether you are catering for a large or small gathering, your plan of action will be the same: make a list of the dishes you want to serve, highlighting dishes that will freeze successfully, and therefore can be prepared in advance. Read through the recipes, plan when to cook each one, and start to make shopping lists. Take account of the time you have in hand, and of any ingredients that may need to be ordered well ahead. Remember that many ingredients will store well in the freezer, if necessary. If you have a formal dinner party in mind, think also about whether you will need to buy any glasses, crockery, napkins or other table linen.

CHOOSING THE DISHES

When selecting the menu, the main rule of thumb is to keep the dishes simple and within your capabilities. Tempting though it may be to try out something new and elaborate, you will be far better off choosing dishes that have gone down well in the past and can be relied upon to work.

As a general guideline, try to achieve a balance of flavours, textures and colours in the food you serve. When it comes to specific dishes, the 'wet' and 'dry' rule is a good one to follow: a 'wet' course, such as a soup or casserole, should precede a 'dry' one, such as grilled fish or steak, or an apple tart. Aim, too, for balance in the 'weight' of the courses. A thick soup, followed by steak and kidney pie and a steamed pudding may be traditional country fare, but is far too filling for the majority of appetites.

Another point to consider is variety and a balance of flavours throughout the courses. If you're serving fish as a main course, for example, don't choose fish for the starter – a chilled soup or a salad would be better instead. Similarly, one course based on a vegetable or fruit (such as avocado or melon), and one based on meat or fish makes a well-balanced combination. Fruit puddings go well with most menus, but if fruit was served in either of the first courses, it is best to choose an alternative – a chocolate-based recipe, say – for dessert. Avoid creamy desserts if either of the preceding courses have been served with a cream sauce.

Up to three levels of food can be prepared simultaneously without any intermingling of flavours in your Circotherm oven, so for example Roast Eye Fillet of Lamb and Old English Apple Pie pose absolutely no problem when cooked together.

Bearing in mind how health-conscious most people are today, avoid putting together a meal that consists of several rich courses. If your main dish is heavy and filling, for example, serve it with lightly cooked vegetables or a salad and keep your starter and dessert simple, and refreshing.

Last, but not least, plan the menu so that you leave plenty of time to be with your guests. A dish that needs very careful timing will not allow for the fact that guests may not be punctual or that people linger over their food longer than you had anticipated.

FREEZING AND MICROWAVING

While planning your menu, think carefully about freezing and microwaving as helpful aids. Dishes suitable for freezing can be cooked well in advance, and stored. Remember to make a note of how much thawing and final cooking time each dish needs, and to label frozen packages carefully. After cooking, cool food for freezing as quickly as possible, then freeze immediately, making use of the 'fast freeze' facility if your freezer has one. Before freezing a casserole, line the dish with foil so that it can be frozen and then removed and the dish can be used again. Pack foods in bags or rigid containers.

A microwave oven is useful for thawing or last-minute reheating. Decant the food into microwave-proof dishes that will fit in your microwave oven, and always reheat until the food is piping hot to avoid any risk of food poisoning.

DRINKS

What you give your guests to drink is just as important as the food. The time of the day and the season will give you guidelines. Pimms and other long, cool drinks, chilled white wine and fruit wine cups are welcome for summer, a warm glass of mulled wine makes an attractive winter drink.

If you are giving a dinner party, you will need to think in terms of pre-dinner drinks, then wines with the meal, followed by liqueurs and coffee.

Pre-dinner drinks

An aperitif should stimulate the palate and the appetite. It is best to avoid sweet drinks such as sweet sherry and many cocktails, and spirits, as these will deaden both the appetite and the taste buds. Good choices are dry sherry or Madeira, dry vermouths and dry white wines, still or sparkling.

Matching food and wine

Try to match the quality and style of the wine to the quality and style of the food, ie. serve a light wine with light food, a full-bodied one with full-flavoured dishes. For suggestions for wines to serve with different foods, see below:

Soups: Good quality dry white wines with fish soups; dry (fino) sherry, Madeira and light red wines with consommés, meat and game soups.

Salads, vegetarian dishes and cold meats: Any dry to medium white wine, but particularly Muscadet, Chablis and Sauvignon Blanc.

Fish and shellfish: Any light or medium dry white wine for fish, particularly Muscadet, Mosel, and Australian or Californian Chardonnay; white Burgundies and Chardonnays for shellfish.

Red meat and game: Full-bodied rosés such as Tavel or Rioja, and any full-bodied red such as Burgundy or Rioja.

White meat (not stuffed or served with a heavy sauce): Any light dry wine such as Pouilly Fuissé: (*served in a richer manner*) a light Bordeaux or Chianti Classico.

Cheese: Port, or, for mild cheeses, a light-medium white wine such as Sancerre, or a claret; for full-flavoured cheese, a mature red wine such as a good Burgundy.

Desserts: Any sweet white wine, particularly Asti Spumante, sweet Sauternes or Monbazillac.

Soups & Starters

Previous page: Chicken and Beef Satay with Peanut Sauce (see page 24); Layered Fish Terrine (see page 21); Iced Tomato and Herb Soup (see page 13)

SERVING IDEA

Curried Potato and Apple Soup is delicately spiced, with a sweet flavour of apples. Serve with crisp poppadoms and chilled lager for an informal supper or lunch.

COOK'S TIPS

It is important to fry the curry powder in step 2 of *Curried Potato and Apple Soup*, or the spices will taste raw in the finished soup.

Natural yogurt has a tendency to curdle when stirred into very hot liquids. This problem can be overcome if the yogurt is brought to room temperature and stirred well before use.

CURRIED POTATO AND APPLE SOUP

SERVES 4

50 g (2 oz) butter or margarine
4 medium old potatoes, peeled and diced
2 eating apples, peeled, cored and diced
10 ml (2 level tsp) curry powder
1.1 litres (2 pints) vegetable stock or water
salt and freshly ground pepper
150 ml (¼ pint) natural yogurt, at room temperature

1 Melt the butter or margarine in a large saucepan. Add the potatoes and apples and fry gently for about 10 minutes until lightly coloured, shaking the pan and stirring frequently.

2 Add the curry powder, and fry gently for 1-2 minutes, stirring. Pour in the stock or water and bring to the boil. Add salt and pepper to taste. Lower the heat, cover the pan and simmer for 20-25 minutes or until the potatoes and apples are really soft.

3 Sieve the soup or purée it in a blender or food processor, then return to the rinsed-out pan.

4 Stir the yogurt until smooth, then pour half into the soup. Heat through, stirring constantly, then taste and adjust the seasoning.

5 Pour the hot soup into warmed individual bowls and swirl in the remaining yogurt. Serve immediately.

CHESTNUT AND ROASTED GARLIC SOUP

SERVES 4

225 g (8 oz) dried chestnuts, soaked overnight
4 large garlic cloves, unpeeled
three 425 g (15 oz) cans game or beef consommé
pinch freshly grated nutmeg
salt and freshly ground pepper
120 ml (8 tbsp) Greek natural yogurt
5 ml (1 tsp) curry paste
coriander leaves, to garnish

1 Drain the chestnuts and place in a medium saucepan. Cover with cold water. Bring to the boil and simmer for about 20 minutes until tender. Drain.

2 Place the garlic cloves with the chestnuts on a baking tray and roast in the oven at 170°C Circotherm for 15-20 minutes or until the garlic is soft to the touch and the chestnuts are browning. Cool slightly, then pop the garlic cloves out of their skins.

3 Place the garlic, chestnuts and consommé in a blender or food processor and process until smooth. Pour into a saucepan, bring almost to the boil and season to taste with nutmeg, salt and pepper. Simmer very gently for 5 minutes to allow the flavours to blend. If necessary, add a little water to thin.

4 Mix the yogurt with the curry paste. Serve the soup in warmed bowls with a dollop of yogurt, garnished with coriander leaves.

a small amount at a time in a blender or food processor and process to form a smooth purée. Transfer to a bowl and chill for 2 hours.

3 To serve, core and seed the remaining green pepper, then dice very finely. Pour the purée into a serving bowl and add a few ice cubes. Serve garnished with diced pepper and croûtons.

ICED TOMATO AND HERB SOUP

──────── SERVES 4 ────────

450 g (1 lb) ripe tomatoes
1 small onion, skinned and sliced
20 ml (4 tsp) tomato purée
411 g (14½ oz) can chicken consommé
30 ml (2 tbsp) chopped fresh herbs e.g. basil, coriander, parsley
salt and freshly ground pepper
25 g (1 oz) fresh white breadcrumbs
150 ml (¼ pint) soured cream
basil leaves, to garnish

1 Roughly chop the tomatoes and process them with the onion, tomato purée, consommé and herbs until smooth.

2 Rub the tomato mixture through a nylon sieve into a saucepan. Heat gently to remove the frothy texture, then add plenty of salt and pepper.

3 Pour the soup into a large serving bowl and stir in the breadcrumbs. Chill for at least 2 hours.

4 Stir the soured cream until smooth, then swirl it into the chilled soup. Float the basil leaves on top and serve.

Left: Gazpacho

SERVING IDEA

Chilled soup such as *Iced Tomato and Herb Soup* makes an elegant starter for a summer dinner party. However, it could also be served as a starter in a winter menu.

SERVING IDEA

There are numerous variations of the famous Spanish chilled soup *Gazpacho* with its colourful garnishes, and you will find that each Spanish cook has his or her own favourite recipe. Some versions have lots of tomatoes, some have lots of cucumber, and some are crushed vegetables, with hardly any liquid. Nowadays, *Gazpacho* is eaten as a sophisticated starter, but originally the soup was created by workers in the fields who made it simply by crushing fresh raw vegetables in wooden bowls with wooden spoons.

GAZPACHO

──────── SERVES 4 ────────

2 small green peppers
1 medium cucumber
450 g (1 lb) fully ripe tomatoes
50-100 g (2-4 oz) onions, skinned
1 garlic clove, skinned
45 ml (3 tbsp) vegetable oil
425 g (15 oz) can tomato juice
30 ml (2 tbsp) tomato purée
1.25 ml (¼ level tsp) salt
green pepper, ice cubes and croûtons, to serve

1 Remove the core and seeds from one green pepper and chop roughly with the cucumber, tomatoes, onions and garlic.

2 Mix all the ingredients in a bowl, then put

ICED TZAZIKI SOUP

SERVES 4

1 medium cucumber, peeled
450 ml (¾ pint) Greek natural yogurt
1 small garlic clove, skinned and crushed
30 ml (2 tbsp) chopped fresh mint
350 ml (12 fl oz) chicken stock
salt and freshly ground pepper
mint leaves, to garnish

1 Quarter the cucumber lengthways and discard the seeds, using a teaspoon. Finely dice the cucumber, cutting several strips at a time.
2 Pour the yogurt into a bowl and stir in the cucumber, garlic and chopped mint.
3 Stir in the chicken stock and season to taste. Chill for 2-3 hours. Serve garnished with mint.

CHINESE CABBAGE AND PRAWN SOUP

SERVES 4

30 ml (2 tbsp) vegetable oil
50 g (2 oz) French beans, trimmed and cut into 5 cm (2 inch) lengths
1 large carrot, scrubbed and cut into matchstick strips
1 small turnip, peeled and cut into matchstick strips
1.1 litres (2 pints) chicken stock
30 ml (2 tbsp) soy sauce, preferably naturally fermented shoyu
1.25 ml (¼ tsp) sweet chilli sauce
30 ml (2 tbsp) medium dry sherry
30 ml (1 level tbsp) light muscovado sugar
175 g (6 oz) Chinese leaves, finely shredded
75 g (3 oz) peeled cooked prawns

1 Heat the oil in a saucepan and gently cook the beans, carrot and turnip for 5 minutes.
2 Add the stock, soy sauce, chilli sauce, sherry and sugar. Simmer for 15 minutes or until the vegetables are just tender.
3 Add the Chinese leaves and prawns and cook for 2-3 minutes until the leaves are tender but still crisp. Serve immediately.

Chinese Cabbage and Prawn Soup

CREAM OF CARROT WITH ORANGE SOUP

SERVES 4-6

25 g (1 oz) butter or margarine
700 g (1½ lb) carrots, peeled and sliced
225 g (8 oz) onions, skinned and sliced
1 litre (1¾ pints) chicken or ham stock
salt and freshly ground pepper
1 orange

1 Melt the butter in a saucepan, add the vegetables and cook gently for 10 minutes until softened slightly.
2 Add the stock and bring to the boil. Lower the heat, cover and simmer for about 40 minutes, or until the vegetables are tender.
3 Sieve or purée the vegetables with half of the stock in a blender or food processor. Add this mixture to stock remaining in the pan. Season to taste with salt and pepper.
4 Meanwhile, pare half of the orange rind thinly, using a potato peeler, then cut it into shreds. Cook the shreds in gently boiling water until tender.
5 Finely grate the remaining orange rind into the soup. Stir well to combine with the ingredients in the pan.
6 Squeeze the juice of the orange into the pan. Reheat the soup gently, then taste and adjust the seasoning. Drain the shreds of orange rind and use to garnish the soup just before serving. Serve hot.

WATERCRESS SOUP

SERVES 4

100 g (4 oz) butter or margarine
1 medium onion, skinned and chopped
2 bunches watercress
50 g (2 oz) plain flour
750 ml (1¼ pints) chicken stock
300 ml (½ pint) milk
salt and freshly ground pepper

1 Melt the butter in a saucepan, add the onion and cook gently for 10 minutes until soft but not coloured.
2 Meanwhile, wash and trim the watercress, leaving some of the stem, then chop roughly.
3 Add chopped watercress to the onion, cover the pan with a lid and cook gently for a further 4 minutes.
4 Add the flour and cook gently, stirring, for 1-2 minutes. Remove from the heat and gradually blend in the stock and milk. Bring to the boil, stirring constantly, then simmer for 3 minutes. Season to taste with salt and pepper.
5 Sieve or purée the soup in a blender or food processor. Return to the rinsed-out pan and reheat gently, without boiling. Taste and adjust the seasoning, if necessary. Serve hot.

COOK'S TIP

Cream of Carrot with Orange Soup is an economical soup made from everyday ingredients, but the orange juice and rind give it a delicious and distinctive flavour.

MENU SUGGESTION

Watercress Soup makes a delicious starter for a winter dinner party. Follow it with roast game such as *Pheasant au Porto* (see page 80) and end with a fruity dessert such as *Oranges in Caramel* (see page 135) or *Pears Poached in Ginger Syrup* (see page 133).

COOK'S TIPS

Follow these few guidelines to help you to prepare mussels.

● Scrub the shells very thoroughly with a stiff vegetable brush to remove all traces of dirt and sand.

● Scrape off barnacles with a sharp knife and remove the 'beard' which protrudes between the two shells.

● Discard any that are open or which do not close when given a sharp tap against a work surface. This may seem rather wasteful but it is a very important part of the preparation process – any mussel that remains open cannot be alive and should not be cooked.

● Steam or cook the drained mussels according to individual recipes, allowing 5-10 minutes cooking time over high heat. Always cover the pan and shake frequently during cooking. Do not cook for longer than this or the mussels will toughen and become coarse and rubbery.

● At the end of cooking, discard any mussels that haven't opened.

Opposite: Stuffed Plaice Fillets; Mussels with Garlic and Parsley

STUFFED PLAICE FILLETS
───── SERVES 6 ─────

3 large double plaice fillets, skinned
75 g (3 oz) butter
5 ml (1 tsp) lemon juice
125 g (4 oz) mushrooms, wiped
175 g (6 oz) leeks, trimmed and washed
50 g (2 oz) long-grain rice, cooked and drained
30 ml (2 tbsp) chopped fresh tarragon or 10 ml (2 tsp) dried
salt and freshly ground pepper

1 Cut each plaice into two long fillets.

2 Place one fillet, skinned side out, round the inside of each of six buttered ramekins.

3 Make the lemon butter. Beat together 50 g (2 oz) of the butter and the lemon juice. Wrap in greaseproof paper and chill.

4 Meanwhile, finely chop the mushrooms and leeks. Melt the remaining butter in a frying pan, add the vegetable and cook gently until softened. Remove from the heat and stir in the rice and tarragon. Season to taste.

5 Spoon the vegetable mixture into the centre of each ramekin, pressing down well.

6 Cover the ramekins with buttered foil, place in a roasting tin and pour hot water into the tin to come halfway up the sides of the ramekins. Bake in the oven at 160°C Circotherm for about 15 minutes.

7 To serve, invert the ramekins on to serving plates. With the dishes still in place, pour off any excess liquid. Remove the dishes and serve hot, with a knob of lemon butter on top.

MUSSELS WITH GARLIC AND PARSLEY
───── SERVES 6 ─────

1.8 kg (4 lb) mussels in their shells, cleaned (see left)
150 ml (10 tbsp) fresh breadcrumbs
150 ml (10 tbsp) fresh parsley
2 garlic cloves, skinned and finely chopped
freshly ground black pepper
100 ml (4 fl oz) olive oil
60 ml (4 tbsp) grated Parmesan cheese
French bread, to serve

1 Place the cleaned mussels in a large saucepan. Cover and cook over high heat for 5-10 minutes until the mussels are open, shaking the pan frequently. Discard any mussels that have not opened. Shell the mussels, reserving one half of each empty shell.

2 Strain the mussel liquid through a sieve lined with absorbent kitchen paper. Mix together the breadcrumbs, parsley, garlic and plenty of pepper. Add the oil and 60 ml (4 tbsp) of the mussel liquid. Blend well together. Taste and adjust the seasonings.

3 Place the mussels in their shells on two baking sheets. With your fingers, pick up a good pinch of the breadcrumb mixture and press it down on each mussel, covering it well and filling the shell. Sprinkle with grated Parmesan cheese.

4 Bake in the oven at 180°C Circotherm for 10 minutes. Serve with French bread.

SERVING IDEA

Serve *Ramekins of Baked Crab* with triangles of crisp hot granary toast for an informal dinner party starter. Alternatively, serve them for a tasty lunch or supper snack.

SERVING IDEA

Serve luxurious *Avocado with Prawns and Smoked Salmon* for a special dinner party, with thinly sliced brown bread and butter.

MICROWAVE

Ramekins of Baked Crab
Put the butter and onion in a dish, cover and cook on HIGH for 4 minutes, stirring once or twice. Complete step 2 and spoon the mixture into six ramekins. Arrange the ramekins around the edge of a large, shallow round dish and cook, uncovered, on HIGH for 3 minutes until piping hot all the way through and the cheese has melted. Place under a hot grill until golden brown.

RAMEKINS OF BAKED CRAB

SERVES 6

25 g (1 oz) butter or margarine
50 g (2 oz) onion, skinned and finely chopped
225 g (8 oz) white crab meat or white and brown mixed
50 g (2 oz) fresh brown breadcumbs
10 ml (2 tsp) French mustard
150 ml (¼ pint) natural yogurt
45 ml (3 tbsp) single cream or milk
cayenne pepper
salt
about 40 g (1½ oz) Cheddar cheese
lime slices and sprigs of parsley, to garnish (optional)

1 Melt the butter or margarine in a saucepan, add the onion and fry gently until brown.

2 Flake the crab meat, taking care to remove any membranes or shell particles. Mix it into the cooked onion and add the breadcrumbs. Mix well together. Stir in the mustard, yogurt and cream. Sprinkle generously with cayenne pepper, then add salt to taste.

3 Spoon the mixture into six 75 ml (3 fl oz) individual ramekins or individual soufflé dishes. Grate the cheese thinly over the surface of each dish. Stand the dishes on a baking sheet. Cook in the oven at 150°C Circotherm for 25-30 minutes, or until really hot. Garnish with lime slices and parsley, if liked.

AVOCADO WITH PRAWNS AND SMOKED SALMON

SERVES 4

60 ml (4 tbsp) mayonnaise
60 ml (4 tbsp) fromage frais or Greek natural yogurt
30 ml (2 tbsp) snipped chives
10 ml (2 tsp) lemon juice
few drops of Tabasco sauce
salt and freshly ground pepper
100 g (4 oz) smoked salmon
100 g (4 oz) peeled prawns, thawed and thoroughly dried if frozen
2 ripe avocados
lemon wedges and 4 unpeeled prawns (optional), to garnish

1 Make the dressing. Put the mayonnaise in a bowl with the fromage frais or yogurt, chives, lemon juice and Tabasco sauce to taste. Add plenty of salt and pepper, then whisk vigorously with a fork to combine all the ingredients together.

2 Cut the smoked salmon into bite-sized pieces. Chop the prawns roughly. Add to the dressing and fold gently to mix.

3 Just before serving, halve and stone the avocados. Scoop out the flesh and chop into small pieces.

4 Fold the avocado into the fish mixture. Spoon into the avocado shells, garnish with lemon wedges and prawns, if wished, and serve immediately.

ANCHOVY EGG TARTLETS

SERVES 6

350 g (12 oz) Shortcrust Pastry made with 350 g (12 oz) flour (see page 189)
6 eggs, chilled
12 canned anchovy fillets, soaked in milk for 30 minutes, drained and finely chopped
pinch of sugar
salt and freshly ground pepper
90 ml (6 tbsp) single cream
small sprig of fresh tarragon or 1.25 (¼ tsp) dried
2.5 ml (½ tsp) lemon juice
sprigs of dill and strips of anchovy, to garnish

1 Roll out the shortcrust pastry thinly on a lightly floured surface. Cut or stamp out six rounds. Carefully line six 7.5 cm (3 inch) tartlet tins. Chill in the refrigerator for 30 minutes.
2 Bake the tartlets blind (see right) in the oven at 170°C Circotherm for 15-20 minutes or until pale golden.
3 Turn the pastry cases out of the tins on to a wire rack and leave to cool for 20 minutes.
4 Not more than 10 minutes before serving, softly poach the eggs for 2 minutes. Drain and place on greaseproof paper. Trim neatly and cover with dampened greaseproof paper.
5 To serve, spread the base of each tartlet with the chopped anchovy fillets. Sprinkle with sugar and season to taste. Place one egg in each tartlet, then stand them on a baking sheet. Warm gently in the oven at 160°C Circotherm for about 3 minutes.
6 Meanwhile, put the cream in a saucepan with a small sprig of tarragon (or the dried tarragon), the lemon juice and salt and pepper to taste. Warm gently.
7 Spoon the warmed cream mixture around the warmed tartlets or over the eggs and garnish with sprigs of dill and thin anchovy strips. Serve immediately.

PRAWN AND GRUYÈRE COCOTTES

SERVES 6

15 g (½ oz) butter
15 ml (1 tbsp) olive or vegetable oil
1 small onion, skinned and finely chopped
4 rashers of back bacon, rinded and chopped
350 g (12 oz) peeled prawns, thawed and thoroughly dried if frozen
150 ml (¼ pint) soured cream
1 egg, beaten
salt and freshly ground pepper
100 g (4 oz) Gruyère cheese, grated

1 Melt the butter with the oil in a heavy-based saucepan, add the onion and fry gently for 5 minutes until soft but not coloured.
2 Add the bacon and fry until turning colour, stirring frequently.
3 Transfer the mixture to the bowl, add the prawns, soured cream and egg and salt and pepper to taste. Mix well.
4 Divide the mixture equally between six cocottes or 100 ml (4 fl oz) ramekins. Sprinkle with the Gruyère cheese. Bake in the oven at 160°C Circotherm for 20 minutes until bubbling. Serve hot.

COOK'S TIPS

Baking blind is essential for little tartlet cases such as the ones in *Anchovy Egg Tartlets* because the filling is only warmed gently for 3 minutes in in the oven, rather than being cooked with the pastry cases from the beginning. To bake blind, simply prick the base of each tartlet with the prongs of a fork, then line with foil and fill with baking beans. The weight of the beans acts like a filling and prevents the pastry from bubbling up during baking. Remove the foil and beans after 10-15 minutes, then return the empty cases to the oven for a further 5 minutes or so, until the cases are crisp and lightly coloured.

Anchovy Egg Tartlets

MICROWAVE

Spicy Prawns
Put the onion, garlic, tomatoes, ginger, coriander, cumin, vinegar and tomato purée in a medium bowl. Cook on HIGH for 10 minutes or until thickened and reduced, stirring occasionally. Stir in the prawns. Cook on HIGH for 2-3 minutes or until the prawns are heated through, stirring once. Season to taste with salt and pepper. Garnish with coriander.

Sesame Prawn Toasts

SESAME PRAWN TOASTS

SERVES 8

175 g (6 oz) peeled prawns, thawed and thoroughly dried if frozen
2 spring onions, trimmed and roughly chopped
2.5 cm (1 inch) piece of fresh root ginger, peeled and roughly chopped
2 garlic cloves, skinned and roughly chopped
30 ml (2 level tbsp) cornflour
10 ml (2 tsp) soy sauce
10 ml (2 tsp) anchovy essence
12 slices stale white bread from a small loaf, crusts removed
25-40 g (1-1½ oz) sesame seeds
about 600 ml (1 pint) vegetable oil for deep frying
soy sauce for dipping
sprigs of dill, to garnish (optional)

1 Put prawns, spring onions, ginger and garlic in a food processor. Add the cornflour, soy sauce and anchovy essence and work to a thick paste.
2 Spread the bread slices evenly with the paste, then cut each slice into four triangles. Sprinkle with sesame seeds and press down with your fingers so that they adhere to the paste. Chill the triangles in the refrigerator for at least 30 minutes.
3 Heat the oil in a wok to 190°C (375°F) or until a cube of stale bread turns golden in 30 seconds. With a slotted spoon, lower a batch of the bread slices, paste side down, into the hot oil. Deep fry for 2-3 minutes, turning for the last minute. Lift out with the slotted spoon, shake off the excess oil, then drain on absorbent kitchen paper and keep warm while frying the remainder.
4 Place a bowl of soy sauce in the centre of a large tray or platter. Arrange the toasts around the bowl. Garnish the tray or platter with sprigs of dill, if using. Serve immediately.

SPICY PRAWNS

SERVES 4

30 ml (2 tbsp) vegetable oil
1 small onion, skinned and finely chopped
1 garlic clove, skinned and chopped
2.5 cm (1 inch) piece of fresh root ginger, peeled and grated
2.5 ml (½ level tsp) ground coriander
20 ml (4 level tsp) ground cumin
3 large tomatoes, roughly chopped
15 ml (1 tbsp) red wine vinegar
5 ml (1 tsp) tomato purée
450 g (1 lb) peeled prawns
salt and freshly ground pepper
chopped fresh coriander, to garnish

1 Heat the oil in a saucepan, add the onion, garlic and ginger and cook until the onion has softened.
2 Add the spices and tomatoes and cook to a purée.
3 Add the remaining ingredients, except the garnish, and simmer until heated through. Season to taste with salt and pepper. Garnish with chopped coriander and serve hot with poppadoms.

LAYERED FISH TERRINE

—————— SERVES 10-12 ——————

700 g (1½ lb) whiting, sole, plaice or hake, skinned and chilled
3 egg whites, chilled
salt and freshly ground pepper
15 ml (1 tbsp) lemon juice
30 ml (2 tbsp) chopped fresh tarragon
30 ml (2 tbsp) chopped fresh dill
300 ml (½ pint) double cream, chilled
25 g (1 oz) butter for greasing tin
450 g (1 lb) piece of fresh salmon tail, filleted and skinned
15 ml (1 tbsp) green peppercorns, drained
300 ml (½ pint) smetana or soured cream
a little milk
30 ml (2 tbsp) snipped chives (optional)
sprigs of dill, to garnish

1 Trim the white fish, remove any bones and cut into small pieces. Work in a blender or food processor until finely minced. Alternatively, put the fish through a mincer and mince finely.

2 Add the egg whites and pepper to the fish and process or beat until completely incorporated. Turn into a bowl, cover with cling film and chill for at least 30 minutes.

3 Stir in the lemon juice, tarragon and dill and process or beat again, gradually adding the double cream. Add salt to taste, cover and refrigerate again for at least 30 minutes.

4 Meanwhile, grease a 1.1 litre (2 pint) terrine or loaf tin with the butter and line the base with greaseproof paper.

5 Cut the salmon into chunky strips, about 1 cm (½ inch) square and the length of the loaf tin or terrine. Cover and chill in the refrigerator until required.

6 Carefully stir the green peppercorns into the fish mixture. Spoon a third of the fish mixture into the terrine and spread out evenly to cover the bottom. Lay half of the salmon strips on top, leaving a 1 cm (½ inch) border all the way round. Cover this with half of the remaining fish mixture, levelling it carefully.

7 Repeat the salmon layer, using the remaining salmon strips. Finally cover with the remaining fish mixture and smooth the top.

8 Cover the terrine with buttered foil and place in a roasting tin and pour hot water into the tin to come halfway up the sides of the terrine. Bake in the oven at 160°C Circotherm for 45 minutes or until a skewer inserted into the centre comes out clean.

9 Transfer the terrine to a wire rack and leave to cool for 2 hours at room temperature. Remove from the rack, cover with cling film and chill for at least 4 hours.

10 When ready to serve the terrine, mix the smetana or soured cream with a little milk to make a thin sauce. Add the chives, if using, and season to taste with salt and pepper.

11 Turn the terrine out on to a plate and wipe with absorbent kitchen paper to remove any butter or liquid. Slice thickly. Flood individual serving plates with the sauce, and place a slice of terrine in the centre. Garnish with dill.

MENU SUGGESTION

Layered Fish Terrine makes an impressive first course for a dinner party. Serve with a chilled dry white wine such as a French Muscadet or an Italian Orvieto Secco. Follow with an elegant main course such as *Pork with Peppercorns* (page 67) and crisp green beans or mange tout. *Snowcap Iced Pudding* (page 160) would make a spectacular finale for dessert.

COOK'S TIP

Red lumpfish – often referred to as 'mock caviar' – can be added to *Layered Fish Terrine*. Real caviar is the salted hard roe of the sturgeon, and is extremely expensive because it is so rare, and mostly fished in the Caspian Sea. Lumpfish, which are found in the waters off Iceland and Greenland, are more common, and so the roe is far less expensive. It is available in jars at most supermarkets and delicatessens, coloured either red or black, and is useful as a tasty and unusual garnish.

Veal, Wine and Apricot Pâte makes a delicious dinner party starter. Serve with Melba toast (see below) and a chilled dry white wine such as a Muscadet.

COOK'S TIP

To make Melba toast to serve with *Veal, Wine and Apricot Pâte*, simply remove the crusts from thin slices of white or brown bread, then toast the bread lightly on both sides. Place the toast on a board and split through the middle, working carefully with a sharp knife and using a sawing action. Pop the bread back under the grill, untoasted side facing upwards, and grill until the toast becomes crisp and the edges curl up. Remove from the heat, leave until cold, then store in an airtight tin.

SERVING IDEA

Pork and Herb Pâté has a strong flavour. Serve with crusty French bread and butter as a starter, with a full-bodied French wine to drink.

Opposite: Veal, Wine and Apricot Pâte

VEAL, WINE AND APRICOT PÂTE

SERVES 6

| 700 g (1½ lb) pie veal |
| 25 g (1 oz) no soak dried apricots |
| 100 ml (4 fl oz) dry white wine |
| 225 g (8 oz) pork fat |
| ½ small bunch of watercress, washed and trimmed |
| 2 garlic cloves, skinned and crushed |
| 2 eggs |
| 50 g (2 oz) fresh white breadcrumbs |
| 2.5 ml (½ level tsp) ground allspice |
| 7.5 ml (1½ level tsp) salt |
| freshly ground pepper |

1 Cut the pie veal into pieces and put in a shallow dish with the apricots. Pour over the wine, cover and chill overnight.
2 The next day, drain the veal and apricots, reserving the marinade. Finely mince the veal and apricots with the pork fat. Chop half of the watercress and reserve the rest for garnishing.
3 Put the minced mixture in a large bowl with the reserved marinade and the remaining ingredients. Mix well together.
4 Spoon the mixture into a 1.4 litre (2½ pint) terrine or loaf tin and press down well. Cover and place in a roasting tin, then pour boiling water into the tin to come halfway up the sides of the terrine. Cook in the oven at 150°C Circotherm for about 1¼ hours until firm.
5 When the pâte is cooked, remove from the roasting tin, uncover and spoon off the excess fat. Leave to cool slightly, then place a piece of greaseproof paper on top. Place heavy weights on top, then chill in the refrigerator overnight.
6 Turn the pâte out and leave at room temperature for 30 minutes. Garnish before serving.

PORK AND HERB PÂTÉ

SERVES 4-6

| 225 g (8 oz) streaky bacon rashers, rinded |
| 1 medium onion, skinned |
| 1 garlic clove, skinned |
| 300 g (10 oz) pig's liver |
| 450 g (1 lb) belly pork, rinded, with any bones removed |
| 10 ml (2 tsp) chopped fresh sage |
| 15 ml (1 tbsp) chopped fresh marjoram |
| 15 ml (1 tbsp) chopped fresh parsley |
| 2.5 ml (½ level tsp) ground mace |
| salt and freshly ground pepper |

1 Stretch the rashers with a knife. Use to line the base and sides of a 1.1 litre (2 pint) loaf tin.
2 Roughly chop the onion, garlic, liver and belly pork. Mince together.
3 Place the mixture in a large bowl with the herbs and mace and season to taste. Mix well.
4 Press the mixture into the loaf tin and cover tightly with foil. Place in a roasting tin and pour in hot water to come halfway up the sides of the loaf tin. Bake in the oven at 160°C Circotherm for about 1½ hours, or until a skewer inserted into the centre comes out hot to the touch.
5 Remove the loaf tin from the roasting tin, drain off the liquid and place heavy weights on top of the foil. Leave until cold, then chill overnight. Turn out and slice before serving.

Serve rich, creamy *Chicken Liver Pâté* with Melba toast (see Cook's Tip, page 22) and a dry red wine.

Serve *Spicy Spareribs* as a first course for a Chinese-style supper party.

CHICKEN LIVER PÂTÉ

SERVES 8

100 g (4 oz) butter
1 medium onion, skinned and chopped
1 garlic clove, skinned and crushed
450 g (1 lb) chicken livers, cleaned and dried
75 ml (5 tbsp) double cream
15 ml (1 tbsp) tomato purée
15 ml (1 tbsp) brandy
salt and freshly ground pepper
pink peppercorns and fresh bay leaves, to garnish

1 Melt half of the butter in a saucepan, add the onion and garlic and fry gently for 5 minutes. Add the chicken livers and cook for 5 minutes.
2 Cool slightly, then add the cream, tomato purée, brandy and plenty of salt and pepper.
3 Purée the mixture in a blender or food processor, then spoon into a serving dish.
4 Melt the remaining butter gently. Pour the butter over the pâté and leave to cool. Garnish with peppercorns and bay leaves and chill.

SPICY SPARERIBS

SERVES 4

1.8 kg (4 lb) pork spareribs
1 medium onion, skinned and sliced
350 ml (12 fl oz) tomato juice
45 ml (3 tbsp) cider vinegar
30 ml (2 tbsp) clear honey
10 ml (2 level tsp) salt
5 ml (1 level tsp) paprika
3.75 ml (¾ level tsp) chilli powder

1 Separate the spareribs into sections of two or three ribs. Place in a shallow dish. Mix all the remaining ingredients together and pour over the ribs. Cover and marinate in the refrigerator for 2 hours.
2 Place the spareribs under a preheated grill. Brush with the marinade. Grill for 20 minutes, brushing occasionally with the marinade and turning. Heat the marinade and serve as a sauce.

CHICKEN AND BEEF SATAY WITH PEANUT SAUCE

SERVES 4

350 g (12 oz) chicken breast fillets
350 g (12 oz) flash-fry steak
5 ml (1 tsp) coriander seeds
5 ml (1 level tsp) cumin seeds
1 medium onion, skinned and chopped
60 ml (4 tbsp) lime or lemon juice
30 ml (2 tbsp) soy sauce
2 garlic cloves, skinned and crushed
30 ml (2 tbsp) vegetable oil
5 ml (1 level tsp) ground turmeric
5 ml (1 level tsp) five-spice powder
salt
100 g (4 oz) crunchy peanut butter
100 g (4 oz) creamed coconut, crumbled
300 ml (½ pint) boiling water
20 ml (4 tsp) lemon juice
15 ml (1 level tbsp) soft brown sugar
2.5-5 ml (½-1 level tsp) chilli powder

1 Prepare the satay. Using a sharp knife, cut the chicken and the steak into small chunks.

2 Heat a small frying pan, add the coriander and cumin and fry over dry heat for 1-2 minutes, stirring constantly. Remove from the heat and pound to a fine powder with a mortar and pestle.

3 Put the pounded spices in a blender or food processor with the onion, lime juice, 15 ml (1 tbsp) soy sauce, garlic, vegetable oil, turmeric, five-spice powder and a pinch of salt. Work for a few seconds, then pour over the meat. Cover and leave to marinate for 4 hours, turning the meat occasionally during this time.

4 Thread the meat on oiled wooden sticks, keeping the chicken and beef separate if liked. Grill for 10-15 minutes, turning frequently and basting with any remaining marinade.

5 Meanwhile, make the peanut sauce. Put the peanut butter, coconut, water, lemon juice, 15 ml (1 tbsp) soy sauce, sugar and chilli powder in a pan and bring slowly to the boil, stirring constantly. Lower the heat and simmer gently for about 5 minutes until the coconut has dissolved and the sauce thickens. Taste and adjust the seasoning according to taste.

6 Serve the satay sticks hot on a platter, with a small bowl of peanut sauce for dipping.

BAKED STUFFED MUSHROOMS
SERVES 4

4 rashers of pancetta (see right) or unsmoked streaky bacon, rinded
12 large cup mushrooms
75 g (3 oz) fresh white breadcrumbs
1 egg, beaten
30 ml (2 tbsp) chopped fresh parsley
150 ml (¼ pint) dry white wine
salt and freshly ground pepper
90 ml (6 tbsp) freshly grated Parmesan cheese
15 g (½ oz) butter

1 Make the stuffing mixture. Fry the pancetta in a heavy-based pan until the fat runs, then continue frying until beginning to brown. Remove from the pan and leave to cool for 5 minutes.

2 Meanwhile, carefully remove the stalks from each of the mushrooms, leaving the cups intact.

3 Chop the stalks finely, then put them in a bowl with the breadcrumbs, egg, parsley and 15 ml (1 tbsp) of the wine.

4 With kitchen scissors, snip the cooled pancetta finely into the breadcrumb mixture. Mix well, adding seasoning to taste. Take care not to add too much salt if using pancetta, as this can be quite salty.

5 Place the mushrooms in a single layer in a buttered ovenproof dish and top with the stuffing mixture. Sprinkle with the Parmesan cheese and dot with the butter.

6 Pour remaining wine into the dish and bake at 160°C Circotherm for 20-25 minutes.

MENU SUGGESTION

Serve *Baked Stuffed Mushrooms* as a starter followed by *Osso Bucco* (page 64), then *Zabaglione* (page 141).

COOK'S TIPS

It is important to buy the right kind of mushrooms for *Baked Stuffed Mushrooms*. Button mushrooms are far too small to stuff and they have very little flavour for a dish such as this one. The cup mushrooms specified in this recipe are cultivated in much the same as button mushrooms, but they are larger and slightly stronger in flavour. Do not confuse them with the large open mushrooms which would be too strong in flavour and too flat to hold the stuffing.

Pancetta is salted raw belly of pork which looks rather like streaky bacon and can be bought in long rasher form or rolled up from Italian delicatessens or large supermarkets.

Ideal vegetables for dipping in *Aubergine Dip* are celery, carrots and courgettes, cut into sticks. Tiny button mushrooms and florets of cauliflower or broccoli are also good.

Tahini is a paste of finely ground sesame seeds, which is available from health food shops.

Artichoke Hearts à la Grecque

ARTICHOKE HEARTS À LA GRECQUE

SERVES 6

75 ml (5 tbsp) olive oil
15 ml (1 tbsp) white wine vinegar
10 ml (2 tsp) tomato purée
1 large garlic clove, skinned and crushed
7.5 ml (1½ tsp) chopped fresh thyme or basil
salt and freshly ground pepper
175 g (6 oz) button onions, skinned
5 ml (1 tsp) caster sugar
225 g (8 oz) small button mushrooms, wiped
two 400 g (14 oz) cans artichoke hearts

1 Make the dressing. Place 45 ml (3 tbsp) of the oil, the vinegar, tomato purée, garlic, thyme and salt and pepper to taste in a bowl and whisk together until well blended.

2 Blanch the onions in boiling water for 5 minutes, then drain well. Heat the remaining oil, add the onions and sugar and cook for 2 minutes.

3 Add the mushrooms and toss over a high heat for a few seconds. Tip the contents of the pan into the dressing. Drain the artichoke hearts, rinse and dry. Add the hearts to the dressing and toss together. Cover and chill.

AUBERGINE DIP

SERVES 4

2 large aubergines, total weight about 700 g (1½ lb)
2 garlic cloves, skinned and crushed
10 ml (2 level tsp) ground cumin
150 ml (¼ pint) natural yogurt
10 ml (2 level tsp) ground coriander
15 ml (1 tbsp) tahini (see Cook's Tip)
about 30 ml (2 tbsp) lemon juice
salt and freshly ground pepper
crudités, to serve

1 Prick the aubergines with a fork and place in a baking dish. Bake at 170°C Circotherm for 1 hour or until soft. Leave to cool slightly.

2 Skin and roughly chop the aubergines. Purée with the remaining ingredients in a blender or food processor until smooth. Season and add a little more lemon juice if necessary.

3 Turn the mixture into a serving bowl and chill. Serve as a dip with a selection of fresh vegetable crudités.

GRILLED CHICORY WITH PEARS AND HAZELNUTS

SERVES 8

4 large or 8 small heads of chicory,
halved and cored

olive oil for basting

2 ripe pears, halved, cored and sliced

45 ml (3 tbsp) hazelnut oil

15 ml (1 tbsp) chopped fresh thyme or
5 ml (1 tsp) dried thyme

freshly ground pepper

50 g (2 oz) hazelnuts, toasted and chopped

sprigs of fresh thyme, to garnish

crusty Italian bread, to serve

1 Brush the chicory all over with olive oil. Place in a grill pan, cut side up, and cook under a really hot grill (as near to the heat as possible) for about 3-4 minutes (2-3 minutes for smaller heads) or until just beginning to char and soften. Turn, baste with more oil and cook for a further 2-3 minutes (1-2 minutes for smaller heads).
2 Carefully turn the chicory again and top with slices of pear. Brush with hazelnut oil, sprinkle on the thyme, season with pepper and grill for 5-6 minutes (4-5 minutes for smaller heads). The chicory will be very soft, so carefully transfer it to warmed plates, scatter with the hazelnuts, garnish with extra sprigs of thyme and drizzle with the remaining hazelnut oil. Serve with crusty Italian bread.

SPANAKOPITTES

MAKES 60

30 ml (2 tbsp) olive oil

1 small onion, skinned and chopped

1 garlic clove, skinned and crushed

227 g (8 oz) packet frozen chopped spinach,
thawed and squeezed dry

75 g (3 oz) Feta cheese, crumbled

1 egg, beaten

freshly ground pepper

175 g (6 oz) large sheets frozen filo pastry, thawed

100-150 g (4-5 oz) butter, melted

1 Heat the oil in a saucepan, add the onion and garlic and fry gently for 5 minutes until soft. Remove the pan from the heat and stir in the spinach, cheese, egg and pepper to taste.
2 Cut the pastry widthways into strips 15 cm (6 inches) long and 5 cm (2 inches) wide. Place on waxed paper and cover with a slightly damp tea towel.
3 Brush one strip of the pastry with melted butter and place 5 ml (1 tsp) of the spinach mixture at the end of the strip.
4 Fold one corner of the strip diagonally over the filling, so the short edge lies on top of the long edge and forms a right angle.
5 Continue folding the pastry at right angles until you reach the end of the strip, forming a neat triangular package. Repeat to make 60.
6 Place the packages seam side down in a large baking or roasting tin, and brush with melted butter. Bake in the oven at 180°C Circotherm for about 20 minutes until golden. Serve hot.

SERVING IDEA

Spanakopittes (Greek savoury pasties) are delicious on their own as a first course. Follow with a Greek-style main course such as grilled minced lamb kebabs, and a mixed salad of tomatoes, black olives and crumbled feta cheese. Finish the meal with refreshing slices of ripe melon.

Fish & Shellfish

Previous page: Kettle-cooked Sea Bass (see page 32); Monkfish and Mussel Brochettes (see page 42); Italian Fish Stew (see page 46)

(see page 32); (see page 42); (see page 46)

MICROWAVE

Plait of Salmon and Courgettes
Put the vermouth and saffron into a medium bowl and cook on HIGH for 2-3 minutes until just boiling. Add 50 g (2 oz) of the butter or margarine and the cream and cook on HIGH for 4-5 minutes until slightly thickened. Set aside while cooking the fish. Cook the fish parcels on HIGH for about 5 minutes or until the fish is just cooked. Carefully remove from the microwave and arrange on four plates. Meanwhile, cook the sauce on HIGH for 2-3 minutes or until hot. Season to taste with salt and pepper, then spoon around the salmon and courgette plaits. Serve immediately.

BAKED TROUT WITH BACON AND APPLE

SERVES 2

2 trout, about 350 g (12 oz) each, gutted
25 g (1 oz) long-grain white rice
salt and freshly ground pepper
1 small eating apple
15 ml (1 tbsp) vegetable oil
50 g (2 oz) onion, skinned and finely chopped
50 g (2 oz) streaky bacon, cut into small pieces
grated rind of ½ orange
100 ml (4 fl oz) dry white wine
45 ml (3 tbsp) orange juice
few sprigs of dill or 5 ml (1 level tsp) dried dill weed
45 ml (3 tbsp) double cream
sprigs of dill, to garnish

1 If using whole trout, cut off the head, tail and fins. Place flesh side down on a board and press firmly along the backbone to release. Turn over and ease out the backbone. Rinse, drain and dry the fish.
2 Cook the rice in boiling salted water until tender. Drain and cool. Peel, quarter, core and roughly chop the apple.
3 Heat the oil in a small frying pan. Add the onion and bacon and fry together for 2-3 minutes until just beginning to brown. Stir in the apple and continue to fry for 1 minute longer. Turn into a bowl and mix in the rice and grated orange rind and season well.
4 Place the trout side by side in a medium-sized shallow ovenproof dish. Stuff with the rice mixture and secure with wooden cocktail sticks. Pour the wine, mixed with the orange juice, around the fish. Add a few sprigs of dill.
5 Cover tightly, then bake at 160°C Circotherm for 25-30 minutes or until the fish is just cooked.
6 Lift the fish onto a serving dish and remove the cocktail sticks. Strain the juices into a small saucepan. Add the cream, then bring to the boil and bubble for a few minutes to thicken slightly. Adjust the seasoning, pour over the fish and garnish with dill sprigs.

PLAIT OF SALMON AND COURGETTES

SERVES 4

3 large long courgettes
900 g (2 lb) piece of fresh salmon, cut from the middle
75 g (3 oz) butter
150 ml (¼ pint) dry white vermouth
large pinch of saffron strands
150 ml (¼ pint) double cream
salt and freshly ground pepper

1 Top and tail the courgettes, then cut lengthways into 0.5 cm (¼ inch) slices. You need 12 middle slices to make the plaits. Cut the green outer slices into thin strips and reserve for the sauce.
2 Cut the salmon either side of the central bone to make two pieces. To remove the skin, put the fish, skin side down on a flat board. Starting at one corner of the thinner end, insert a sharp knife between the skin and the flesh. Using a

sawing action, carefully remove the skin, keeping the flesh in one piece. Repeat with the second piece of salmon. Discard both the skin and the central bone.

3 Cut six strips about 1.5 cm (¾ inch) wide from each piece of salmon, cutting against the grain. Cut the four thickest strips in half horizontally to make a total of 16 strips.

4 Cut out four large pieces of greaseproof paper and grease with 15 g (½ oz) of the butter. Place four of the salmon strips close together on one of the pieces of greaseproof paper to make a square. Working at right angles to the salmon, take one courgette slice and weave it under and over the strips of salmon. Repeat with two more courgette slices to make a neat square of plaited salmon and courgette. Repeat with the remaining salmon and courgette on the other pieces of paper to make four plaits.

5 Arrange them on a baking sheet, dot with 15 g (½ oz) butter, fold together the edges of the paper to completely enclose the salmon. Cook in the oven at 150°C Circotherm for about 20 minutes or until the fish is cooked.

6 Meanwhile, put the vermouth and saffron into a saucepan and bring to the boil. Add the remaining butter, cream and reserved courgette strips and cook over high heat for 7-8 minutes until slightly thickened. Season to taste with salt and pepper.

7 To serve, unwrap the salmon plaits, spoon some of the sauce around each one and serve immediately while piping hot.

Red Mullet Baked in Paper

RED MULLET BAKED IN PAPER

——— SERVES 2 ———

2 red mullet, about 225 g (8 oz) each, cleaned, with the livers reserved, and scaled
30 ml (2 tbsp) olive oil
15 ml (1 tbsp) chopped fresh parsley
1 small onion, skinned and sliced
50 g (2 oz) mushrooms, finely sliced
finely grated rind and juice of 1 lemon
salt and freshly ground pepper

1 Cut two squares of greaseproof paper, each large enough to wrap one fish. Place the fish on top and put a liver in each cavity, brush with oil, then add half remaining ingredients to each fish. Fold the paper to make secure parcels.

2 Place the parcels on a baking sheet and bake in the oven at 160°C Circotherm for about 30 minutes, or until the fish is tender. Serve the fish in their parcels.

MICROWAVE

Red Mullet Baked in Paper
Put the parsley, onions, mushrooms, lemon juice and rind, oil and pepper in a bowl, cover and cook on HIGH for 6 minutes until softened, stirring once or twice. Fill the fish cavities with the stuffing, then wrap in the greaseproof paper squares. Cook on HIGH for 3 minutes. Turn the parcels over and cook for a further 2 minutes. Leave to stand for 2 minutes before serving.

COOK'S TIP

To make French bread croûtes to serve with *Cod in White Wine*, cut the bread into thin slices and fry in vegetable oil until golden brown.

MICROWAVE

Cod in White Wine
Put the butter, courgettes, onion, pepper, flour and paprika in a bowl and cook, uncovered, on HIGH for 3 minutes. Stir the mixture, cover and cook on HIGH for a further 10 minutes until tender, stirring once or twice. Add the cod, 200 ml (7 fl oz) wine, the tomatoes, basil, garlic and seasoning. Cover and cook on HIGH for 12 minutes, stirring once or twice.

KETTLE-COOKED SEA BASS
SERVES 8

1.6-1.8 kg (3½-4 lb) sea bass, gutted with head and tail left on
1 large bunch spring onions, trimmed
2 celery sticks, trimmed
5 cm (2 inch) piece of fresh root ginger, peeled
vegetable oil for brushing
60 ml (4 tbsp) soy sauce
60 ml (4 tbsp) dry sherry
salt and freshly ground pepper
30 ml (2 tbsp) vegetable oil, 15 ml (1 tbsp) sesame oil, 30 ml (2 tbsp) soy sauce, 5 ml (1 tsp) caster sugar and 8 spring onions, trimmed and finely shredded, to serve

1 Wash the fish inside and out, then dry thoroughly. With kitchen shears or scissors, cut the tail into a 'V' shape.
2 Finely shred the spring onions and slice the celery and root ginger into very thin matchstick shapes.
3 Pour water under the rack of a fish kettle and place half of the spring onion, celery and ginger on the rack. Brush the outside of the fish lightly with oil, then place over the flavourings on the rack. Sprinkle the remaining spring onions, celery and ginger over the fish, then sprinkle with the soy sauce and sherry, and season to taste, with salt and pepper.
4 Cover the fish kettle with its lid, bring the water slowly to the boil, then simmer for 20 minutes, or until the flesh of the fish is opaque when tested near the bone.
5 To serve, heat the vegetable and sesame oils in a wok or heavy frying pan, add the soy sauce and sugar and stir well to mix. Add the shredded spring onions and stir to coat them in the liquid.
6 Discard the flavourings from on top and transfer the fish to a warmed large serving plate. Arrange the freshly cooked spring onion over the fish in a criss-cross pattern and drizzle with the cooking liquid. Serve immediately, garnished with shreds of spring onion.

COD IN WHITE WINE
SERVES 8

50 g (2 oz) butter or margarine
450 g (1 lb) courgettes, thinly sliced
2 large onions, skinned and sliced
1 red pepper, seeded and cut into strips
30 ml (2 level tbsp) plain flour
15 ml (1 level tbsp) paprika
300 ml (½ pint) dry white wine
397 g (14 oz) can tomatoes
15 ml (1 tbsp) chopped fresh basil or 5 ml (1 tsp) dried
1 garlic clove, crushed
salt and freshly ground pepper
1.1 kg (2½ lb) cod fillets, skinned and cut into 5 cm (2 inch) pieces
basil leaves and French bread croûtes (see Cook's Tip)

1 Melt the butter in a large frying pan, add the courgettes, onions, pepper, flour and paprika and fry gently for 3-4 minutes, stirring.
2 Stir in the wine, tomatoes, basil, garlic and seasoning. Bring to the boil.

3 In a large ovenproof dish, layer the fish and sauce mixture, seasoning well.

4 Cover the dish and cook at 150°C Circotherm for 50-55 minutes. Garnish with basil leaves and French bread croûtes.

VARIATION

Use haddock or other firm white fish instead of the cod fillets.

FRICASSÉE OF MONKFISH WITH CORIANDER
——— SERVES 6 ———

700 g (1½ lb) monkfish fillets
450 g (1 lb) halibut cutlets
150 ml (¼ pint) dry vermouth
1 small onion, skinned and sliced
salt and freshly ground pepper
100 g (4 oz) small button mushrooms, wiped
40 g (1½ oz) butter
45 ml (3 level tbsp) plain flour
30 ml (2 tbsp) chopped fresh coriander
60 ml (4 tbsp) single cream
sprigs of coriander, to garnish

1 Cut the monkfish and halibut into large, fork-sized pieces, discarding skin and bone.

2 Place the fish in a medium saucepan, cover with cold water and bring slowly to the boil. Strain the fish in a colander and then rinse off any scum.

Cod in White Wine

3 Return the fish to the rinsed-out pan and pour over the dry vermouth with 300 ml (½ pint) water. Add the onion, season to taste with salt and pepper and bring to the boil. Cover the pan, reduce the heat, and simmer gently for 8-10 minutes or until the fish is just tender and beginning to flake.

4 Add the mushrooms after 6 minutes of the cooking time. Strain off the cooking liquid and reserve for the sauce.

5 Melt the butter in a separate saucepan and stir in the flour followed by the cooking liquid. Bring the sauce slowly to the boil, stirring all the time, and bubble for 2 minutes until thickened and smooth.

6 Stir in the coriander, cream, mushrooms, onion and fish and adjust the seasoning. Warm through gently, being careful not to break up the pieces of fish. Serve hot, garnished with sprigs of coriander.

COOK'S TIP

Monkfish fillets and steaks taste very like lobster, but cost a fraction of the price. Monkfish hasn't always been a popular fish because of its ugly appearance when whole. For this reason it is almost always sold without its head, which is its ugliest part. Many fishmongers also fillet and skin it before offering it for sale.

Monkfish has always been popular in Mediterranean countries, particularly Spain where it is called *rape* and France where it is known as *lotte de mer* or *baudroie*. The Spanish like to serve it cold in the same way as lobster, or hot with potatoes and tomatoes; the French braise it in white wine or serve it *en brochette* (on skewers).

SERVING IDEA

Serve *Buttered Salmon Steaks* with new potatoes and a special green vegetable such as mange tout, petits pois or broccoli. The ideal wine to serve would be a crisp, dry white such as a French Muscadet or Italian Verdicchio.

MICROWAVE

Buttered Salmon Steaks
Complete step 1. Place the salmon steaks in a shallow round dish with the thickest part towards the edge of the dish. Spread the butter mixture over the top and spoon over 15 ml (1 tbsp) wine. Cover and cook on HIGH for 3-4 minutes.

Opposite: Seafood Pilaki;
Plait of Salmon and Courgettes
(see page 30)

BUTTERED SALMON STEAKS
SERVES 2

50 g (2 oz) butter, softened

finely grated rind and juice of ½ lemon

10 ml (2 tsp) chopped fresh tarragon

2 fresh salmon steaks, about 175 g (6 oz) each

30 ml (2 tbsp) dry white wine

freshly ground pepper

sprigs of tarragon and lemon wedges, to serve

1 In a small bowl, cream together the butter, lemon rind and juice and the tarragon.

2 Cut two pieces of foil, each one large enough to wrap around a salmon steak. Grease the foil with half of the butter mixture.

3 Place the salmon steaks on the buttered foil and dot with the remaining butter. Spoon the wine over the steaks and sprinkle with pepper to taste.

4 Fold the foil around the steaks, keeping the parcels quite loose. Place the parcels on a baking sheet and bake in the oven at 150°C Circotherm for 20 minutes, or until the fish is firm.

5 Unwrap the salmon steaks, place on warmed individual serving plates and pour over the juices from the foil packets. Serve immediately, garnished with tarragon sprigs and lemon wedges.

SEAFOOD PILAKI
SERVES 8

30 ml (2 tbsp) olive oil

2 garlic cloves, skinned and crushed

1 large onion, skinned and chopped

2 celery sticks, trimmed and chopped

3 large carrots, sliced

finely grated rind and juice of 1 lemon

397 g (14 oz) can chopped tomatoes

700 g (1½ lb) monkfish fillet, trimmed and cut into chunks

450 g (1 lb) cleaned squid, cut into rings

900 g (2 lb) mussels in their shells, cleaned (see page 16)

chopped fresh parsley

salt and freshly ground pepper

sprigs of parsley, to garnish

1 Heat the oil in a large heavy-based pan. Add the garlic, onion, celery, carrots and lemon rind and cook for about 5 minutes, stirring.

2 Add the lemon juice and the tomatoes with their juice, cover and cook on a low heat for about 25 minutes, or until the vegetables are very tender. Stir occasionally and add a little water if the liquid is evaporating too rapidly.

3 Add the fish and squid and a little water. Re-cover and cook for 3-5 minutes or until the fish is just tender. Arrange the mussels on the top, cover the pan again and cook for about 5 minutes, stirring occasionally. The mussels should have opened; discard any that remain shut. Stir in plenty of parsley and season to taste. Garnish with parsley and serve hot or cold.

MICROWAVE

Salmon with Hollandaise Sauce

Arrange the salmon with the thinner ends pointing towards the centre in a large shallow dish. Pour over the wine, cover and cook on HIGH for 5-6 minutes, or until tender. Leave to stand, covered, while making the sauce. To make the sauce, put the butter in a large bowl and cook on HIGH for 1 minute, or until just melted (do not cook for any longer or the butter will be too hot and the mixture will curdle). Add the egg yolks and the vinegar and whisk together until well mixed. Cook on HIGH for 1 minute, whisking every 15 seconds until thick enough to coat the back of a spoon. Season with a little salt and pepper. Transfer the salmon to four serving plates and serve immediately with the sauce.

SALMON WITH HOLLANDAISE SAUCE

SERVES 4

4 salmon steaks, about 225 g (8 oz) each
60 ml (4 tbsp) medium dry white wine
30 ml (2 tbsp) white wine vinegar
2 egg yolks
100 g (4 oz) butter, cut into small pieces
salt and freshly ground white pepper

1 Place the salmon in a shallow ovenproof dish and pour over the wine. Cover and cook in the oven at 150°C Circotherm for 25-30 minutes.

2 Meanwhile, make the sauce. Put the vinegar into a saucepan with 15 ml (1 tbsp) water. Boil gently until the liquid has reduced by half. Set aside until cool.

3 Put the egg yolks and vinegar into a double saucepan or a bowl set over a pan of very gently simmering water and whisk until the mixture is thick and fluffy. Gradually add the butter, a piece at a time, whisking briskly until each piece has been absorbed by the sauce and the sauce is the consistency of mayonnaise. Season to taste with salt and pepper.

4 Transfer the salmon to four serving plates and serve immediately with the sauce.

SPICED GRILLED HALIBUT

SERVES 4

4 halibut steaks, about 175 g (6 oz) each
75 ml (5 tbsp) Greek or thick set natural yogurt
2 garlic cloves, skinned and crushed
1 medium onion, skinned and finely chopped
15 ml (1 level tbsp) paprika
5 ml (1 level tsp) garam masala
5 ml (1 level tsp) ground coriander
5 ml (1 level tsp) ground cumin
salt and freshly ground pepper
2.5 ml (½ level tsp) ground turmeric
1 red chilli, seeded and finely chopped
5 ml (1 level tsp) grated fresh root ginger
juice of 1 lemon
lemon wedges and chopped fresh coriander, to garnish

1 Wash the halibut steaks under cold running water, drain and then place in a large shallow flameproof dish.

2 Put all the remaining ingredients, except those for the garnish, into a blender or food processor and purée until smooth. Pour over the fish. Cover and leave to marinate in a cool place for 24 hours, turning occasionally.

3 Cook the fish under a preheated hot grill, basting occasionally with the marinade, until the fish flakes easily when tested with a fork.

4 Serve the fish hot, garnished with lemon wedges and coriander.

MARINATED SOLE AND CITRUS FRUIT

SERVES 4

8 sole fillets, 100 g (4 oz) each, skinned
finely grated rind and juice of 1 lime
finely grated rind and juice of 1 lemon
finely grated rind and juice of 1 orange
30 ml (2 tbsp) dry white wine
45 ml (3 tbsp) olive oil
30 ml (2 tbsp) chopped fresh parsley
1 shallot or small onion, skinned and finely chopped
salt and freshly ground pepper
lime, lemon and orange wedges, to garnish

1 Fold the sole fillets in half crossways and place in a single layer in a shallow ovenproof dish. Mix the lime, lemon and orange rinds and juices with the wine, oil, parsley and shallot. Season to taste with salt and pepper and spoon over the fish. Cover and leave to marinate for at least 30 minutes.
2 Cover the fish tightly with foil. Bake in the oven at 170°C Circotherm for about 25 minutes, or until tender.
3 Transfer the fish to a warmed serving dish and spoon over a little of the cooking liquid. Garnish with fruit wedges and serve with boiled rice and a green vegetable.

HADDOCK AND MUSHROOM PUFFS

SERVES 4

25 g (1 oz) butter
225 g (8 oz) mushrooms, wiped
30 ml (2 tbsp) double cream
5 ml (1 tsp) lemon juice
20 ml (4 tsp) capers, chopped
15 ml (1 tbsp) snipped fresh chives or 5 ml (1 tsp) dried
salt and freshly ground pepper
500 g (1 lb 2 oz) ready prepared puff pastry
450 g (1 lb) haddock fillet, skinned
1 egg

1 Melt the butter in a saucepan, add the mushrooms and cook until soft. Stir in the cream, lemon juice, capers and chives and season to taste with salt and pepper. Mix well.
2 Roll out the pastry on a floured surface to a 40.5 cm (16 inch) square. Cut into four squares, trim the edges and reserve the trimmings.
3 Place the squares on dampened baking sheets. Divide the fish into four and place diagonally across the pastry squares. Spoon the mushroom mixture over the top.
4 Brush the edges of each square lightly with water. Bring the four points of each square together and seal the edges to form a parcel.
5 Decorate with pastry trimmings and make a small hole in the centre. Chill for 30 minutes.
6 Beat the egg with a pinch of salt and use to glaze the pastry. Bake in the oven at 180°C Circotherm for 20-30 minutes, or until the pastry is golden brown and well risen. Serve hot.

MICROWAVE

Marinated Sole and Citrus Fruit
Follow step 1, but place the sole in a round shallow dish, arranged like the spokes of a wheel with the thickest part on the outside. Leave to marinate, then cover and cook on HIGH for 8 minutes.

Haddock and Mushroom Puffs

37

PARSLEY FISH PIE

——— SERVES 4 ———

900 g (2 lb) potatoes, peeled
450 ml (¾ pint) milk, plus 90 ml (6 tbsp)
65 g (2½ oz) butter or margarine
salt and freshly ground pepper
450 g (1 lb) haddock fillets
1 bay leaf
6 peppercorns
1 medium onion, skinned and finely sliced
45 ml (3 level tbsp) plain flour
2 eggs, hard-boiled and chopped
150 ml (¼ pint) single cream
30 ml (2 tbsp) chopped fresh parsley
100 g (4 oz) cooked peeled prawns
1 egg, beaten, to glaze

1 Boil the potatoes, drain and mash without any liquid. Heat 90 ml (6 tbsp) of the milk and 25 g (1 oz) butter and beat into the potatoes. Season to taste with salt and pepper.

2 Rinse and drain the fish. Place in a pan and pour over 450 ml (¾ pint) milk, then add the bay leaf, peppercorns, onion and a pinch of salt. Bring just to the boil and simmer for 5-7 minutes until just tender.

3 Lift from the pan, flake the flesh and remove the skin and bones. Strain the cooking liquid and reserve.

4 Make the sauce. Melt the remaining butter in a pan, stir in the flour and cook gently for 1 minute, stirring. Remove the pan from the heat and gradually stir in the reserved cooking liquid. Bring to the boil, stirring, until sauce thickens, then cook for a further 2-3 minutes. Season to taste with salt and pepper.

5 Add the eggs to the sauce with the cream, fish, parsley and prawns. Check the seasoning, and spoon the mixture into a 1.8 litre (3 pint) pie dish.

6 Spoon the potatoes into a piping bag and pipe across the fish mixture. Alternatively, spoon the potato over the fish and roughen the surface with a fork.

7 Brush with the beaten egg and bake in the oven at 170°C Circotherm for 20 minutes until the potato is set. Place under a hot grill until golden brown, if wished.

SALMON EN CROÛTE

——— SERVES 8 ———

500 g (1 lb 2 oz) ready prepared puff pastry
350 g (12 oz) frozen chopped spinach, thawed and squeezed dry
150 g (5 oz) full fat soft cheese with garlic and herbs
salt and freshly ground pepper
25 g (1 oz) butter or margarine
100 g (4 oz) spring onions, roughly chopped
100 g (4 oz) cooked peeled prawns
100 g (4 oz) small scallops
1.6 - 1.8 kg (3½ - 4 lb) salmon or sea trout, cleaned, skinned and filleted, about 900 g (2 lb) filleted weight
1 egg, beaten
sprigs of dill, slices of star fruit or orange, to garnish

MICROWAVE

Parsley Fish Pie
Complete step 1. Place the haddock in a shallow dish, pour over the milk, cover and cook on HIGH for 8 minutes. Leave to stand for 2 minutes. Reserve the milk. To make the sauce, put the butter, flour and reserved milk in a large jug and cook, uncovered, on HIGH for 4 minutes, whisking every minute. Mix the sauce with the eggs, cream, fish, parsley and prawns and spoon into a round 1.8 litre (3 pint) pie dish. Pipe over the potato, then cook, uncovered, on HIGH for 3-4 minutes until piping hot all the way through. Place under a hot grill until golden.

1 On a lightly floured surface, roll out half the pastry thinly to a rectangle 38 x 20.5 cm (15 x 8 inches). Place on a large baking sheet and prick all over with a fork. Bake at 170°C Circotherm for about 20 minutes or until golden brown and cooked through. Leave to cool on a wire rack.

2 Beat the spinach into the soft cheese and season to taste with salt and pepper. Melt the butter in a small saucepan and sauté the spring onions for 3-4 minutes until just beginning to soften. Cool, then stir in the prawns and scallops. Season.

3 Return the cooked pastry to a baking sheet and place one fillet on top, skinned side down. Trim the pastry, allowing 1 cm (½ inch) all round. Spread the spinach mixture over the fish, then spread the prawn filling on top and finish with the remaining fillet of salmon, skinned side up.

4 Brush the cooked pastry edge with beaten egg, roll out the remaining pastry thinly and place over the fish to enclose completely. Trim off the excess pastry, leaving about 2.5 cm (1 inch) to tuck under all round. Decorate with a lattice made from the trimmings. Glaze all over with beaten egg. Make two small holes to allow steam to escape, then bake at 170°C Circotherm for 45 minutes until well risen and golden. Garnish and serve warm.

SKATE WITH BLACK BUTTER

SERVES 4

700-900 g (1½-2 lb) skate wings
salt
50 g (2 oz) butter
15 ml (1 tbsp) white wine vinegar
10 ml (2 tsp) capers
10 ml (2 tsp) chopped fresh parsley

1 Put the fish in a saucepan and cover with salted water. Bring to the boil, then simmer for 10-15 minutes until tender. Drain and place on a warm serving dish. Cover and keep warm.

2 Melt the butter in a saucepan, cook until it turns golden brown, add the vinegar and capers and cook for a further 2-3 minutes. Pour over the fish, sprinkle with parsley and serve immediately.

VARIATION

Skate in Pepper Butter

Prepare the skate as described in the recipe above. Melt 75 g (3 oz) butter in a saucepan, add 30 ml (2 tbsp) black peppercorns, crushed, 1 small garlic clove, crushed, and 5 ml (1 level tsp) dried sage. Stir over a medium heat for about 1 minute until the butter is golden brown. Pour over the skate and serve immediately.

Skate with Black Butter

BAKED RED SNAPPER

— SERVES 2 —

2 red snapper, about 550 g (1¼ lb) each, cleaned
100 g (4 oz) butter or margarine
1 large bunch of watercress, about 100 g (4 oz), washed and finely chopped
100 g (4 oz) spring onions, trimmed and finely chopped
salt and freshly ground pepper
2 garlic cloves, skinned and crushed
sprigs of parsley or coriander, to garnish

1 Place the fish in a buttered shallow ovenproof dish. Melt half the butter in a frying pan, add the watercress and onions and fry gently for 1-2 minutes until softened.
2 Remove from the heat and season to taste with salt and pepper. Spoon the mixture into the cavity of each fish.
3 Melt the remaining butter in a saucepan. Stir in the crushed garlic, then pour the mixture over the fish. Bake in the oven at 170°C Circotherm for about 30 minutes. Place under a hot grill for 3-4 minutes until well browned. Garnish with sprigs of parsley or coriander.

MOULES MARINIÈRES

SERVES 4 AS A STARTER
OR 2 AS A MAIN COURSE

25 g (1 oz) butter or margarine
1 medium onion, skinned and finely chopped
1.1-1.4 kg (2½-3 lb) mussels in their shells, cleaned (see page 16)
1 small garlic clove, skinned and crushed
300 ml (½ pint) medium dry white wine
1 bay leaf
salt and pepper
15-30 ml (1-2 tbsp) chopped fresh parsley
30-45 ml (2-3 tbsp) double cream (optional)

1 Melt the butter in a large heavy-based saucepan, add the onion and fry gently until lightly brown. Add the mussels, garlic, wine, bay leaf, salt and plenty of pepper.
2 Cover, bring to the boil, and cook for 3-5 minutes until the mussels open, shaking the pan frequently.
3 Pour off the cooking juices into a small saucepan, discarding the bay leaf, if wished, and boil until reduced by about one third.
4 Lift the mussels out of the pan and discard any that have not opened. Transfer the mussels to a warmed soup tureen or individual soup bowls, cover and keep warm.
5 Return the juices to the heat and bring to the boil, stirring constantly. Adjust the seasoning and add the parsley and cream, if using. Pour over the mussels and serve immediately.

MICROWAVE

Baked Red Snapper
Put 25 g (1 oz) butter, the watercress and onions in a bowl, cover and cook on HIGH for 4-5 minutes until soft, stirring once or twice. Season, then stuff the fish with the watercress mixture and place in a shallow dish. Cut the remaining butter into pieces and place along the length of the fish. Sprinkle the garlic over the top. Cover and cook on HIGH for 8 minutes, turning the fish over after 4 minutes.

Opposite: Moules Marinières;
Baked Red Snapper

Scallops in Creamy Basil Sauce

SCALLOPS IN CREAMY BASIL SAUCE
SERVES 4

900 g (2 lb) shelled scallops, thawed if frozen
30 ml (2 tbsp) vegetable oil
15 g (½ oz) butter
1 small onion, skinned and crushed
2 garlic cloves, skinned and crushed
150 ml (¼ pint) dry white wine
20 ml (4 tsp) chopped fresh basil
salt and freshly ground pepper
150 ml (¼ pint) double cream
sprigs of basil, to garnish

1 Cut the scallops (including the coral) into fairly thick slices. Pat dry with absorbent kitchen paper and set aside.

2 Heat the oil and butter in a large frying pan, add the onion and garlic and fry gently for 5 minutes until soft and lightly coloured.

3 Add the scallops to the pan and toss to coat in the oil and butter. Stir in the wine and basil and season to taste with salt and pepper.

4 Fry scallops over moderate heat for 10 minutes until they are tender, turning them constantly so that they cook evenly on all sides. Do not overcook or they will become tough.

5 Remove the scallops from the liquid with a slotted spoon and set aside on a plate. Boil the liquid until reduced by about half, then stir in the cream a little at a time and simmer until the sauce is thick.

6 Return the scallops to the pan and heat gently. To serve, taste and adjust the seasoning, and serve garnished with basil sprigs.

MONKFISH AND MUSSEL BROCHETTES
SERVES 6

36 mussels, cooked (see page 16)
18 streaky bacon rashers, rinded and halved
900 g (2 lb) monkfish fillets, skinned, boned and cut into 42 cubes
50 g (2 oz) butter or margarine, melted
60 ml (4 tbsp) chopped fresh parsley
grated rind and juice of 1 lime or lemon
4 garlic cloves, skinned and crushed
salt and freshly ground pepper
shredded lettuce, bay leaves and lime or lemon wedges, to garnish
saffron rice, to serve (optional)

1 Using a sharp knife, shell the mussels, discarding the shells.

2 Roll the bacon rashers up neatly. Thread the cubed fish, mussels and bacon alternately on to six oiled kebab skewers.

3 Mix together the melted butter, parsley, lime rind and juice and garlic and season to taste with salt and pepper. (Take care when seasoning with salt as both the mussels and the bacon are naturally salty.)

4 Place the brochettes on an oiled grill. Brush with the butter mixture, then grill under a moderate grill for 15 minutes, turning frequently and brushing with the butter mixture.

5 Arrange the hot brochettes on a serving platter lined with shredded lettuce. Garnish with bay leaves and lime wedges and serve at once with saffron rice, if wished.

SKEWERED SCALLOPS WITH BACON
SERVES 2

8 large fresh or frozen shelled scallops, thawed if frozen
4 rashers of streaky bacon, rinded
15 ml (1 tbsp) chopped fresh basil or tarragon or 5 ml (1 tsp) dried
30 ml (2 tbsp) olive or vegetable oil
2 medium tomatoes, skinned
5 ml (1 tsp) wine vinegar
salt and freshly ground pepper
sprigs of basil, to garnish

1 If necessary, remove and discard the tough white 'muscle' from each scallop, which is found opposite the orange coral. Separate the corals.

2 With a sharp knife, lightly score the scallops on each side in a lattice pattern.

3 Stretch the bacon rashers with the back of a knife and divide each rasher in two.

4 Wrap the bacon around the corals. Thread the scallops, horizontally, and corals alternately on to two kebab skewers. Place in a foil-lined grill pan.

5 Mix basil with 15 ml (1 tbsp) of the oil and brush over the scallops and bacon. Cook under a hot grill for 5 minutes on each side until the scallops are just cooked and the bacon golden, brushing with more oil and basil when turning the skewers over.

6 Slice each tomato into six wedges and arrange on the side of two individual serving plates. Whisk the remaining oil and the vinegar together and season to taste with salt and pepper.

7 When the scallops are cooked, place a skewer on each plate and spoon the dressing over the tomatoes. Garnish with basil and serve.

SPANISH COD WITH MUSSELS
SERVES 4

900 g (2 lb) mussels in their shells, cleaned (see page 16)
150 ml (¼ pint) dry white wine
700 g (1½ lb) cod fillet, skinned and cut into chunks
2 medium onions, skinned and very thinly sliced
1 red pepper, seeded and very thinly sliced
1-2 garlic cloves, skinned and crushed
450 g (1 lb) tomatoes, skinned and chopped
1.25 ml (¼ tsp) Tabasco sauce, or to taste
1 bay leaf
salt and freshly ground pepper

1 Put the mussels and wine in a large saucepan. Cover and cook for 4-5 minutes or until all the mussels have opened, shaking the pan occasionally. Drain, reserving the cooking liquid. Shell all but eight mussels.

2 Layer the cod and onions, peppers, garlic and tomatoes in a casserole, then add the Tabasco sauce and bay leaf and season to taste. Pour over the reserved cooking liquid.

3 Cover and cook in the oven at 160°C Circotherm for 45 minutes. Discard the bay leaf and add the shelled mussels. Cover and cook for a further 15 minutes. Serve immediately, garnished with chopped parsley and the mussels in their shells.

SERVING IDEA

Serve *Skewered Scallops with Bacon* on a bed of saffron rice, with side salads of curly endive, radicchio and chopped red or green peppers. A chilled dry white Bordeaux wine such as Entre-Deux-Mers goes well with scallops.

GLAZED SEAFOOD PLATTER

SERVES 8

450 g (1 lb) haddock fillet, skinned
900 g (2 lb) halibut fillet, skinned
175 g (6 oz) Florence fennel
600 ml (1 pint) dry white white
300 ml (½ pint) fish stock
1 bay leaf
450 g (1 lb) queen scallops, cleaned
225 g (8 oz) fresh shelled mussels
225 g (8 oz) cooked peeled prawns
75 g (3 oz) butter
75 g (3 oz) plain flour
2 egg yolks
300 ml (½ pint) double cream
salt and freshly ground pepper
100 g (4 oz) Emmenthal cheese, coarsely grated

1 Cut the fish fillets into bite-sized pieces. Remove the feathery tops from the fennel, finely chop and reserve. Cut the fennel into thin slices.
2 Place the fish and fennel in a large shallow pan and pour on the wine, stock and bay leaf. Bring to the boil, cover and simmer for 7-8 minutes or until the fish is just cooked.
3 With a slotted spoon, remove the fish and fennel from the cooking liquid and arrange in a single layer on two large heatproof platters. Add the scallops and mussels to the cooking liquid, return to the boil and immediately remove. Scatter over the fish with the prawns.
4 Cover the platters with foil and keep warm in the oven at 150°C Circotherm. Melt the butter in a medium saucepan. Stir in the flour and cook, stirring, for 1-2 minutes. Strain in the poaching liquid, bring to the boil, stirring all the time, then simmer for 2-3 minutes.
5 Heat the grill. Beat the egg yolks and cream into the sauce. Season. Spoon evenly over the seafood and sprinkle with cheese. Place the platters under the grill until golden brown. Serve garnished with the reserved fennel tops.

MONKFISH WITH LIME AND PRAWNS

SERVES 4

550 g (1¼ lb) monkfish fillets, skinned, boned and cut into 5 cm (2 inch) pieces
30 ml (2 level tbsp) seasoned flour
30 ml (2 tbsp) vegetable oil
1 small onion, skinned and chopped
1 garlic clove, skinned and chopped
225 g (8 oz) tomatoes, skinned and chopped
150 ml (¼ pint) dry white wine
juice of 1 lime
pinch of sugar
salt and freshly ground pepper
100 g (4 oz) peeled prawns
chopped parsley and lime rind, to garnish

1 Coat the fish in seasoned flour. Heat the oil in a flameproof casserole, add the onion and garlic and fry gently for 5 minutes until softened. Add the fish and fry for 5 minutes until golden.
2 Stir in the tomatoes, wine and lime juice, sugar and seasoning. Bring to the boil.
3 Add the prawns, cover and cook in the oven at 160°C Circotherm for 15 minutes until the monkfish is tender. Garnish and serve.

MENU SUGGESTION

Serve Glazed Seafood Platter with mixed long-grain and wild rice and *Fennel and Tomato Salad* (see page 124). For a starter, serve *Spanakopittes* (see page 27) or *Artichokes à la Grècque* (see page 26). *Summer Pudding* (see page 130) makes a light end to this meal.

QUICK PAELLA
— SERVES 4-6 —

60 ml (4 tbsp) olive oil

about 450 g (1 lb) boneless chicken meat, skinned and cut into bite-sized cubes

1 medium onion, skinned and chopped

2 garlic cloves, skinned and crushed

1 large red pepper, cored, seeded and sliced into thin strips

3 tomatoes, skinned and chopped

400 g (14 oz) Italian risotto (arborio) rice

1.2 litres (2¼ pints) boiling chicken stock

5 ml (1 level tsp) paprika

2.5 ml (½ level tsp) saffron powder

salt and freshly ground pepper

225 g (8 oz) mussels, cooked (see page 16)

lemon wedges, peeled prawns and mussels in their shells (optional), to serve

1 Heat the oil in a large, deep frying pan, add the cubes of chicken and fry over moderate heat until golden brown on all sides. Remove from the pan with a slotted spoon and set aside.
2 Add the onion, garlic and red pepper to the pan and fry gently for 5 minutes until softened. Add the tomatoes and fry for a few more minutes until the juices run, then add the rice and stir to combine with the oil and vegetables.
3 Pour in 1 litre (1¾ pints) of the boiling stock (it will bubble furiously), then add half the paprika, the saffron powder and season to taste with salt and pepper. Stir well, lower the heat and add the chicken.
4 Simmer, uncovered, for 30 minutes until the chicken is cooked through, stirring frequently during this time to prevent the rice from sticking. When the mixture becomes dry, stir in a few tablespoons of boiling stock. Repeat as often as necessary to keep the paella moist.
5 To serve, fold in the mussels and heat through. Taste and adjust the seasoning, then garnish with lemon wedges, peeled prawns, mussels in their shells, if wished, and a sprinkling of the remaining paprika.

FRITTO MISTO DI MARE
— SERVES 6 —

450 g (1 lb) squid, cleaned

225 g (8 oz) whitebait

4 small red mullet, cleaned and heads and tails removed, cut into chunks

225 g (8 oz) firm, white fish fillets, e.g. cod, haddock or sole, skinned, and cut into long thin strips

8-12 large prawns, peeled

60 ml (4 level tbsp) seasoned flour

vegetable oil for deep-frying

sprigs of parsley and lemon wedges, to garnish

1 Slice the body of the squid into rings 0.5 cm (¼ inch) thick and the tentacles into 1 cm (½ inch) pieces. Toss all the fish in seasoned flour to coat.
2 Heat the oil in a deep-fat fryer to 190°C (375°F). Add the fish pieces a few at a time and fry until crisp and golden brown. Drain on absorbent kitchen paper and keep each batch warm while frying the rest.
3 Divide the fish between six warmed plates and garnish with lemon wedges and parsley.

Quick Paella

SERVING IDEA

Quick Paella is ideal for a substantial supper dish with fresh crusty bread and a mixed green salad.

45

MENU SUGGESTION

Serve *Seafood Saffron Risotto* with fresh crusty bread, a salad and a bottle of chilled white wine – a dry Soave or Frascati would go well with the seafood in this risotto. Serve *Iced Tzaziki Soup* (see page 14) for a starter, and *Individual Apple Soufflés* (see page 141) for dessert.

COOK'S TIP

When making a risotto, follow the instructions carefully, adding the liquid a little at a time. The rice should absorb each amount of liquid before you add the next. Don't worry if you do not need to add all the liquid specified.

SEAFOOD SAFFRON RISOTTO
— SERVES 4-6 —

good pinch of saffron strands

45 ml (3 tbsp) olive oil

30 ml (2 tbsp) butter or margarine

1 onion, skinned and chopped

2 garlic cloves, skinned and crushed

½ green pepper, finely chopped

½ red pepper, finely chopped

400 g (14 oz) Arborio (Italian risotto) rice

about 600 ml (1 pint) hot fish or chicken stock

120 ml (8 tbsp) dry white wine

1 bay leaf

salt and freshly ground pepper

350-450 g (12 oz-1 lb) frozen shelled cooked scampi or jumbo prawns, thawed and thoroughly drained and dried

24 cooked mussels, shelled (see page 16)

a few mussels in shells, to garnish

freshly grated Parmesan cheese, to serve

1 Soak the saffron strands in 150 ml (¼ pint) boiling water for at least 30 minutes.

2 Meanwhile, heat the oil and half the butter in a heavy-based pan, add the onion, garlic and peppers and fry gently for 5 minutes until soft.

3 Add the rice and stir until coated in the oil and butter. Pour in a few spoonfuls of the stock and the wine, then add the saffron liquid.

4 Add the bay leaf and salt and pepper to taste and simmer gently, stirring frequently, until all the liquid is absorbed by the rice.

5 Add a few more spoonfuls of stock and simmer again until it is absorbed. Continue adding stock in this way for about 15 minutes, stirring frequently until the rice is tender.

6 Melt the remaining butter in a separate pan, add the scampi and toss gently for about 5 minutes until they change colour.

7 Remove the bay leaf from the risotto, then stir in the scampi and juices and the mussels. Warm through, taste and adjust seasoning. Turn into a warmed serving dish. Top with whole mussels and serve with Parmesan cheese.

ITALIAN FISH STEW
— SERVES 8 —

good pinch of saffron strands

about 1.8 kg (4 lb) mixed fish fillets (red mullet, bream, brill, monkfish, plaice or cod), skinned

20-24 Mediterranean prawns, cooked

120 ml (8 tbsp) olive oil

2 large onions, skinned and finely chopped

4 garlic cloves, skinned and crushed

4 slices of drained canned pimiento, sliced

900 g (2 lb) tomatoes, skinned, seeded and chopped

4 anchovy fillets, drained

300 ml (½ pint) dry white wine

4 bay leaves

90 ml (6 tbsp) chopped fresh basil

salt and freshly ground pepper

20-24 mussels in their shells, cleaned (see page 16)

8 slices of toast

1 Soak the saffron in a little boiling water.

2 Meanwhile, cut the fish into chunky bite-sized pieces. Peel most of the prawns, reserving some for garnishing.

3 Heat the oil in a large saucepan, add the onion, garlic and pimiento and fry for 5 minutes.
4 Add the tomatoes and anchovies and stir to break them up. Add the wine and 300 ml (½ pint) water, bring to the boil, then lower the heat and add the bay leaves and half the basil. Simmer, uncovered, for 20 minutes.
5 Add the firm fish to the tomato mixture, then strain in the saffron water and season to taste. Cook for 10 minutes, then add the delicate-textured fish and cook for a further 5 minutes.
6 Add prawns and mussels, cover and cook for 5 minutes until mussels open. Put the toast in eight bowls and spoon over stew. Garnish.

PRAWN PURIS
SERVES 8

30 ml (2 tbsp) vegetable oil
1 medium onion, skinned and finely chopped
2 garlic cloves, skinned and crushed
450 g (1 lb) peeled cooked prawns, thawed and thoroughly dried if frozen
5-10 ml (1-2 tsp) chilli powder, to taste
8 ripe tomatoes, skinned, seeded and roughly chopped
150 ml (¼ pint) coconut milk (see right)
10 ml (2 tsp) lime or lemon juice
salt and freshly ground pepper
chopped fresh coriander, to garnish
PURIS
225 g (8 oz) plain wholemeal flour
pinch of salt
10 ml (2 tsp) vegetable oil
vegetable oil for deeping frying

1 Heat the oil in a heavy flameproof casserole, add the onion and cook gently, stirring frequently, for 5-7 minutes until softened. Add the garlic, prawns and chilli powder, increase the heat to moderate and stir fry for 2-3 minutes. Remove with a slotted spoon and set aside.
2 Add the tomatoes and coconut milk to the casserole and bring to the boil, stirring. Simmer until the tomatoes are broken up and the sauce is thickened, stirring frequently, then return the prawn mixture and its juices to the pan and stir well to mix. Add the lime or lemon juice and salt and pepper to taste, then remove from the heat.
3 To make the puris, put the flour, salt and oil in a bowl and mix together. Gradually stir in 100-150 ml (3½-5 fl oz) tepid water to make a fairly stiff dough. Knead on a floured surface for at least 5 minutes, until smooth and elastic, then return to the bowl, cover with a damp cloth and leave to rest for 15 minutes.
4 Divide the dough into 8 equal parts and roll each one out to a round about 12.5 cm (5 inches) in diameter. Cover each one as you finish rolling, to prevent drying out.
5 Heat about 5 cm (2 inches) oil in a deep, heavy frying pan until hot. Add the puris one at a time and deep fry for about 10-15 seconds on each side until puffed and golden. Remove with a slotted spoon, drain on absorbent kitchen paper and keep warm.
6 Return the prawn mixture to the heat and bring quickly to the boil, stirring. Place a puri on each of 8 plates and top with the prawn mixture. Sprinkle with chopped fresh coriander and serve immediately.

COOK'S TIPS

To make coconut milk for *Prawn Puris*, put half of a 200 g (7 oz) packet creamed coconut in a heatproof measuring jug and pour in boiling water to come up to the 600 ml (1 pint) mark. Stir until dissolved. This makes 600 ml (1 pint).

If you prefer not to deep fry the puris for *Prawn Puris*, you can make chapatis instead. Simply cook each round of dough on a hot griddle or frying pan for a few seconds on each side, then hold the chapati with tongs over a gas flame until it puffs up. Spread with butter or ghee before serving.

Meat Dishes

Previous page: Loin of Pork with Fruit Stuffing (see page 66); Duck with Raspberries (see page 83); Boeuf à la Bourguignonne (see page 57)

MENU SUGGESTION

Raan is a spectacular dish to serve, either for a dinner party or for a special Sunday roast. Saffron rice makes a good accompaniment. Alternatively, serve with *Curried Spinach and Potatoes (Sag aloo)*, (see page 121).

RAAN

SERVES 8

2.35 kg (5¼ lb) leg of lamb

5 cm (2 inch) cinnamon stick, broken into small pieces

6 cardamom pods, split

6 whole cloves

15 ml (1 level tbsp) cumin seeds

450 ml (¾ pint) natural yogurt

5 cm (2 inch) piece of fresh root ginger, peeled and roughly chopped

4-6 garlic cloves, skinned and roughly chopped

2 fresh green chillies, roughly chopped

thinly pared rind of ½ lemon

30 ml (2 tbsp) lemon juice

10 ml (2 level tsp) ground turmeric

10 ml (2 level tsp) salt

slivered almonds, sultanas and sprigs of coriander, to garnish

1 Remove and discard the membrane and any fat from around the lamb. With a sharp pointed knife, make deep slashes in the lamb, especially near the bone.

2 Put the cinnamon, cardamom, cloves and cumin seeds in a heavy frying pan and dry fry over moderate heat for 2-3 minutes, stirring constantly. Remove from the pan and crush in a mortar and pestle.

3 Transfer the crushed spices to a blender or food processor, add all the remaining ingredients, except the garnish, and work together.

4 Place the lamb, meaty side uppermost, in a roasting tin. Pour the marinade over the lamb, spreading it so that is seeps down into the cuts. Cover and marinate in the refrigerator for at least 48 hours, turning the meat over after 24 hours and spooning over the marinade.

5 When ready to cook, uncover the lamb, turn the meat the right way up and spoon over the marinade. Allow the lamb to come to room temperature.

6 Roast the lamb in the oven at 180°C Circotherm for 20 minutes. Remove from the oven, spread with the marinade in the pan, then lower the oven temperature to 160°C Circotherm and return the lamb to the oven. Roast for a further 30 minutes.

7 Remove the lamb from the oven. Lower the oven temperature to 140°C Circotherm. Cover the lamb with foil, return to the oven and roast for a further 2 hours or until very tender.

8 Remove the lamb from the oven and transfer to a warmed serving dish. Leave to rest, covered, for 10 minutes. Meanwhile, place the roasting pan on the hob and gradually pour in 450 ml (¾ pint) boiling water, stirring vigorously with a metal spoon to scrape up as much of the sediment from the meat and marinade as possible. Boil the liquid rapidly for about 5 minutes, stirring constantly, until reduced slightly, then strain into a warmed jug or gravy boat.

9 Arrange the almonds and sultanas in a floral pattern over the lamb and garnish with sprigs of coriander. Serve hot or warm, with the gravy handed separately.

ROAST EYE FILLET OF LAMB WITH CANDIED LEMONS AND HONEY

— SERVES 8 —

4 small, thin-skinned lemons
4 fillets of lamb, about 900 g (2 lb) total weight
MARINADE
30 ml (2 tbsp) chopped fresh rosemary
2 bay leaves
2 garlic cloves, skinned and crushed
2.5 cm (1 inch) piece fresh root ginger, peeled and thinly sliced
150 ml (¼ pint) clear honey
75 ml (5 tbsp) vegetable oil
salt and freshly ground pepper
sprigs of fresh thyme, rosemary and bay leaves, to garnish

1 Mix together all the marinade ingredients. Add the strained juice of two of the lemons. Place the remaining two lemons in a small saucepan and cover with cold water. Bring to the boil, cover and simmer for 7-10 minutes or until the lemons are just beginning to soften. Leave them to cool and then cut into thickish slices, discarding any pips.

2 Place the lamb fillets in a shallow, non-metallic dish, add the lemon slices and the marinade, cover and leave in the refrigerator overnight.

3 Remove the lamb from the marinade and place on a rack above the roasting tin and roast at 180°C Circotherm for 20-25 minutes. This produces a medium rare roast.

4 About 5 minutes before the end of the cooking time, bring the marinade and lemon slices to the boil in a small saucepan. Simmer, stirring occasionally for about 5 minutes or until syrupy. Carefully add any pan juices from the lamb. Adjust the seasoning.

5 Serve lamb thickly sliced with the candied lemon slices. Pour over the remaining honey sauce and garnish with sprigs of fresh thyme, rosemary and bay leaves.

Roast Eye Fillet of Lamb with Candied Lemons and Honey

SERVING IDEA

Serve *Roast Eye Fillet of Lamb with Candied Lemons and Honey* for a special occasion serve for Sunday lunch, with carrots and green beans tossed in chopped herbs, and new potatoes with melted butter.

51

CROWN ROAST OF LAMB

SERVES 6

2 best end necks of lamb, chined,
each with 6 cutlets

15 g (½ oz) butter

1 medium onion, skinned and chopped

3 celery sticks, chopped

2 eating apples, cored and chopped

100 g (4 oz) fresh breadcrumbs

30 ml (2 tbsp) chopped fresh mint

grated rind and juice of ½ lemon

1 egg

salt and freshly ground pepper

15 ml (1 tbsp) plain flour

450 ml (¾ pint) lamb or beef stock

sprigs of parsley, to garnish

1 Trim each cutlet bone to a depth of 2.5 cm (1 inch). Trim off most of the fat.

2 Bend joints around, fat side inwards, making small incisions on the outside to enable it to bend. Sew together using fine string to form a crown. Cover the exposed bones with foil.

3 Melt the butter in a saucepan and cook the onion, celery and apples until brown. Stir in the breadcrumbs, mint, lemon rind and juice and egg. Season to taste and cool. Weigh the joint, then fill the centre with the stuffing.

4 Place the joint in a small roasting tin. Roast at 160°C Circotherm for 25 minutes per 450 g (1 lb) plus 25 minutes. Baste occasionally and cover with foil if necessary.

5 Transfer the joint to a warmed serving dish and keep warm. Drain off all but 30 ml (2 tbsp) of the fat in the roasting tin, then add the flour and blend well. Cook for 2-3 minutes, stirring continuously. Add the stock and boil for 2-3 minutes. Adjust the seasoning and serve hot with the joint. Garnish with sprigs of parsley.

FRENCH ROAST RACKS OF LAMB WITH ROSEMARY AND GARLIC
SERVES 6

3 best end necks of lamb, chined, each with 6 cutlets, trimmed of excess fat

3 garlic cloves, skinned and crushed

60 ml (4 tbsp) wholegrain mustard

30 ml (2 tbsp) olive or vegetable oil

30 ml (2 tbsp) chopped fresh rosemary or 15 ml (1 tbsp) dried

60-90 ml (4-6 tbsp) fresh white breadcrumbs

salt and freshly ground pepper

1 With a sharp, pointed knife, trim the fat off the ends of the cutlets to expose about 5 cm (2 inches) of bone. Place the racks, fat side up, in an oiled roasting tin.
2 Mix the garlic, mustard, oil, rosemary, breadcrumbs and salt and pepper to taste together in a small bowl. Spread this mixture over the lamb fat to cover it evenly.
3 Roast in the oven at 160°C Circotherm for 25 minutes for pink lamb, 35 minutes for medium and 45 minutes for well done.
4 Transfer the racks to a carving dish or board, leave to stand for 10-15 minures at room temperature, then carve into individual cutlets.

MUSTARD-COATED LEG OF LAMB
SERVES 6

75 ml (5 tbsp) Dijon mustard

5 ml (1 tsp) dried rosemary

2 garlic cloves, skinned and crushed

15 ml (1 tbsp) soy sauce

salt and freshly ground pepper

15 ml (1 tbsp) olive or vegetable oil

1.8 kg (4 lb) leg of lamb

300 ml (½ pint) lamb or beef stock

1 Put the mustard, rosemary, garlic, soy sauce, salt and pepper in a bowl and mix well together.
2 Gradually whisk in the oil, drop by drop, to make a thick creamy consistency.
3 Spread the mustard mixture all over the lamb and put in a large shallow dish. Cover and marinate in the refrigerator for 6-8 hours.
4 Put lamb fat side up on a rack in a roasting tin. Roast in the oven at 160°C Circotherm for 1¾-2 hours. Transfer the lamb to a warmed serving dish and keep hot.
5 Pour the stock into the roasting tin and stir to loosen the sediment. Bring to the boil, then simmer, stirring until sauce reduces slightly. Serve the lamb carved into slices, with the sauce handed separately.

SERVING IDEA

With its spicy coating of mustard and soy sauce, *Mustard-coated Leg of Lamb* makes an unusual alternative to an ordinary Sunday joint. Serve with roast potatoes cooked in the oven at the same time, and lightly cooked courgettes or mange tout.

MICROWAVE

Crown Roast of Lamb
Complete steps 1 and 2. To prepare the stuffing, put the butter, onion, celery and apples in a large bowl. Cover and cook on HIGH for 7-8 minutes, until softened. Complete step 3. Cook, uncovered, on HIGH for 10 minutes per 450 g (1 lb). Turn round halfway through cooking. Wrap the crown in foil and stand for 10 minutes before garnishing and serving.

Opposite: Crown Roast of Lamb

COOK'S TIP

Spiced Kidneys with Mushrooms are delicious with chanterelle mushrooms but brown cap or oyster mushrooms are good, too.

MICROWAVE

Lamb and Spinach Lasagne
To cook the spinach in the microwave, put it on a plate or in a bowl, cover and cook on HIGH for 9 minutes.

SERVING IDEA

Lamb and Spinach Lasagne is rich and filling. Serve with a tomato and onion salad dressed with oil, lemon juice and raw onion rings, chopped spring onion or snipped fresh chives.

SPICED KIDNEYS WITH MUSHROOMS
SERVES 8

700 g (1½ lb) lamb's kidneys, skinned
50 g (2 oz) unsalted butter
225 g (8 oz) mushrooms, thickly sliced
30 ml (2 tbsp) green peppercorn mustard (Maille)
15 ml (1 tbsp) wholegrain mustard
dash of Worcestershire sauce
5 ml (1 tsp) anchovy paste or essence
300 ml (½ pint) double cream
salt and freshly ground pepper
chopped fresh parsley, to garnish

1 Halve the kidneys and using scissors, snip out the white cores. Heat the butter in a frying pan until foaming. Add the kidneys in batches and cook briskly until brown. Remove from the pan with a slotted spoon and transfer to a sieve to drain out the bitter juices.

2 Fry the mushrooms in the same pan, stirring occasionally, until just tender, then add to the sieve.

3 Add the mustards, Worcestershire sauce and anchovy paste to the pan. Cook over moderate heat, stirring for 1-2 minutes. Stir in the cream and bring to the boil. Return the kidneys and mushrooms to the pan with any juices. Stir to coat with the sauce and simmer for 5 minutes. Season to taste and transfer to a warm serving dish. Sprinkle with plenty of chopped parsley.

LAMB AND SPINACH LASAGNE
SERVES 6

450 g (1 lb) fresh spinach, washed
30 ml (2 tbsp) vegetable oil
1 medium onion, skinned and chopped
450 g (1 lb) minced lamb
227 g (8 oz) can tomatoes
1 garlic clove, skinned and crushed
30 ml (2 tbsp) chopped fresh mint
5 ml (1 level tsp) ground cinnamon
freshly grated nutmeg
salt and freshly ground pepper
50 g (2 oz) butter or margarine
50 g (2 oz) plain flour
900 ml (1½ pints) milk
150 ml (¼ pint) natural yogurt
12 sheets oven-ready lasagne
175 g (6 oz) Cheddar cheese, grated

1 Put the spinach in a saucepan with only the water that clings to the leaves and cook gently for about 4 minutes. Drain well and chop finely.

2 Heat the oil in a large saucepan, add the onion and fry gently for 5 minutes until softened. Add the lamb and brown well, then drain off all the fat.

3 Stir in the spinach with the tomatoes and their juice, the garlic, mint and cinnamon. Season with nutmeg, salt and pepper to taste. Bring to the boil and simmer, uncovered, for about 15 minutes. Leave to cool while making the white sauce.

4 Melt the butter in a saucepan, add the flour and cook gently, stirring, for 1-2 minutes.

Remove from the heat and gradually blend in the milk. Bring to the boil, stirring constantly, then simmer for 3 minutes until thick and smooth. Add the yogurt and season to taste.

5 Spoon one-third of the meat mixture over the base of a rectangular baking dish.

6 Cover with four sheets of lasagne and spread over one-third of the white sauce. Repeat these layers twice more, finishing with the sauce, which should completely cover the lasagne. Sprinkle the cheese on top.

7 Stand the dish on a baking sheet. Bake in the oven at 160°C Circotherm for about 45-50 minutes or until the top is well browned and bubbling. Serve hot.

Tajine

TAJINE

SERVES 4-6

15 ml (1 tbsp) vegetable oil
30 ml (2 tbsp) butter
1.1 kg (2½ lb) boned leg of lamb, cubed
1 medium onion, skinned and sliced
5 ml (1 level tsp) ground ginger
5 ml (1 level tsp) ground cinnamon
1.25 ml (¼ level tsp) powdered saffron
salt and freshly ground pepper
225 g (8 oz) dried apricots or mixed dried fruit, soaked and stoned if necessary
25 g (1 oz) sesame seeds (optional)
sprigs of mint, to garnish

1 Heat the oil with the butter in a flameproof casserole. Add the lamb, onion, spices and seasoning and stir well to mix. Fry, stirring, over moderate heat until the meat cubes are browned on all sides.

2 Pour enough water into the casserole to just cover the meat, then bring slowly to boiling point, stirring constantly.

3 Cover the casserole with a lid and simmer gently for 1 hour to prevent sticking.

4 Add the dried fruit and stir well to mix with the meat, then continue cooking for a further 30 minutes or until the lamb is tender and the liquid has reduced to a thick sauce.

5 Meanwhile, spread the sesame seeds out in a grill pan, if using, and toast under a moderate grill until they start colouring. Shake the pan constantly to avoid scorching.

6 When the lamb is tender, taste and adjust the seasoning, if necessary. Transfer to a warmed serving dish, garnish with the sesame seeds and sprigs of mint and serve at once.

SERVING IDEA

Serve *Tajine* – a Middle Eastern spiced lamb and fruit casserole – with saffron rice or couscous and a yogurt and cucumber salad.

SERVING IDEA

Serve *Spiced Beef with Horseradish* with Brussels sprouts and mashed potato.

SERVING IDEA

Serve *Bobotie* with boiled rice and crisp poppadoms. Mango chutney and lime pickle also go well with it, and ice-cold beer or lager is the ideal drink.

SPICED BEEF WITH HORSERADISH
SERVES 6

1.1 kg (2½ lb) stewing beef
vegetable oil
450 g (1 lb) onions, skinned and sliced
225 g (8 oz) button mushrooms, wiped
1 garlic clove, crushed
25 g (1 oz) plain flour
2.5 ml (½ level tsp) ground ginger
5 ml (1 level tsp) medium-hot curry powder
5 ml (1 level tsp) dark muscovado sugar
600 ml (1 pint) beef stock
30 ml (2 tbsp) Worcestershire sauce
salt and freshly ground pepper
30 ml (2 level tbsp) creamed horseradish
45 ml (3 tbsp) chopped fresh parsley, to garnish

1 Trim the beef of any excess fat and cut into 5 cm (2 in) pieces.
2 Heat 30 ml (2 tbsp) oil in a 4 litre (7 pint) flameproof casserole. Brown the meat one-third at a time. Drain on absorbent kitchen paper.
3 Lower the heat, add the onions, mushrooms and garlic with another 30 ml (2 tbsp) oil. Sauté, stirring occasionally, for 3-4 minutes. Stir in the flour, spices and sugar and cook, stirring, for a further 1-2 minutes. Add the stock, sauce and seasoning.
4 Return all the meat to the casserole, bring to the boil, then cover and cook at 150°C Circotherm for about 2-2½ hours or until the meat is tender.
5 Stir in the horseradish, adjust the seasoning and sprinkle with parsley.

BOBOTIE
SERVES 4

50 g (2 oz) slice of bread, with the crusts removed
300 ml (½ pint) milk
40 g (1½ oz) butter or margarine
2 medium onions, skinned and finely chopped
1 cooking apple, cored and chopped
15 ml (1 tbsp) mild curry powder
700 g (1½ lb) minced beef
30 ml (2 tbsp) raisins
25 g (1 oz) flaked almonds
15 ml (1 tbsp) lemon juice
salt and freshly ground pepper
2 bay leaves
3 eggs

1 Put the bread in a bowl, pour in the milk, and leave to soak. Meanwhile, melt the butter in a saucepan, add the onions and fry for about 5 minutes until beginning to soften. Add the apple and curry powder and fry, stirring, for a further 2-3 minutes.
2 Turn the onion mixture into a bowl, add the meat, raisins, almonds and lemon juice and season to taste with salt and pepper. Mix until well combined.
3 Squeeze the milk from the bread, reserving the milk, and stir the bread into the meat mixture.
4 Place the bay leaves on the bottom of a 1.8 litre (3½ pint) pie dish. Fill with the meat and bread mixture.

5 Whisk the eggs together with the reserved milk and pour over the meat, stirring gently to distribute the custard mixture.

6 Bake in the oven at 160°C Circotherm for 1 hour 10 minutes or until the custard has set and the top browned. Serve hot.

BOEUF À LA BOURGUIGNONNE
SERVES 6

225 g (8 oz) piece of streaky bacon
30 ml (2 tbsp) beef dripping or vegetable oil
1.4 kg (3 lb) chuck steak, trimmed of excess fat and cut into 5 cm (2 inch) cubes
45 ml (3 tbsp) plain flour
salt and freshly ground pepper
1 medium carrot, peeled and diced
1 leek, trimmed and thinly sliced
1 medium onion, skinned and finely chopped
1-2 garlic cloves, skinned and crushed
300 ml (½ pint) red Burgundy wine
750 ml (1¼ pints) beef stock
1 bouquet garni
18 button (pickling) onions, skinned
40 g (1½ oz) butter
30 ml (2 tbsp) olive oil
225 g (8 oz) button mushrooms, wiped and halved or quartered, if large
chopped fresh parsley, to garnish

1 Cut the piece of bacon into thin strips, about 4 cm (1½ inches) long, discarding the rind. Place the strips in a heavy flameproof casserole and heat gently until the fat runs.

2 Increase the heat and fry the bacon strips until they become crisp and golden brown. Remove with a slotted spoon and drain on absorbent kitchen paper.

3 Melt the dripping with the bacon fat in the casserole, add the beef and fry in batches over moderate to high heat until sealed and browned on all sides.

4 Sprinkle in the flour and salt and pepper to taste and continue frying for 2-3 minutes, stirring. Remove with a slotted spoon and drain on absorbent kitchen paper.

5 Lower heat, add the vegetables and garlic and fry gently for about 10 minutes until softened, stirring frequently. Return the bacon and beef to the casserole, pour in the wine and 600 ml (1 pint) of the stock. Bring slowly to the boil. Add the bouquet garni, cover tightly and cook in the oven at 140°C Circotherm for 3 hours or until the meat is very tender.

6 Meanwhile, put the button onions in a heavy-based frying pan with half of the butter and oil and the remaining beef stock. Simmer gently for about 20 minutes until the onions are tender and the liquid absorbed. Shake the pan frequently and watch carefully to make sure that the onions do not catch and burn on the bottom of the pan. Transfer to a plate.

7 Melt the remaining butter and oil together in the frying pan, add the mushrooms and sauté quickly until lightly coloured. Remove from the heat and set aside with the onions.

8 Add the onions and mushrooms to the meat and heat through gently. Taste and adjust the seasoning, then turn into a warmed serving dish. Garnish and serve immediately.

SERVING IDEA

Boeuf à la Bourguignonne is the perfect main course for a dinner party, as it can be made in advance and reheated. It is also easy to double up the quantity for large numbers. In France, it is traditionally served with plain steamed or boiled potatoes, followed by a tossed green salad. Serve with a red Burgundy.

COOK'S TIP

To make a traditional bouquet garni for *Boeuf à la Bourguignonne*, tie a bay leaf, a sprig of parsley, a sprig of thyme and a few peppercorns in a small piece of muslin. Other fresh herbs can be used if these are unavailable.

57

FILET DE BOEUF EN CROÛTE

SERVES 6

1.4 kg (3 lb) fillet of beef
2 garlic cloves, skinned, and cut into thin slivers (optional)
15 g (½ oz) butter
30 ml (2 tbsp) olive oil
30 ml (2 tbsp) brandy
500 g (1 lb 2 oz) ready prepared puff pastry, thawed if frozen
100 g (4 oz) smooth liver pâté
salt and freshly ground pepper
beaten egg, to glaze
15 ml (1 level tbsp) plain flour
450 ml (¾ pint) beef stock
45 ml (3 tbsp) Madeira, port or dry sherry
sprigs of parsley, to garnish

1 Trim any fat off the beef and tie into a neat, regular shape with trussing thread or string.

2 With a sharp pointed knife, make shallow incisions all over the meat at regular intervals. Insert the garlic slivers into the incisions.

3 Melt the butter with the oil in a flameproof casserole. Add the meat and fry over moderate heat until well browned and sealed on all sides, then roast in the oven at 170°C Circotherm for 15 minutes.

4 Warm the brandy in a small separate pan or a ladle. Remove the meat from the oven, pour over the brandy and ignite.

5 When the flames have died down, lift the meat out of the casserole and set aside on a plate until cold. Reserve the juices in the casserole for the gravy.

6 Meanwhile, roll out the pastry on a lightly floured surface to a rectangle measuring 45 × 30 cm (18 × 12 inches).

7 Remove the thread or string from the cold meat. Soften the pâté with a knife, then spread over the top and sides of the meat. Sprinkle with salt and pepper.

8 Place the meat on the pastry, pâté side down. Wrap the pastry around the meat, sealing the joins with water.

9 Invert the meat and place join side down on a dampened baking sheet. Decorate with any left-over pastry trimmings, sticking them on with water. Brush all over the pastry with beaten egg.

10 Bake in the oven at 170°C Circotherm for 55 minutes if you like beef pink or 1 hour 10 minutes for well done.

11 Meanwhile, make the gravy. Add the flour to the casserole, then gradually add the stock, reserved cooking liquid and Madeira, stirring. Bring to the boil, stirring to scrape up any sediment in the pan. Boil until reduced slightly, then remove from the heat and taste and adjust the seasoning, if necessary.

12 At the end of the cooking time, turn off the oven and leave the meat to 'rest' for 15 minutes before serving. Reheat the gravy at the last moment and pour into a sauceboat. Transfer the fillet in pastry to a serving plate and garnish with sprigs of parsley. Carve the meat at the table.

SERVING IDEA

Serve *Filet de Boeuf en Croûte* with classic French accompaniments such as *French Beans in Soured Cream with Paprika* (see page 106).

Opposite: Filet de Boeuf en Croûte

BRAISED BEEF

——— SERVES 6 ———

1.4 kg (3 lb) piece of silverside
2 carrots, peeled
2 parsnips, peeled
3 celery sticks
2 small turnips, peeled
2 medium onions, skinned
30 ml (2 tbsp) vegetable oil or dripping
75 g (3 oz) streaky bacon rashers, rinded
1 bay leaf
salt and freshly ground pepper
300 ml (½ pint) beef stock
300 ml (½ pint) cider
15 g (½ oz) butter
15 ml (1 level tbsp) plain flour
chopped fresh parsley, to garnish (optional)

Braised Beef

1 Tie up the meat to form a neat joint. Cut the carrots and parsnips into slices about 1 cm (½ inch) thick, halving them if large. Cut the celery and turnips into similar-sized pieces. Cut the onions in half and slice thickly.

2 Heat the oil in a deep 3.4 litre (6 pint) flame-proof casserole. Chop the bacon, add to the pan and fry until beginning to brown. Remove with a slotted spoon and reserve.

3 Reheat the oil in the casserole for a few seconds. Add the meat and fry until browned all over, then remove from the casserole and set aside.

4 Add the vegetables to the casserole and fry over high heat. Return the bacon to the casserole, add the bay leaf and plenty of salt and pepper.

5 Place the joint in the centre of the bed of vegetables. Pour in the stock and cider and bring to the boil. Fit a piece of foil over the meat and vegetables to form a 'tent' then cover with a close-fitting lid.

6 Cook the joint in the oven 150°C Circo-therm for about 2 hours. Halfway through the cooking time, turn the joint over and re-cover firmly. Test the meat after 2 hours; if it is done, a fine skewer will glide easily and smoothly into the joint.

7 Lift the joint on to a board and cut into slices no more than 0.5 cm (¼ inch) thick. Remove the vegetables from the casserole with a slotted spoon and place on a shallow serving dish. Arrange the meat over the vegetables, cover with foil and place in a low oven.

8 Knead together the butter and flour. Skim off

the excess fat from the cooking juices, then stir in pieces of the butter and flour.

9 Place the casserole on top of the hob and bring to the boil, stirring. Boil rapidly until reduced and thickened, then taste and adjust the seasoning. Spoon a little gravy over the meat and sprinkle with parsley, if wished. Serve the remaining gravy separately in a sauceboat.

ROAST BEEF WITH YORKSHIRE PUDDING
— SERVES 6 —

1.4 kg (3 lb) boned and rolled sirloin rib, rump or topside
50 g (2 oz) beef dripping (optional)
freshly ground pepper
5 ml (1 level tsp) mustard powder
125 g (4 oz) plain flour
pinch of salt
1 egg
200 ml (7 fl oz) milk
25 g (1 oz) lard or dripping or 30 ml (2 tbsp) vegetable oil
300 ml (½ pint) hot stock or vegetable water

1 Weigh the meat and calculate the cooking time, allowing 15 minutes per 450 g (1 lb) plus 15 minutes for rare beef, 20 minutes per 450 g (1 lb) plus 20 minutes for medium beef or 25 minutes per 450 g (1 lb) plus 25 minutes for well-done.

2 Put the meat into a shallow roasting tin, preferably on a grid, with the thickest layer of fat uppermost and the cut sides exposed to the heat. Smear with dripping if the meat is lean. Grind pepper all over the meat and sprinkle with the mustard powder.

3 Roast the joint in the oven at 160°C Circotherm for the calculated time, basting occasionally with the juices from the tin. Forty-five minutes before the end of the cooking time, cover the joint with foil and place on the bottom shelf of the oven. Increase the oven temperature to 180°C Circotherm.

4 While the beef is cooking, make the Yorkshire pudding. Mix the flour and salt in a bowl, make a well in the centre and break in the egg.

5 Add half of the milk and, using a wooden spoon, gradually work in the flour. Beat the mixture until smooth, then add the remaining milk and 100 ml (3½ fl oz) water. Beat until well mixed, then leave to stand for 45 minutes.

6 Put the fat in a small roasting or other baking tin and place in the oven for about 15 minutes until the fat shows a haze.

7 Pour in the batter and return to the oven to cook for 40-45 minutes, until risen and golden brown. Do not open the oven door for 30 minutes.

8 After 30 minutes, transfer the meat to a serving dish, cover and place on the lowest shelf in the oven. Pour the fat from the roasting tin, leaving the sediment behind. Pour in the stock and stir to scrape up the sediment. Place the tin on top of the hob, bring to the boil, stirring, then simmer for 2-3 minutes. Season to taste. Serve with the meat and Yorkshire pudding.

COOK'S TIP

When making the Yorkshire pudding for *Roast Beef with Yorkshire Pudding*, it is very important that the fat is really hot before the batter is poured into the tin. The tin with the fat in can be put on the floor of the oven while the meat is cooking until the fat shows a haze. If preferred, the meat can be covered with foil and placed on the floor of the oven while the Yorkshire pudding is cooking.

61

SERVING IDEA

Keema Curry with Peas is very quick to prepare. Serve it for an informal supper party with parathas or puris (there are excellent packet mixes available), mango chutney and lime pickle.

COOK'S TIP

Ghee is clarified butter, which is available from Asian stores or you can make your own (see Cook's Tip, page 78).

KEEMA CURRY WITH PEAS

SERVES 4

45 ml (3 tbsp) ghee or butter
1 medium onion, skinned and finely chopped
1-2 garlic cloves, skinned and crushed
700 g (1½ lb) minced beef
4 medium tomatoes, skinned and roughly chopped
15 ml (1 level tbsp) tomato purée
20 ml (4 level tsp) ground coriander
10 ml (2 level tsp) ground cumin
7.5 ml (1½ level tsp) ground fenugreek
2.5 ml (½ tsp) chilli powder
5 ml (1 level tsp) salt
350 g (12 oz) frozen peas
juice of ½ lemon
45 ml (3 tbsp) chopped fresh coriander
10 ml (2 tsp) garam masala
150 ml (¼ pint) natural yogurt

1 Heat the ghee in a heavy-based saucepan, add the onion and garlic and fry gently for about 5 minutes until soft and lightly coloured

2 Add the minced beef in batches and fry until browned, pressing the meat with a wooden spoon to remove any lumps.

3 Add the tomatoes, tomato purée, coriander, cumin, fenugreek, chilli powder and salt and stir well to mix. Pour in 300 ml (½ pint) water and bring to the boil, stirring. Lower the heat, cover and simmer for 30 minutes.

4 Pour 150 ml (¼ pint) water into the pan and bring to the boil. Add the peas, cover the pan and simmer for a further 10 minutes or until the peas are just tender.

5 Remove the curry mixture from the heat and stir in the lemon juice, fresh coriander and garam masala. Cover the pan and leave to stand for 5 minutes. Stir the yogurt into the curry and serve immediately.

STEAK AU POIVRE

SERVES 4

30 ml (2 tbsp) black peppercorns
4 sirloin, rump or fillet steaks, about 100-175 g (4-6 oz) each and 2.5 cm (1 inch) thick
25 g (1 oz) butter
15 ml (1 tbsp) olive or vegetable oil
30 ml (2 tbsp) brandy
150 ml (¼ pint) double cream
salt

1 Crush the peppercorns coarsely using a pestle and mortar, or on a board with a rolling pin.

2 Trim the steaks, then place the steaks on the peppercorn mixture. Press hard to encrust the surface of the meat. Turn over and repeat with the other side.

3 Melt the butter with the oil in a frying pan, add the steaks and fry until sealed on all sides. Reduce the heat and continue cooking for 7-10 minutes or until cooked to your liking.

4 Remove the steaks from the pan and keep warm. Stir the brandy into the pan, remove from the heat and set it alight. Keep the pan off the heat until the flames have died down.

5 Stir in cream, add salt to taste, then return to the heat and reheat gently. Pour over the steaks and serve immediately.

SIRLOIN STEAKS WITH MUSTARD

— SERVES 4 —

50 g (2 oz) wholegrain mustard

15 g (½ oz) plain flour

4 sirloin steaks, about 175 g (6 oz) each

30 ml (2 tbsp) chopped fresh parsley

30 ml (2 tbsp) chopped fresh thyme

1 Mix together the wholegrain mustard and the flour, then spread a quarter of the mixture on top of each of the steaks.

2 Line a grill pan with foil, sprinkle with herbs and put the steaks on top. Grill for 5-15 minutes, turning them frequently until the steaks are cooked to taste (see the chart on the right). Serve at once.

COOKING TIMES FOR STEAKS

(Total in Minutes)

Thickness	2 cm (¾ in)	2.5 cm (1 in)	4 cm (1½ ins)
Rare	5	6-7	10
Medium rare	9-10	10	12-14
Well done	12-15	15	18-20

Sirloin Steaks with Mustard

Serve *Osso Bucco* for an informal supper party. *Avocado with Prawns and Smoked Salmon* (see page 18) would make a good first course, with *Exotic Fruit Salad* (see page 131) to finish the meal. In Milan, *Osso Bucco* itself is traditionally accompanied by *Risotto alla Milanese* (see page 119), a deliciously creamy rice dish made from Italian Arborio rice, chicken or beef stock, butter, onion and grated Parmesan cheese. Follow with a crisp green salad to refresh the palate before serving the dessert.

SERVING IDEA

Paupiettes de Veau can be prepared up to the cooking stage (step 4) up to 24 hours in advance. Serve them with a special potato dish such as *Crispy Potato Galette* (see page 118), and steamed green vegetables. Look for varieties of baby vegetables such as baby savoy cabbage and baby cauliflowers.

64   *Opposite: Paupiettes de Veau*

OSSO BUCCO
SERVES 4

1.75 kg (3½ lb) veal knuckle (veal shin, hind cut), sawn into 5 cm (2 inch) lengths
50 g (2 oz) plain flour
salt and freshly ground pepper
25 g (1 oz) butter
30 ml (2 tbsp) olive oil
1 medium onion, skinned and very finely chopped
1 medium carrot, peeled and very finely chopped
1 celery stick, trimmed and very finely chopped
2 garlic cloves, skinned and crushed
2 canned anchovy fillets
300 ml (½ pint) dry white wine
300 ml (½ pint) veal stock
30 ml (2 tbsp) tomato purée
thinly pared rind and juice of 1 lemon
10 ml (2 tsp) chopped fresh marjoram or 5ml (1 tsp) dried
1 bay leaf
45 ml (3 tbsp) chopped fresh parsley
finely grated rind of 1 lemon

1 Coat the pieces of veal in the flour seasoned with salt and pepper. Melt the butter with the oil in a large flameproof casserole, add the veal a few pieces at a time and fry over moderate heat until browned on all sides. Remove with a slotted spoon and set aside to drain on absorbent kitchen paper.

2 Lower the heat, add the chopped vegetables to the casserole with half of the garlic and fry gently for about 10 minutes, stirring frequently. Add the anchovies and stir to combine.

3 Add the wine, stock, tomato purée, pared lemon rind and juice, marjoram and bay leaf. Bring to the boil, stirring, then return the veal to the casserole.

4 Cover the pan tightly and simmer for 1½-2 hours, turning the veal occasionally and basting with the sauce.

5 Remove the veal with a slotted spoon and arrange on a warmed serving dish or plate. Discard the pared lemon rind and bay leaf and taste and adjust seasoning.

6 Mix the remaining garlic with the parsley and grated lemon rind. Spoon the sauce over the pieces of veal and sprinkle each one with the garlic, parsley and lemon mixture. Serve immediately.

PAUPIETTES DE VEAU
SERVES 4

4 veal escalopes, about 100 g (4 oz) each
100 g (4 oz) butter
1 medium onion, skinned and finely chopped
175 g (6 oz) cooked ham, chopped
finely grated rind and juice of ½ lemon
50 g (2 oz) fresh breadcrumbs
15 ml (1 tbsp) chopped fresh parsley and marjoram or 5 ml (1 tsp) dried
salt and freshly ground pepper
1 egg, beaten
150 ml (¼ pint) dry white wine
15 ml (1 level tbsp) plain flour
chopped fresh parsley

1 Place each veal escalope between two sheets of damp greaseproof paper and bat out thinly with a rolling pin.

2 Melt 40 g (1½ oz) of the butter in a frying pan, add the onion and cook over gentle heat for about 10 minutes until soft but not coloured. In a bowl, mix together the ham, half of the lemon rind and juice, the breadcrumbs, herbs and salt and pepper to taste. Mix in the onion and beaten egg.

3 Spread the stuffing over the pieces of veal and roll up. Tie each roll with thin string.

4 Melt another 40 g (1½ oz) of the butter in a shallow flameproof casserole. When foaming, add the paupiettes and brown them quickly all over. Pour in the wine and 150 ml (¼ pint) water, the remaining lemon rind and juice and salt and pepper to taste. Cover the casserole and simmer gently for 25-30 minutes until the meat is tender.

5 When the paupiettes are cooked, lift them out of the casserole and place on a serving dish. Carefully remove the string, cover and keep warm while making the sauce.

6 Put the flour and the remaining butter on a small plate and work to a paste called a beurre manié. Bring cooking liquid to the boil, then gradually whisk in the beurre manié to thicken the sauce slightly. Taste and adjust seasoning.

7 Pour the sauce over the paupiettes and garnish them with the chopped fresh parsley. Serve immediately.

LOIN OF PORK WITH FRUIT STUFFING

──────── SERVES 8 ────────

1.8 kg (4 lb) loin of pork, boned
10 ml (2 level tsp) ground allspice
salt and freshly ground pepper
4 garlic cloves, skinned
150 g (5 oz) mixed dried fruit (e.g. pears, prunes, apricots, figs)
50 g (2 oz) fresh cranberries or frozen cranberries, thawed
300 ml (½ pint) full-bodied red wine
2-3 bay leaves
30 ml (2 tbsp) bottled cranberry sauce
fresh bay leaves, to garnish

1 Lay the meat flat, fat side down. Slice lengthways, two-thirds through the thick side of the 'eye' of the meat.
2 Open up the joint like a book. Rub the allspice into the flesh, with salt and pepper to taste.
3 Cut the garlic cloves into thin slivers, then place at regular intervals along the length of the meat. Chop the dried fruit finely, mix with the cranberries, then place on top of the garlic on the pork joint.
4 Form the joint into a roll and tie at close intervals. Weigh the joint and calculate the cooking time, allowing 35 minutes per 450 g (1 lb) plus 35 minutes. Put the joint in a large flameproof casserole or roasting tin and place over moderate heat. Fry the joint in its own fat until browned on all sides, then pour in the wine. Add the bay leaves and seasoning.
5 Bring to the boil, then cover and cook in the oven at 140°C Circotherm for the calculated cooking time. Baste frequently and turn the joint round in the liquid every 30 minutes.
6 Place the joint on a warmed serving dish and leave to stand in a warm place for 15 minutes before carving. Transfer the casserole or tin to the top of the hob. Discard the bay leaves, then boil the cooking liquid to reduce slightly. Stir in the cranberry sauce and heat through, then pour into a gravy boat or jug. Slice the pork and garnish with fresh bay leaves.

FILET DE PORC CHASSEUR

──────── SERVES 6 ────────

1 kg (2¼ lb) pork fillet or tenderloin
vegetable oil for frying
65 g (2½ oz) butter
2 medium onions, skinned and chopped
225 g (8 oz) button mushrooms
30 ml (2 tbsp) plain flour
300 ml (½ pint) beef stock
150 ml (¼ pint) dry white wine
salt and freshly ground pepper
twelve 1 cm (½ inch) slices of French bread
chopped fresh parsley, to garnish

1 Cut the pork fillet into bite-sized pieces. Heat 30 ml (2 tbsp) of the oil in a frying pan, add the pork and brown quickly. Transfer to a casserole.
2 Melt 50 g (2 oz) of the butter in the frying pan, add the onions and fry for 5 minutes.
3 Add the mushrooms to the pan, increase the heat and fry for 1-2 minutes, tossing constantly.

SERVING IDEA

Filet de Porc Chasseur is an excellent main course for a dinner party. The garnish of French bread slices is an unusual serving idea, which makes the dish quite substantial. Suitable vegetable accompaniments would be mange tout, courgettes or French beans.

Remove with a slotted spoon and place over the meat in the casserole.

4 Blend the flour into the juices in the pan, with the remaining butter. Cook, stirring, for 1-2 minutes, then gradually blend in the stock, wine and salt and pepper. Simmer for 2-3 minutes. Pour into the casserole.

5 Cover and cook in the oven at 150°C Circotherm for about 45 minutes or until the pork fillet is tender.

6 Meanwhile, heat a little oil in a frying pan, add the French bread slices and fry until golden brown on each side. Drain well on absorbent kitchen paper.

7 Serve the pork hot, sprinkled liberally with chopped fresh parsley and garnished with the French bread.

PORK WITH PEPPERCORNS

——— SERVES 6 ———

30 ml (2 tbsp) fresh green peppercorns or dried black peppercorns
6 large pork chops
50 g (2 oz) butter or margarine
30 ml (2 level tbsp) plain flour
90 ml (6 tbsp) dry sherry
300 ml (½ pint) pineapple juice
salt
12 cooked prunes, drained and stoned
sprig of parsley, to garnish

1 If using dried peppercorns, crush in a pestle and mortar. Trim the chops of excess fat and brown well in the hot butter in a frying pan.

Pork with Peppercorns

Place side by side in a shallow ovenproof dish.

2 Stir flour into pan with sherry, pineapple juice, peppercorns and salt and bring to the boil. Stir in the prunes and spoon over the chops. Cover the dish tightly and cook in the oven at 160°C Circotherm for 50 minutes. Garnish with parsley and serve.

67

Serve *Lemon-roasted Pork with Garlic and Basil* with the rich potato dish *Swiss Chalet Potatoes with Cream and Cheese* (see page 112), which complements the flavour of the lamb, and could be prepared the night before.

LEMON-ROASTED PORK WITH GARLIC AND BASIL

SERVES 4

12 garlic cloves, peeled
2 pork fillets, about 350 g (12 oz) each
grated rind and juice of 2 lemons
90 ml (6 tbsp) chopped fresh basil or parsley
salt and freshly ground pepper
2-3 fresh bay leaves
30 ml (2 tbsp) vegetable oil
sautéed shallots, to serve
fresh herbs, bay leaves and lemon slices, to garnish

1 Blanch the garlic cloves in boiling water for 2 minutes.

2 Trim pork of excess fat. Make a deep cut lengthways into each fillet and open out flat. Sprinkle on the lemon rind and basil. Cut any large garlic cloves in half. Lay them evenly down the middle of each fillet and season.

3 Close the fillets and tie loosely at 2.5 cm (1 inch) intervals with string. Place in a shallow non-metallic dish with the bay leaves and the strained juice of all the lemons. Cover and marinate in the refrigerator overnight.

4 Remove the pork and reserve the marinade. Heat the oil in a saute pan and brown the meat. Transfer to a shallow roasting tin with the marinade. Season to taste with salt and pepper, then cook in the oven at 170°C Circotherm for 35 minutes, basting frequently.

5 Serve the pork sliced on a bed of sautéed shallots. Garnish with herbs, bay leaves and lemon slices.

PORK AND HERB BEAN POT

SERVES 8

275 g (10 oz) pinto, black-eye or white haricot beans
550 g (1¼ lb) boned leg of pork
550 g (1¼ lb) fresh pork streaky rashers
225 g (8 oz) garlic sausage, cut in one piece
vegetable oil
25 g (1 oz) butter or margarine
450 g (1 lb) onions, sliced
3 sticks celery, sliced
2 garlic cloves, crushed
30 ml (2 tbsp) each chopped fresh thyme and rosemary or 10 ml (2 tsp) dried
30 ml (2 tbsp) chopped fresh parsley
397 g (14 oz) can chopped tomatoes
salt and pepper
750 ml (1¼ pints) light stock
4 juniper berries, lightly crushed
175 g (6 oz) fresh wholemeal breadcrumbs

1 Soak the beans overnight in cold water.

2 Trim the boned pork of any excess fat and cut into 4 cm (1½ inch) pieces. Cut the rind and any excess fat from the pork streaky rashers, then thickly slice the flesh. Cut the garlic sausage into similar-sized pieces.

3 Heat 15 ml (1 tbsp) oil and the butter in a 5.1 litre (9 pint) deep, flameproof casserole. Sauté the pork pieces and the bacon, about one-third at a time, until golden brown. Remove and drain on absorbent kitchen paper.

4 Lower the heat and add the onions, celery and garlic with a little more oil if necessary.

Sauté, stirring continuously, for 3-4 minutes until the vegetables are beginning to soften.

5 Set aside about half of the chopped herbs. Drain the beans and spoon one-third in a layer over the vegetables. Add a layer of pork and garlic sausage, a layer of the remaining herbs and a layer of chopped tomatoes. Continue until all the beans, pork and garlic sausage, herbs and tomatoes have been used. Season the stock slightly and stir in with the juniper berries; pour into the casserole. Bring slowly to the boil, cover and cook at 150°C Circotherm for 2 hours.

6 Mix together the breadcrumbs and reserved herbs and sprinkle over the casserole. Leave uncovered and cook in the oven at 170°C Circotherm for 30 minutes until the breadcrumbs are golden and the meat and beans tender.

RICOTTA CHEESE AND HAM PIE
SERVES 4-6

225 g (8 oz) Shortcrust Pastry, made with 225 g (8 oz) flour (see page 189)
beaten egg, to glaze and seal
175 g (6 oz) ricotta or cottage cheese
175 g (6 oz) curd or cream cheese
50 g (2 oz) Parmesan or Romano cheese, grated
225 g (8 oz) cooked ham, diced
2 eggs
2.5 ml (½ tsp) dried oregano
salt and freshly ground pepper

1 Roll out two-thirds of the pastry to a 25 cm (10 inch) circle, about 0.3 cm (⅛ inch) thick.

2 Line a 20.5 cm (8 inch) spring-release cake

Ricotta Cheese and Ham Pie

tin with the pastry circle. Trim the pastry to the top edge of the tin and brush it with some of the beaten egg to glaze.

3 Put the cheeses in a bowl with the ham, eggs and oregano and season to taste. Mix well.

4 Spoon the mixture into the pastry case and fold the edges over the filling. Brush with more beaten egg to glaze.

5 Roll out the remaining pastry to a 20.5 cm (8 inch) circle and cut a decorative design in it if you wish. Place it over the filling, sealing the edge by pressing lightly on to the pastry below. Brush the top with the remaining beaten egg.

6 Bake in the oven at 160°C Circotherm for 1 hour or until a knife inserted in the centre comes out clean. Leave to cool completely.

VARIATION

Add 450 g (1 lb) packet frozen chopped spinach, thawed and squeezed dry, to the filling mixture.

SERVING IDEA

Ricotta Cheese and Ham Pie makes an excellent summer lunch dish. The flavour of the different cheeses is quite strong, so salad accompaniments should have definite flavours. Fennel, chicory and spring onions will all hold their own against the sharpness of the cheese. Serve with a robust red wine such as a Chianti or Valpolicella.

HONEY AND MUSTARD-GLAZED GAMMON

SERVES 8-10

1.8 kg (4 lb) middle gammon joint
450 g (1 lb) mixed dried fruit
juice of 1 orange
juice of 1 lemon
10 ml (2 tsp) ground mixed spice
60 ml (4 tbsp) honey
15 ml (1 tbsp) French mustard

Honey and Mustard-glazed Gammon

1 Weigh the gammon and calculate the cooking time, allowing 25 minutes per 450 g (1 lb), plus 25 minutes. Put the gammon in a large saucepan and cover with cold water. Bring slowly to the bowl, then drain off the water.

2 Cover the gammon with fresh cold water. Add the dried fruit, fruit juices and mixed spice and bring slowly to the boil again. Lower the heat, cover and simmer for half the calculated cooking time. Discard the cooking liquid, reserving the dried fruit.

3 Transfer the gammon to a roasting tin. Cover and roast at 160°C Circotherm for the other half of the calculated cooking time.

4 Strip off the skin. Mix together the honey and mustard and spread over the exposed fat of the gammon. Increase the oven temperature to 180°C Circotherm and roast for 10-15 minutes until well glazed, basting the gammon every 5 minutes. Remove the gammon from the oven and leave until completely cold, basting from time to time while it is cooling.

5 Place the gammon on a serving platter and surround with the reserved dried fruit, sliced if necessary. Serve cold.

VARIATIONS

Decorate the gammon with a few halved Maraschino cherries, securing each one with a long-stemmed clove.

Garnish with salad and some of the dried fruit, if preferred.

CHICKEN WITH COCONUT AND CORIANDER

SERVES 4

50 g (2 oz) creamed coconut
1 garlic clove, skinned and crushed
30 ml (2 tbsp) lemon juice
15 ml (1 tbsp) vegetable oil
10 ml (2 level tsp) each ground coriander and cumin
salt and freshly ground pepper
1 bunch spring onions
60 ml (4 tbsp) chopped fresh coriander
8 boneless chicken thighs, about 550 g (1¼ lb) total weight
slices of lemon and lime
mixed long-grain, white and wild rice, to serve

1 Chop the coconut and dissolve in 200 ml (7 fl oz) boiling water. Mix in the garlic, lemon juice, oil and spices and season to taste with salt and pepper. Cool.

2 Finely chop the spring onions, reserving the green tops.

3 Open up the chicken thighs and stuff with half the fresh coriander, the chopped onions and seasoning. Reshape. Thread one or two thighs onto each wooden skewer with a slice of lemon and lime. Place in a shallow non-metallic dish. Pour over the coconut mixture, cover and marinate in the refrigerator overnight.

4 Place the chicken on the wire rack over the roasting tin and cook on 190°C Circotherm for about 35 minutes, basting with remaining marinade until cooked.

5 Stir the remaining coriander, snipped onion tops and plenty of seasoning through the cooked rice to serve with the chicken.

CHICKEN THIGHS WITH WATERCRESS AND ORANGE

SERVES 4

8 chicken thighs, about 800 g (1¾ lb) total weight
15 ml (1 level tbsp) plain flour
1 small bunch watercress
3 oranges
about 30 ml (2 tbsp) vegetable oil
225 g (8 oz) onion, thinly sliced
300 ml (½ pint) chicken stock
salt and freshly ground pepper

1 Toss the chicken thighs in the flour. Rinse, drain and finely chop the watercress. Peel and slice two of the oranges. Cover.

2 Heat the oil in a shallow flameproof casserole. Add the chicken and lightly brown. Remove from the pan.

3 Stir the onion into the pan, adding a little more oil if necessary. Fry gently until golden. Add the watercress and stir over a moderate heat for 1-2 minutes.

4 Replace the chicken, add the stock with the grated rind of the remaining orange and 75 ml (5 tbsp) juice. Season, then cover and simmer for 20-25 minutes until the chicken is tender.

5 Stir in the oranges slices and simmer for 1-2 minutes. Adjust the seasoning and serve.

COOK'S TIP

The method of cooking *Chicken with Coconut and Coriander* is called thermo grilling, and is ideal for small pieces of meat as it ensures they cook evenly on all sides without having to be turned over during cooking.

71

Opposite: Middle Eastern Stuffed Chicken; Normandy Chicken

NORMANDY CHICKEN
SERVES 4

30 ml (2 tbsp) vegetable oil
40 g (1½ oz) butter
4 chicken portions
6 eating apples
salt and freshly ground pepper
300 ml (½ pint) dry cider
60 ml (4 tbsp) Calvados
60 ml (4 tbsp) double cream (optional)

1 Heat the oil with 25 g (1 oz) of the butter in a large flameproof casserole. Add the chicken portions and fry over moderate heat until golden brown on all sides. Remove from the pan and drain on absorbent kitchen paper.
2 Peel two apples, core and slice them and two more apples. Add to pan and fry gently, tossing constantly, until lightly coloured.
3 Return the chicken portions to the pan, placing them on top of the apples. Sprinkle with salt and pepper to taste, then pour in the cider. Bring to the boil, then cover and cook in the oven at 160°C Circotherm for 45 minutes or until the chicken portions are tender.
4 Meanwhile, peel, core and slice the remaining apples. Melt the 15 g (½ oz) butter in a frying pan, add the apple slices and toss to coat in the fat. Fry until lightly coloured, then spoon them over the chicken.
5 Warm the Calvados gently in a ladle or small pan, then ignite and pour over the chicken and apples. Serve as soon as the flames have died down, drizzled with cream, if liked.

MIDDLE EASTERN STUFFED CHICKEN
SERVES 6

75 g (3 oz) butter
1 small onion, skinned and finely chopped
1-2 garlic clove, skinned and crushed
50 g (2 oz) blanched almonds, roughly chopped
50 g (2 oz) long-grain rice
salt and freshly ground pepper
50 g (2 oz) stoned prunes, chopped
50 g (2 oz) dried apricots, chopped
2.5 ml (½ level tsp) ground cinnamon
1.8 kg (4 lb) chicken

1 Melt one-third of the butter in a heavy-based saucepan, add the onion and garlic and fry gently until soft and lightly coloured. Add the almonds and fry until turning colour, then add the rice and stir fry until the grains become opaque and well coated in butter.
2 Pour 150 ml (¼ pint) water over the rice (it will bubble furiously), then add salt and pepper to taste. Cover and simmer for 15 minutes or until all the water has been absorbed by the rice.
3 Remove the pan from the heat and stir in 25 g (1 oz) butter with the dried fruit and cinnamon. Taste and adjust the seasoning.
4 Stuff the chicken with the rice mixture, then truss with thread or fine string. Brush with the remaining butter and sprinkle liberally with salt and pepper.
5 Roast in the oven at 160°C Circotherm for 2 hours until the chicken is brown and the juices run clear when the thickest part of the thigh is pierced with a skewer. Serve hot.

CHICKEN MARENGO

SERVES 4

4 chicken portions
50 g (2 oz) plain flour
100 ml (4 fl oz) olive oil
50 g (2 oz) butter
1 medium onion, skinned and sliced
30 ml (2 tbsp) brandy
salt and freshly ground pepper
450 g (1 lb) tomatoes, skinned, or 397 g (14 oz) can tomatoes, with their juice
1 garlic clove, skinned and crushed
150 ml (¼ pint) chicken stock
100 g (4 oz) button mushrooms
chopped fresh parsley, to garnish

1 Coat the chicken portions in the flour. Heat the oil in a large frying pan and fry the chicken on both sides for 5-10 minutes until golden brown. Remove from the frying pan and place, skin side up, in a large saucepan or flameproof casserole together with 25 g (1 oz) butter.
2 Add the onion to the oil in the frying pan and cook for 5 minutes until soft.
3 Sprinkle the chicken joints with the brandy and salt and pepper and turn the joints over.
4 Roughly chop the tomatoes. Add to chicken with the onion, garlic and stock. Cover and simmer for 1 hour until chicken is tender.
5 Ten minutes before serving, melt the remaining butter in a pan and cook the mushrooms for about 5 minutes. Drain and add to the chicken.
6 When the chicken joints are cooked, transfer them to a warmed serving dish. If the sauce is too thin, boil briskly to reduce. Spoon sauce over chicken and serve garnished with parsley.

POT ROAST CHICKEN WITH PEPPERS

SERVES 4

15 ml (1 tbsp) olive oil
25 g (1 oz) butter or margarine
1.6 kg (3½ lb) oven-ready chicken
1 red, green and yellow pepper
3 celery sticks
1 whole bulb of garlic
1 lemon
10 ml (2 level tsp) ground paprika
12 black olives
1 or 2 sprigs fresh thyme or rosemary
150 ml (¼ pint) white wine
150 ml (¼ pint) chicken stock
salt and freshly ground pepper
45 ml (3 tbsp) double cream

1 Heat the oil and butter in a medium flameproof casserole over moderate heat. Add the chicken and brown on all sides.
2 Meanwhile, chop the peppers, discarding core and seeds. Roughly slice the celery. Halve the bulb of garlic and the lemon.
3 Lift the chicken out of the casserole and add the peppers and celery with the garlic, lemon and paprika. Stir over a moderate heat for 1-2 minutes.
4 Replace the chicken with the olives and herbs. Pour round the wine and stock and season lightly. Bring to the boil, cover tightly and bake

at 160°C Circotherm for 1-1¼ hours or until the chicken is quite tender.

5 Lift the chicken out of the juices with a slotted spoon and cut into portions. Place on a serving dish together with the vegetables, discarding the garlic, lemon and rosemary sprigs.

6 Add the cream to the juices and bubble down over a moderate heat until slightly thickened. Adjust seasoning. Spoon a little sauce over the chicken. Serve the remaining sauce separately.

MARINATED CHICKEN WITH PEPPERS AND MARJORAM

———— SERVES 2 ————

2 chicken breast fillets, skinned

1 garlic clove, skinned and crushed

10 ml (2 tsp) lemon juice

pinch of sugar

45 ml (3 tbsp) olive or vegetable oil

15 ml (1 tbsp) chopped fresh marjoram or
5 ml (1 tsp) dried

1 small onion, skinned and thinly sliced into rings

salt and freshly ground pepper

1 small red pepper

1 small yellow pepper

50 g (2 oz) black olives, halved and stoned

15 ml (1 tbsp) capers

fresh marjoram, to garnish

1 Cut the chicken breasts into slices, and put in a shallow ovenproof dish.

2 Put the garlic, lemon juice and sugar in a small bowl and blend together. Gradually whisk in the oil. Stir in the marjoram and onion rings

and season to taste with salt and pepper. Pour over the chicken, cover and leave to marinate for at least 30 minutes.

3 Meanwhile, core and seed the peppers and cut into large chunks. Put them in a saucepan, cover with boiling water and bring back to the boil. Drain and add to the chicken with the olives and capers. Cover and bake at 170°C Circotherm for 30 minutes. Serve immediately, garnished with fresh marjoram.

———

VARIATION

Add a 397 g (14 oz) can chopped tomatoes with the olives and capers.

———

Marinated Chicken with Peppers and Marjoram

MICROWAVE

Marinated Chicken with Peppers and Marjoram
Marinate the chicken as before. Meanwhile, cut the peppers into chunks. Put into a shallow dish with 30 ml (2 tbsp) water, cover and cook on HIGH for 5-6 minutes or until the peppers are just soft, stirring occasionally. Drain and set aside. Cook the chicken, covered, on HIGH for 5-6 minutes or until tender, turning once. Add the peppers, olives and capers and cook on HIGH for 1-2 minutes or until heated through, stirring once. Serve immediately, garnished with fresh marjoram.

75

STIR-FRIED CHICKEN WITH VEGETABLES

SERVES 4

1 bunch spring onions
3 celery sticks
1 green pepper
100 g (4 oz) cauliflower florets
2 medium carrots
175 g (6 oz) button mushrooms
4 chicken breast fillets
30 ml (2 tbsp) sesame or vegetable oil
10 ml (2 level tsp) cornflour
30 ml (2 tbsp) dry sherry
15 ml (1 tbsp) soy sauce
15 ml (1 tbsp) hoisin sauce
5 ml (1 level tsp) soft brown sugar
75 g (3 oz) unsalted cashew nuts
salt and freshly ground pepper
sprigs of parsley, to garnish

1 Prepare the vegetables. Trim the spring onions and slice them into thin rings. Trim the celery and slice finely.

2 Halve the green pepper, remove the core and seeds and slice the flesh into thin strips. Divide the cauliflower florets into tiny sprigs.

3 Peel the carrots, then grate into thin slivers using the coarse side of a conical or box grater or cut into matchsticks. Wipe the mushrooms and slice them finely.

4 Skin the chicken and cut into bite-sized strips about 4 cm (1½ inches) long with a sharp knife.

5 Heat the oil in a wok or deep frying pan, add the prepared vegetables and stir fry over brisk heat for 3 minutes. Remove the cooked vegetables with a slotted spoon and set aside.

6 In a jug, mix the cornflour to a paste with the sherry, soy sauce and hoisin sauce, then add the sugar and 150 ml (¼ pint) water.

7 Add the chicken strips to the pan and stir fry over moderate heat until lightly coloured on all sides. Pour the cornflour mixture into the pan and bring to the boil, stirring constantly until thickened.

8 Return the vegetables to the pan. Add the cashew nuts and seasoning to taste, and stir fry for a few minutes more. Serve immediately, garnished with sprigs of parsley.

CATALONIAN CHICKEN

SERVES 4-6

8 chicken joints
50 g (2 oz) plus 25 ml (1½ tbsp) plain flour
salt and freshly ground pepper
45 ml (3 tbsp) vegetable oil
12 button onions, skinned
1 garlic clove, skinned and finely chopped
300 ml (½ pint) chicken stock
30 ml (2 tbsp) white wine (optional)
10 ml (2 tsp) tomato purée
225 g (8 oz) dried chestnuts, soaked overnight
225 g (8 oz) piece chorizo sausage

1 Coat the chicken pieces in the 50 g (2 oz) flour liberally seasoned with salt and pepper.

2 Heat 30 ml (2 tbsp) oil in a frying pan, add the chicken joints and fry until well browned.

Stir-fried Chicken with Vegetables

Remove from pan and drain on absorbent kitchen paper.

3 Add the onions and garlic to the pan and fry for 5 minutes until brown, then place in a 1.5-2 litre (3½-4 pint) casserole.

4 Add the remaining 25 ml (1½ tbsp) flour to the frying pan and stir in the chicken stock, white wine and tomato purée. Bring to simmering point.

5 Place the chicken on top of the onions, add the chestnuts and pour the stock over; season. Cover and cook in the oven at 160°C Circotherm for 1 hour until tender.

6 Cut the sausage into thick slices and add to the chicken 10 minutes before the end of the cooking time.

CHICKEN CORDON BLEU
SERVES 4

4 chicken breast fillets, skinned
4 thin slices of boiled ham
4 thin slices of Gruyère cheese
salt and freshly ground pepper
about 25 g (1 oz) plain flour
1 egg, beaten
75 g (3 oz) dried white breadcrumbs
60 ml (4 tbsp) vegetable oil
50 g (2 oz) butter
lemon twists and sprigs of fresh herbs, to garnish

1 Slit along one long edge of each chicken breast, then carefully work the knife to the opposite edge, using a sawing action.

2 Open out the chicken breast, place between two sheets of damp greaseproof paper or cling film and beat with a meat bat or rolling pin to flatten slightly.

3 Place a slice of ham on top of each piece of chicken, then a slice of Gruyère cheese. Fold the chicken fillet over to completely enclose the ham and cheese.

4 Pound the open edge of the parcels so that they stay together, then secure with wooden cocktail sticks.

5 Sprinkle the chicken parcels with salt and pepper to taste, then coat lightly in flour. Dip in the beaten egg, then in the breadcrumbs. Press the breadcrumbs on firmly so that they adhere evenly and completely coat the chicken. Refrigerate for about 30 minutes.

6 Heat oil and butter together in a large heavy-based frying pan (you may need to use two if the chicken parcels are large), then fry the chicken for 10 minutes on each side until crisp and golden. Drain on absorbent kitchen paper, remove the cocktail sticks, then arrange the chicken on a warmed serving platter and garnish with lemon and herbs.

SERVING IDEA

Crunchy on the outside, meltingly delicious on the inside, *Chicken Cordon Bleu* goes well with vegetables such as mushrooms, or French beans, spinach, courgettes and mange tout.

77

SERVING IDEA

Serve *Spiced Chicken with Cashew Nuts* for an informal dinner party with buttered noodles or rice and a vegetable dish such as courgettes and mushrooms tossed together in garlic butter.

COOK'S TIP

In a traditional Indian cookery, ghee is often used to fry foods, as in *Spiced Chicken with Cashew Nuts*. The advantage of using ghee rather than other fats is that it can be heated to a higher temperature without catching and burning, and at the same time it gives a good flavour. You can buy ghee (which is clarified butter) from Asian stores, or make your own clarified butter by heating 225 g (8 oz) unsalted butter in a pan until it melts. Simmer until clear and a creamy residue settles in the base of the pan. Remove from the heat, spoon off the foam on top and leave to cool. Strain off the clear fat (ghee) from the top and discard the residue.

SPICED CHICKEN WITH CASHEW NUTS

SERVES 8

8 chicken breast fillets, skinned
15 g (½ oz) root ginger, peeled and roughly chopped
5 ml (1 tsp) coriander seeds
4 cloves
10 ml (2 tsp) black peppercorns
300 ml (½ pint) natural yogurt
1 medium onion, skinned and roughly chopped
50 g (2 oz) cashew nuts
2.5 ml (½ level tsp) chilli powder
10 ml (2 level tsp) turmeric
40 g (1½ oz) ghee or clarified butter
salt
cashew nuts, chopped and toasted, and chopped fresh coriander, to garnish

1 Make shallow slashes across each of the chicken breasts.

2 Put the ginger in a blender or food processor with the coriander seeds, cloves, peppercorns and natural yogurt and process until the ingredients are blended to a paste.

3 Pour the yogurt mixture over the chicken, cover and marinate in the refrigerator for about 24 hours, turning the chicken once.

4 Put the onion in a blender or food processor with the cashew nuts, chilli powder, turmeric and 150 ml (¼ pint) water. Blend to a paste.

5 Lift the chicken out of the marinade. Heat the ghee or butter in a large sauté pan, add the chicken pieces and fry until the pieces are browned on both sides.

6 Stir in the marinade with the nut mixture and bring slowly to the boil. Season with salt. Cover the pan and simmer for about 20 minutes or until the chicken is tender, stirring occasionally. Taste and adjust the seasoning and garnish with cashew nuts and coriander just before serving.

SPRING CHICKEN FRICASSÉE

SERVES 8

225 g (8 oz) carrots, small young ones if possible
225 g (8 oz) button onions
225 g (8 oz) cauliflower florets
225 g (8 oz) broccoli florets
225 g (8 oz) full fat soft cheese with garlic and herbs
8 chicken breast fillets with skin, about 800 g (1¾ lb) total weight
15 ml (1 level tbsp) plain flour
about 30 ml (2 tbsp) vegetable oil
100 ml (4 fl oz) dry vermouth
300 ml (½ pint) chicken stock
30 ml (2 tbsp) chopped fresh tarragon or 2.5 ml (½ tsp) dried
1 garlic clove, skinned and crushed
salt and freshly ground pepper
60 ml (4 tbsp) single cream
carrot tops, to garnish
brown rice pilaff, to serve

1 Cut the carrots into short fingers. Halve the onions. Blanch the cauliflower and broccoli in salted water for 1-2 minutes only. Drain.

2 Push a little of the soft cheese underneath the

chicken skin and tuck the ends of the breast under to form small, neat rounds. Toss in the flour until coated.

3 Heat the oil in a shallow flameproof casserole. Brown the chicken pieces a few at a time, adding more oil if necessary. Remove with a slotted spoon. Add the carrots and onions and lightly brown on all sides.

4 Return the chicken to the pan and pour in the vermouth and stock. Bring to the boil, stirring in the tarragon, garlic and seasoning.

5 Cover tightly and simmer for about 10 minutes. Stir in the cauliflower and broccoli and cook for another 10 minutes or until the chicken is quite tender.

6 Stir in the cream and simmer for 1-2 minutes. Adjust the seasoning and serve garnished with carrot tops. Accompany with a brown rice pilaff.

DEVILLED POUSSINS

——— SERVES 6 ———

15 ml (1 level tbsp) mustard powder
15 ml (1 level tbsp) paprika
20 ml (4 level tsp) turmeric
20 ml (4 level tsp) ground cumin
60 ml (4 tbsp) tomato ketchup
15 ml (1 tbsp) lemon juice
75 g (3 oz) butter, melted
3 poussins, each weighing about 700 g (1½ lb)
15 ml (1 level tbsp) poppy seeds

1 Measure the mustard powder, paprika, turmeric and cumin into a small bowl. Add the tomato ketchup and lemon juice. Beat well to form a thick, smooth paste. Slowly pour in the melted butter, stirring all the time.

2 Place the poussins on a chopping board, breast side down. With a small sharp knife, cut right along the backbone of each bird through skin and flesh.

3 With scissors, cut through the backbone to open the birds up. Turn birds over, breast side up, and continue cutting along the breast bone which will split the birds into two equal halves.

4 Lie the birds, skin side uppermost, on a large, edged baking sheet. Spread the paste evenly over the surface of the birds and sprinkle with the poppy seeds. Cover loosely with cling film and leave in a cool place for at least 1-2 hours.

5 Uncover the poussins and cook in the oven at 190°C Circotherm for 15 minutes.

6 Reduce the temperature to 160°C Circotherm and cook for a further 20 minutes until the poussins are tender.

7 Remove from the oven and place under a hot grill until the skin is well browned and crisp. Serve immediately.

Devilled Poussins

SERVING IDEA

Serve *Devilled Poussins* for an informal supper party with jacket baked potatoes topped with butter, crumbled crisp bacon, soured cream and herbs. Serve ice-cold lager, beer or cider to drink, and follow with a refreshingly crisp salad of raw vegetables.

Opposite: Pheasant au Porto; Guinea Fowl with Grapes

GUINEA FOWL WITH GRAPES
SERVES 4

1 garlic clove, skinned and finely sliced

sprigs of rosemary

salt and freshly ground pepper

2 prepared guinea fowl

4 streaky bacon rashers, rinded

50 g (2 oz) butter

350 g (12 oz) seedless white grapes

30 ml (2 tbsp) brandy

200 ml (7 fl oz) dry white wine

watercress, to garnish

1 Put a few garlic slices, a sprig of rosemary and seasoning inside each bird. Wrap two bacon rashers round each one and secure with wooden cocktail sticks.

2 Place the guinea fowl breast side down in a casserole with the butter. Season and sprinkle with a little extra rosemary. Cook in the oven at 180°C Circotherm for about 1 hour.

3 Meanwhile, blanch the grapes in boiling water for 2 minutes, then remove the skins with a sharp knife. Put the grapes in a bowl. Spoon over the brandy and leave to marinate, turning from time to time.

4 Bring the wine to the boil in a pan. Turn the guinea fowl over and pour over the wine. Cook, uncovered, for 15 minutes until tender.

5 Transfer the guinea fowl to a warmed serving dish and keep hot. Add the grapes to the sauce and heat through.

6 Pour the sauce over the guinea fowl and garnish with watercress. Cut in half to serve.

PHEASANT AU PORTO
SERVES 6

30 ml (2 tbsp) vegetable oil

3 young pheasants, well wiped

300 ml (½ pint) chicken stock

120 ml (8 tbsp) ruby port

finely grated rind and juice of 2 oranges

50 g (2 oz) sultanas

salt and freshly ground pepper

20 ml (4 level tsp) cornflour

25 g (1 oz) flaked almonds, toasted, to garnish

1 Heat the oil in a large flameproof casserole. When hot, add the pheasants and brown all over.

2 Pour the stock and port over the birds. Add the orange rind and juice with the sultanas and season well. Bring to the boil. Cover tightly and cook in the oven at 150°C Circotherm for 1¼-1½ hours.

3 Remove the birds from the casserole, then joint each pheasant into two or three pieces, depending on size, and arrange on a serving dish; keep warm.

4 Boil the juices with the cornflour mixed to a smooth paste with a little water stirring constantly. Adjust the seasoning and spoon over pheasants. Garnish with toasted almonds.

Right: Roast Duck with Grapefruit

ROAST DUCK WITH GRAPEFRUIT

SERVES 8

100 g (4 oz) fresh white breadcrumbs
225 g (8 oz) minced pork
225 g (8 oz) minced veal
100 g (4 oz) cooked ham
8 stuffed green olives
1 small grapefruit
5 ml (1 tsp) chopped fresh sage or 2.5 ml (½ tsp) dried sage
salt and freshly ground pepper
1 egg
2 kg (4½ lb) duckling, boned
herbs and grapefruit slices, to garnish

BONING A DUCK

Lay the bird on a board breast side up. Using a boning knife, cut off the wings at the second joint and the legs at the first. Turn the bird breast down. Cut through the skin and flesh down the centre of the back from vent to neck. Keeping the knife close to the carcass and slightly flattened to avoid damaging the flesh, work the flesh off the rib cage on one side of the bird until the wing joint is exposed; repeat on the other side. Holding the severed end of one wing joint, scrape the knife over the bone backwards and forwards, working the flesh from the bone. When the wing and socket are exposed, sever the ligaments with the point of the knife and draw out the bone. Repeat with the second wing. Continue working the flesh off the main frame until the leg joint is exposed. Sever the ligaments attaching the bone to the body flesh and break the leg joint by twisting it. Working from the body end of the leg, hold the end of the bone and scrape away the flesh from the thigh. Cut round the joint, scrape the drumstick clean and pull the bone free. Repeat with other leg, then work the flesh from the rest of the main frame, taking care not to cut the skin over the breast bone. Lay the bird out flat ready to spread the stuffing over the cut surface.

1 Place the breadcrumbs, minced pork and veal in a large mixing bowl. Roughly chop the ham and olives and add to the mixture. Grate the rind of the grapefruit and chop the flesh. Add to the mixture with the sage, plenty of seasoning and the egg. Stir well until evenly blended.

2 Spoon a little stuffing into each of the leg cavities of the duckling, pressing in firmly.

3 Mound the remaining stuffing in the centre of the body section. Using a needle and fine string or cotton, sew up the body and wing cavities.

4 Turn the bird over, breast side up, then push it back into shape and secure with skewers.

5 Weigh the duckling and put on the wire rack placed over the roasting tin. Sprinkle with salt. Roast at 160°C Circotherm, allowing 20 minutes per 450 g (1 lb), basting occasionally. Pierce the duckling leg with a fine skewer; if left in for 10 seconds, the skewer with be hot if the centre is cooked.

6 To serve, carefully ease out the string and slice. Garnish with herbs and grapefruit slices.

DUCK WITH RASPBERRIES

SERVES 2

30 ml (2 tbsp) brandy

juice of 2 limes

30 ml (2 tbsp) clear honey

10 ml (2 tsp) green peppercorns

salt and freshly ground pepper

2 duck breasts, about 225 g (8 oz) each

15 g (½ oz) butter

30 ml (2 tbsp) vegetable oil

225 g (8 oz) fresh or frozen raspberries

300 ml (½ pint) rosé wine

blanched julienne shreds of lime zest, to garnish

1 Make the marinade. Mix together the brandy, lime juice and half the honey with half the peppercorns, crushed, and season to taste.

2 Remove the skin from the duck breasts, then place the breasts in a shallow dish. Pour over the marinade and leave to stand for 4 hours. Turn the duck occasionally during this time.

3 Melt the butter with the oil in a frying pan. Remove the duck from the marinade, place in the pan and fry over high heat for a few minutes. Turn the breasts over, and cook for 5 minutes or until tender, but still slightly pink inside.

4 Meanwhile, put the raspberries in a heavy-based pan with the marinade and the wine. Heat gently for a few minutes, then remove about one quarter of the raspberries and set aside.

5 Add the remaining honey to the pan and boil until the liquid is reduced to about half.

6 Strain the sauce through a sieve, pressing the raspberries with the back of a spoon. Return to the rinsed-out pan with reserved raspberries and reheat. Taste and adjust the seasoning.

7 Slice the duck breasts neatly, then arrange on warmed individual serving plates. Pour over the sauce, then sprinkle with the remaining whole peppercorns. Garnish and serve immediately.

CRISPY DUCK WITH MANGE TOUT

SERVES 8

4 duck breast fillets, about 225 g (8 oz) each

45 ml (3 tbsp) vegetable oil

1 bunch spring onions, trimmed and cut into 2.5 cm (1 inch) lengths

1 green pepper, cored, seeded and cut into strips

225 g (8 oz) mange tout, topped and tailed

2 garlic cloves, skinned and crushed

2-3 good pinches five-spice powder

45 ml (3 level tbsp) caster sugar

45 ml (3 tbsp) dark soy sauce

45 ml (3 tbsp) malt vinegar

16 water chestnuts, sliced

40 g (1½ oz) toasted cashew nuts, chopped

1 Place the duck breast fillets skin side up on a rack or trivet in a roasting tin.

2 Bake at 160°C Circotherm for 1 hour. Remove from the oven and cut into thin strips.

3 In a wok or large frying pan, heat the oil. Add the onion, green pepper, mange tout, garlic and five-spice powder and stir fry for 2 minutes. Add the sugar, soy sauce, vinegar and the duckling strips and toss in the sauce to heat through and glaze. Add the water chestnuts and toss through lightly. Serve sprinkled with cashews.

SERVING IDEA

Serve *Duck with Raspberries* for a special dinner party dish. Serve with *Swiss Chalet Potatoes with Cream and Cheese* (see page 112) and a crisply cooked green vegetable such as mange tout or French beans. Chilled rosé wine is the most suitable drink to serve with it.

COOK'S TIP

The five spice powder used in *Crispy Duck with Mange Tout* is a mixture of cloves, cinnamon, fennel seeds, star anise and Szechuan peppercorns. It should be used very sparingly.

A little hoisin sauce or finely chopped fresh ginger may be added to the dish during the final stages, if wished. A few drops of sesame oil added to the finished dish adds an aromatic flavour and sheen.

Sweet and Sour Duck Joints

SERVING IDEA

Quick and easy to make if you have to entertain unexpected guests, *Turkey Scaloppine with Almond Cream* contains a rich combination of turkey, almonds, brandy and cream. A lightly cooked vegetable such as broccoli would provide the perfect contrast, with noodles or buttered new potatoes as an additional accompaniment.

SWEET AND SOUR DUCK JOINTS
SERVES 4

4 duck portions
salt and freshly ground pepper
10 ml (2 level tsp) cornflour
60 ml (4 tbsp) soy sauce
45 ml (3 tbsp) soft brown sugar
45 ml (3 tbsp) honey
45 ml (3 tbsp) wine or cider vinegar
30 ml (2 tbsp) dry sherry
juice of 1 orange
2.5 ml (½ level tsp) ground ginger
spring onions, to garnish

1 Prick the duck portions all over with a fork, then sprinkle liberally with salt and pepper.

2 Place on the rack in the roasting tin and roast in the oven at 160°C Circotherm for about 1 hour until skin is crisp and the juices run clear when the thickest part is pierced with a skewer.

3 Meanwhile, make the sauce. Blend the cornflour to a paste with a little water taken from a measured 150 ml (¼ pint), then mix together all the remaining ingredients in a saucepan with the rest of the water and bring to the boil. Simmer, stirring constantly, for about 5 minutes to allow the flavours to blend and the sauce to thicken slightly. Add salt and pepper to taste.

4 Brush away any excess salt, then trim the duck joints neatly by cutting off any knuckles or wing joints. Arrange the duck on a warmed serving platter and coat with some of the sauce. Garnish with spring onions. Hand the remaining sauce separately.

TURKEY SCALOPPINE WITH ALMOND CREAM
SERVES 4

4 turkey steaks
30 ml (2 tbsp) lemon juice
salt and freshly ground pepper
30 ml (2 tbsp) vegetable oil
50 g (2 oz) blanched almonds, roughly chopped
30 ml (2 tbsp) brandy
150 ml (¼ pint) single cream
1 garlic clove, skinned and crushed
snipped fresh chives, to garnish

1 Place each turkey steak between two sheets of damp greaseproof paper and bat out thinly with a rolling pin. Divide each steak into three pieces. Place in a shallow dish and sprinkle over the lemon juice. Season and leave aside for 15 minutes to marinate.

2 Heat the oil in a sauté pan, add the almonds and fry until brown. Remove from the pan.

3 Add the turkey pieces and sauté for about 3 minutes on each side or until golden brown. Remove from the pan using a slotted spoon and keep warm.

4 Add the brandy to the pan, heat gently, then remove from the heat and ignite the brandy.

5 When the flames have died down, stir in the single cream, crushed garlic and the browned almonds. Return to the heat and warm through – do not boil. Pour the sauce over the turkey steaks and snip fresh chives over the top. Serve immediately while piping hot.

TURKEY MOLE

SERVES 4

100 g (4 oz) butter

30 ml (2 tbsp) vegetable oil

1 green pepper, cored, seeded and chopped

2 garlic cloves, skinned and crushed

4 turkey escalopes

salt and freshly ground pepper

300 ml (½ pint) chicken stock

2.5 ml (½ tsp) aniseed

15 ml (1 tbsp) sesame seeds

pinch of ground cloves

pinch of ground cinnamon

1.25 ml (¼ tsp) coriander seeds

50 g (2 oz) plain chocolate, grated

45 ml (3 tbsp) ground almonds

1.25 ml (¼ level tsp) chilli powder

3 tomatoes, skinned

chopped parsley, to garnish

1 Heat half the butter and oil in a frying pan, add the pepper and garlic and fry gently for 5 minutes. Transfer to blender or food processor.

2 Heat remaining butter and oil and fry the turkey escalopes for 2-3 minutes until brown on all sides. Drain on absorbent kitchen paper and place in an ovenproof casserole.

3 Place all the remaining ingredients, except the garnish, in the blender or food processor with the pepper and garlic and process until smooth.

4 Pour the blended sauce over the turkey and cover. Bake in the oven at 160°C Circotherm for 20 minutes until the turkey is tender. Garnish with chopped parsley.

TURKEY KORMA

SERVES 6-8

50 g (2 oz) blanched almonds

50 g (2 oz) poppy seeds

50 g (2 oz) creamed coconut, crumbled

4 medium onions, skinned and roughly chopped

2.5 cm (1 inch) piece of fresh root ginger, peeled and roughly chopped

2 garlic cloves, skinned

60 ml (4 tbsp) coarsely chopped coriander leaves

15 ml (1 tbsp) chopped fresh mint leaves

30 ml (2 level tbsp) ground coriander

2.5 ml (½ level tsp) chilli powder

5 ml (1 level tsp) ground cloves

10 ml (2 level tsp) turmeric

5-10 ml (1-2 level tsp) salt

45 ml (3 tbsp) lemon juice

45 ml (3 tbsp) ghee or 40 g (1½ oz) butter, melted

1.1 kg (2½ lb) turkey escalopes, cut into bite-sized pieces

120 ml (8 tbsp) natural yogurt

1 Dry roast almonds and poppy seeds in a frying pan until the nuts are golden; transfer to a blender or food processor. Add the coconut, then blend to a paste. Remove and set aside.

2 Place the onions, ginger, garlic, coriander and mint leaves, all the spices, salt and lemon juice in the blender or food processor and blend to a paste. Heat the ghee or butter in a frying pan, add the onion paste and fry over high heat for 5 minutes. Add the turkey and coconut purée, then stir in the yogurt and about 450 ml (¾ pint) water. Bake at 160°C Cirotherm for 40-45 minutes.

SERVING IDEA

Although a mild Indian curry, *Turkey Korma* is spicily rich. Serve with boiled or pilau rice, chutney, pickle and poppadoms.

SERVING IDEA

With its rich and flavoursome sauce, *Turkey Mole* from Mexico needs only a green salad as an accompaniment.

Light
Lunches

Previous page: Spinach and Garlic
Tart (see page 90); Chilled Egg and
Cucumber Mousse (see right);
Spaghetti with Ratatouille Sauce
(see page 98)

Omelette Niçoise

OMELETTE NIÇOISE

SERVES 2

3 eggs

salt and freshly ground pepper

25 (1 oz) unsalted butter

2 tomatoes, skinned and roughly chopped

100 g (4 oz) French beans, cooked and
roughly chopped

10 black olives, stoned

200 g (7 oz) can tuna, drained and flaked

anchovy fillets and sprigs of parsley, to garnish

1 Whisk the eggs in a jug with 60 ml (4 tbsp)
water and plenty of salt and pepper.

2 Melt butter in a non-stick frying pan. When
the butter is foaming, pour in the whisked egg
mixture.

3 Cook the omelette over moderate heat,
lifting it up around the edges with a spatula or
palette knife to allow the liquid egg to run
underneath. When the omelette is almost set,
but still runny on top, allow the underside to
colour a little.

4 Spoon the chopped tomato, beans, olives and
tuna fish on top of the omelette and sprinkle
with salt and pepper to taste.

5 Place the pan under a preheated hot grill for
3-5 minutes to heat the filling.

6 Fold the omelette in half, tilting the pan away
from the handle. Cut the omelette in two, then
turn out on to two warmed plates. Garnish with
fine strips of anchovy and chopped parsley.
Serve immediately.

CHILLED EGG AND CUCUMBER MOUSSE

SERVES 6

1 medium cucumber

4 hard-boiled eggs, shelled

300 ml (½ pint) mayonnaise

salt and freshly ground pepper

mustard powder

15 ml (3 level tsp) powdered gelatine

2 egg whites

fresh chervil, to garnish

1 Cut a 5 cm (2 inch) piece off the cucumber
and reserve. Peel and coarsely grate the remainder, then leave to drain.

2 Finely chop three of the eggs and stir into the
mayonnaise with the drained cucumber. Season
to taste with salt, pepper and mustard powder.

3 Sprinkle the gelatine in 45 ml (3 tbsp) water
in a small bowl and leave to soak. Place the bowl
over a pan of simmering water and stir until
dissolved. Stir into the mayonnaise mixture.

4 Stiffly whisk the egg whites and fold into the
mixture. Spoon into a 1.4 litre (2½ pint) souffle
dish, then refrigerate until set.

5 Serve well chilled, garnished with the
reserved egg and cucumber, finely sliced, and
the chervil.

CHEESE SOUFFLÉ

SERVES 4

15 ml (1 tbsp) grated Parmesan cheese
200 ml (7 fl oz) milk
slices of onion and carrot, 1 bay leaf, 6 black peppercorns, for flavouring
25 g (1 oz) butter or margarine
30 ml (2 level tbsp) plain flour
10 ml (2 level tsp) Dijon mustard
salt and freshly ground pepper
cayenne pepper
4 whole eggs, separated and 1 extra egg white
75 g (3 oz) mature Cheddar cheese or other hard cheese e.g. Gruyère or Stilton, finely grated

1 Butter a 1.3 litre (2¼ pint) soufflé dish. Sprinkle the grated Parmesan into the dish. Tilt the dish, tapping the sides gently until they are evenly coated with cheese.

2 Place the milk in a medium saucepan together with the flavouring ingredients. Bring slowly to the boil, remove from the heat, cover and leave to infuse for 30 minutes. Strain off and reserve the milk.

3 Melt the butter in a medium saucepan, stir in the flour, mustard and seasoning and cook gently for 1 minute, stirring. Remove from the heat and gradually stir in the milk. Bring to the boil slowly and continue to cook, stirring until the sauce thickens. Cool a little.

4 Beat the yolks into the cooled sauce one at a time. Sprinkle the cheese over the sauce, reserving 15 ml (1 tbsp). (At this stage the mixture can be left to stand for several hours if necessary.)

5 Stir in the cheese until evenly blended into the sauce. Whisk the egg whites until they stand in stiff peaks.

6 Mix one large spoonful of egg white into the sauce to lighten its texture. Gently pour the sauce over the remaining egg whites and cut and fold the ingredients together. Do not overmix; fold in very lightly, using a metal spoon or plastic spatula, until the egg whites are just incorporated.

7 Pour the soufflé mixture gently into the prepared dish. The mixture should come about three-quarters of the way up the side of the dish. Smooth the surface of the soufflé with a palette knife and sprinkle over the reserved cheese.

8 Place the soufflé on a baking sheet and cook in the oven at 160°C Circotherm for about 30 minutes. It should be golden brown on the top, well risen and just firm to the touch with a hint of softness in the centre.

VARIATIONS

Ham Soufflé
Omit the cheese and add 75 g (3 oz) cooked ham, or finely chopped pork.

Fish Soufflé
Omit the cheese and add 75 g (3 oz) cooked smoked haddock, finely flaked.

Mushroom Soufflé
Omit the cheese and add 75-100 g (3-4 oz) mushrooms, chopped and cooked in butter until tender.

MICROWAVE

Cheese Soufflé
The sauce can be prepared in the microwave. Put the butter, flour and milk in a medium bowl. Cook on HIGH for 3-5 minutes until boiling and thickened, whisking frequently. Add the mustard and season to taste with salt and pepper. Cool a little, then continue with step 4.

SERVING IDEA

Vegetables in a Potato Crust makes a delicious alternative to quiche for a vegetarian lunch. It is made in the same way as a quiche with the egg, yogurt and curd cheese topping poured over a mixture of vegetables in a potato crust instead of a pastry case.

COOK'S TIP

The pastry case for the *Spinach and Garlic Tart* can be baked in advance and frozen, if wished. Bake blind, then allow it to cool, before wrapping and freezing. Thaw it overnight the day before the lunch party, or early the same day.

VEGETABLES IN A POTATO CRUST

SERVES 6

100 g (4 oz) plain wholemeal flour
50 g (2 oz) butter or margarine
175 g (6 oz) potatoes, peeled and coarsely grated
1 egg yolk
275 g (10 oz) cauliflower, cut into florets
2 carrots, scrubbed and grated
2 spring onions, trimmed and finely chopped
salt and freshly ground pepper
3 eggs
200 ml (7 fl oz) natural yogurt
100 g (4 oz) curd cheese
30 ml (2 tbsp) chopped fresh mixed herbs

1 Put the flour into a bowl and rub in the butter until the mixture resembles fine breadcrumbs. Add the potatoes and egg yolk and mix to a dough. Wrap in cling film and chill for 30 minutes.
2 Meanwhile, blanch the cauliflower florets in a saucepan of boiling water for 5 minutes. Drain thoroughly.
3 Roll out the dough on a lightly floured surface and use to line a 23 cm (9 inch) loose-bottomed flan tin.
4 Mix the cauliflower florets with the carrots and spring onions and season to taste with salt and pepper, then arrange in the flan case.
5 Combine the eggs, yogurt, curd cheese and herbs and beat until well blended. Spoon evenly over the vegetables. Bake at 160°C Circotherm for about 35 minutes. Serve warm.

SPINACH AND GARLIC TART

SERVES 6

250 g (9 oz) Shortcrust Pastry, made with 250 g (9 oz) flour (see page 189)
15 ml (1 tbsp) olive oil
3 small onions, skinned and chopped
1 garlic clove, skinned and crushed
450 g (1 lb) prepared fresh spinach
25 g (1 oz) Parmesan cheese, grated
300 ml (½ pint) double cream
90 ml (6 level tbsp) ground almonds
2 egg yolks
freshly grated nutmeg
salt and freshly ground pepper
25 g (1 oz) pine kernels
25 g (1 oz) piece Parmesan cheese

1 Roll out the pastry and use to line a loose-bottomed 28 cm (11 inch) round, fluted flan tin. Cover and chill for at least 30 minutes.
2 Meanwhile, heat the oil in a very large heavy-based saucepan. Add the onions and garlic and cook, stirring for a couple of minutes. Reduce the heat, cover the pan with a tightly fitting lid and sweat the onion until very soft.
3 Add the spinach and stir to mix with the onion mixture. Re-cover the pan and cook for 4-5 minutes until the spinach is just cooked. Remove from the heat. Stir in the grated Parmesan cheese, cream, almonds and egg yolks. Season generously with nutmeg, salt and pepper.
4 Bake the pastry case blind in the oven at 160°C Circotherm for 15-20 minutes. Remove

the baking beans and greaseproof paper and cook for a further 10 minutes or until the base is cooked through.

5 Spoon the filling into the pastry case and sprinkle with the pine kernels. Stand the tart on a baking sheet and cook at 170°C Circotherm for about 30 minutes until the filling is lightly set. While still warm, coarsely grate over the 25 g (1 oz) Parmesan cheese. Serve warm or cold.

CHEESY SALAMI GRATIN
—— SERVES 4 ——

700 g (1½ lb) potatoes
salt and freshly ground pepper
2 eggs
50 g (2 oz) Parmesan cheese, grated
25 g (1 oz) butter
6 tomatoes, skinned and sliced
100 g (4 oz) Mozzarella cheese
100 g (4 oz) Gruyère cheese, sliced
100 g (4 oz) Italian salami, rinded and chopped
30 ml (2 tbsp) chopped fresh basil or 10 ml (2 tsp) dried

1 Cook the potatoes in their skins in boiling salted water for about 20 minutes or until tender.
2 Drain the potatoes and leave until cool enough to handle, then carefully peel off the skins with your fingers.
3 Mash potatoes in a bowl then add the eggs, Parmesan cheese and salt and pepper to taste. Beat well to mix.
4 Brush the inside of a large gratin dish with some of the butter. Spoon half of the mashed potato in the bottom of the dish. Cover with half of the tomato slices, then half of the Mozzarella and Gruyère cheeses and salami.
5 Sprinkle each layer with basil and salt and pepper to taste, taking care not to add too much salt because the cheeses and salami may be salty. Repeat the layers of potato, tomato, cheese and salami, sprinkling each with the remaining basil and seasoning to taste.
6 Dot with the remaining butter, then bake in the oven at 190°C Circotherm for 25-30 minutes until golden brown and bubbling. Serve hot, straight from the dish.

SERVING IDEA

Cheesy Salami Gratin is very rich and filling. Serve with a crisp and colourful mixed salad.

Cheesy Salami Gratin

AUBERGINES WITH HAM

— SERVES 2 —

two 225 g (8 oz) aubergines
vegetable oil
1 medium onion, skinned
100 g (4 oz) cooked lean ham
50 g (2 oz) butter
1 garlic clove, skinned and crushed
30 ml (2 tbsp) plain flour
10 ml (2 tsp) chopped fresh basil
50 g (2 oz) fresh white breadcrumbs
5 ml (1 level tsp) French mustard
5 ml (1 tsp) lemon juice
60 ml (4 tbsp) single cream
salt and freshly ground pepper
sprigs of basil, to garnish

1 Cut the aubergines in half lengthways, then score the exposed flesh on the cut sides.
2 Brush the aubergines with oil and place, cut sides uppermost, in an ovenproof dish. Add 60 ml (4 tbsp) water, cover with foil or a lid and bake in the oven at 160°C Circotherm for about 30 minutes until the flesh is just tender.
3 With a sharp-edged teaspoon, scoop out as much flesh from the aubergines as possible, leaving the shells intact. Chop the flesh. Finely chop the onion and ham.
4 Melt half the butter in a saucepan, add the onion and fry gently until soft. Add the garlic and aubergine flesh and fry for 2-3 minutes.
5 Sprinkle over the flour and basil and cook for 2-3 minutes, stirring. Add the ham, all but 30 ml (2 tbsp) of the breadcrumbs, the mustard,

lemon juice and cream and season to taste.
6 Fill the aubergine shells with the stuffing. Top with the reserved breadcrumbs and dot with the remaining butter. Bake in the oven at 160°C Circotherm for about 35 minutes. Serve hot, garnished with sprigs of basil.

COURGETTE PASTICCIO

— SERVES 2 —

400 g (14 oz) courgettes, trimmed and coarsely grated
100 g (4 oz) Cheddar cheese, grated
60 ml (4 tbsp) plain wholemeal flour
5 ml (1 tsp) chopped fresh basil
salt and freshly ground pepper
4 egg whites, size 2
225 g (8 oz) can chopped tomatoes
10 ml (2 tsp) tomato purée
50 g (2 oz) button mushrooms, sliced
2.5 ml (½ tsp) dried oregano

1 Combine the courgettes, 75 g (3 oz) of the cheese, the flour, basil and seasoning in a bowl. Whisk the egg whites until frothy but not stiff, then fold into the courgette mixture.
2 Place the mixture in a buttered 23 cm (9 inch) loose-bottomed flan tin and smooth the surface. Bake in the oven at 160°C Circotherm for 25 minutes or until slightly browned.
3 Mix the tomatoes and tomato purée together and spread over the cooked base. Scatter over the mushrooms and sprinkle the remaining cheese and oregano on top. Cook for a further 10-15 minutes. Cut into wedges and serve hot.

SERVING IDEA

Stuffed aubergines make a light main course for an informal lunch party. Serve *Aubergines with Ham* with a mixed salad, French bread and a bottle of full-bodied wine, and follow with a selection of cheeses and grapes, dates or figs.

*Opposite: Courgette Pasticcio;
Aubergines with Ham*

MICROWAVE

Chicken with Tarragon Mayonnaise
Place the chicken breasts in a large round, shallow dish, arranging them like the spokes of a wheel with the thickest part outermost. Scatter the celery over the top, then make the marinade and pour it over. Cover and leave to marinate in a cool place for 3-4 hours, turning once. Cook on HIGH for 12-15 minutes, turning the chicken breasts over halfway through the cooking time. Continue from step 4.

Chicken with Tarragon Mayonnaise

ROASTED PEPPER AND SWEET ONION PIZZA

―――――― SERVES 8 ――――――

4 large yellow or red peppers
olive oil
4 large white or red onions, skinned and sliced
three 283 g (10 oz) packets white bread and pizza mix
two 200 g (7 oz) Mozzarella cheeses, sliced
two 397 (14 oz) cans chopped tomatoes, well drained
6 garlic cloves, skinned and thinly sliced
salt and freshly ground pepper
60 ml (4 tbsp) fresh oregano or basil leaves

1 Grill the peppers under a hot grill until blackened all over. Cover with a damp cloth and leave until cool enough to handle. Carefully peel off the skins. Remove and discard the stalks and seeds. Cut the flesh into thick strips.
2 Heat 60 ml (4 tbsp) olive oil in a frying pan, add the onions and fry gently for 5 minutes until softened but not coloured. Set aside.
3 Make up the pizza dough following the manufacturer's instuctions substituting 60 ml (4 tbsp) oil for a similar amount of the liquid measurement. Divide in two and roll out into thin 30 cm (12 inch) rounds on a floured surface. Place each on a baking sheet.
4 Cover the pizza bases with the Mozzarella. Scatter over the tomatoes, onions and peppers, then the slivers of garlic. Season with salt and pepper, drizzle with olive oil and brush the edges of the pizza with oil. Leave in a warm place for 20-30 minutes or until doubled in size.

5 Bake in the oven at 170°C Circotherm for 25 minutes until golden and bubbling. Scatter with the herbs 5 minutes before the end of the cooking time. Serve immediately.

CHICKEN WITH TARRAGON MAYONNAISE

―――――― SERVES 6 ――――――

6 chicken breast fillets, skinned
2 sticks of celery, washed, trimmed and sliced
200 ml (7 fl oz) medium dry white wine
30 ml (2 tbsp) chopped fresh tarragon or 10 ml (2 tsp) dried
salt and freshly ground pepper
300 ml (½ pint) mayonnaise
sprigs of tarragon, to garnish

1 Place the chicken in a shallow ovenproof dish into which the pieces will just fit. Scatter the celery over the top.
2 To make the marinade, mix the wine, chopped tarragon and seasoning together. Pour the marinade over the chicken.
3 Cover the dish and leave the chicken to marinate in a cool place for 3-4 hours, turning once. Cook, covered, in the oven at 160°C Circotherm for 30-35 minutes or until the chicken is tender.
4 Leave the chicken to cool, covered. Strain off the cooking liquid and boil down until only 90 ml (6 tbsp) remains. Cool and set aside.
5 Stir the reduced cooking liquid into the mayonnaise and spoon over the chicken just before serving. Garnish with tarragon sprigs.

PORK AND MUSHROOM SALAD
SERVES 6

2 pork fillets or tenderloins, about 350 g (12 oz) each, well trimmed
vegetable oil
knob of butter
225 g (8 oz) small button mushrooms
juice of ½ a lemon
1 small onion, skinned and finely sliced
1 small green pepper, seeded and finely shredded
10 green olives, stoned and chopped
150 ml (¼ pint) soured cream
1.25 ml (¼ level tsp) mustard powder
salt and freshly ground pepper
5 ml (1 tsp) chopped fresh marjoram or mint
lemon wedges, to garnish

1 Cut the pork into 1 cm (½ inch) slices on the diagonal, then cut each slice into neat strips, about 5 × 0.5 cm (2 × ¼ inch).

2 Heat a little oil and the butter in a large frying pan, add half the pork and fry quickly to seal the meat. Repeat with the remaining meat, then return it all to the pan. Lower the heat and cook slowly for about 10-15 minutes, until very tender. Using a slotted spoon, lift the meat out of the pan and leave to cool.

3 Add the mushrooms to the pan with 50 ml (2 fl oz) water and the lemon juice. Cook, stirring, for 1-2 minutes. Using the slotted spoon, remove from the pan and leave to cool.

4 Put the onion and green pepper in a saucepan of cold water, bring to the boil and simmer for 1-2 minutes. Drain and cool under cold running water. Stir into the pork with the cooled mushrooms and the olives.

5 Mix the soured cream with the mustard, season to taste with salt and pepper and stir into the pork mixture. Cover and chill for at least 3 hours.

6 Stir the salad well before serving sprinkled with marjoram and garnished with lemon wedges.

CHORIZO AND CHICKPEA STEW
SERVES 4

15 ml (1 tbsp) olive oil
1 large onion, skinned and chopped
1 red pepper, seeded and chopped
2 garlic cloves, skinned and crushed
397 g (14 oz) can chopped tomatoes
350 g (12 oz) piece of chorizo sausage
two 400 g (14 oz) cans chickpeas, drained and rinsed
salt and freshly ground pepper
chopped fresh parsley, to garnish

1 Heat the oil in a heavy-based saucepan. Add the onion, pepper and garlic and cook over a high heat for 2 minutes. Add the tomatoes and simmer for 5 minutes.

2 Cut the sausage into chunks and add to the tomato sauce with the chickpeas. Cover and simmer for about 10 minutes, stirring occasionally. Season to taste with salt and pepper and serve garnished with parsley.

COOK'S TIPS

The topping for *Roasted Pepper and Sweet Onion Pizza* can be prepared in advance to save you time on the day of a lunch party.

The pizza dough can also be made in advance and frozen, if wished. Make up the dough, roll out and open freeze the bases until solid. Overwrap and freeze. Thaw for 1-2 hours at cool room temperature.

SERVING IDEA

Serve *Chorizo and Chickpea Stew* with boiled rice for an easy lunch or supper dish.

Chicken Liver Skewers

CHICKEN LIVER SKEWERS

SERVES 4

2 small oranges
200 ml (7 fl oz) unsweetened orange juice
5 ml (1 tsp) chopped fresh tarragon or 2.5 ml (½ tsp) dried
450 g (1 lb) whole chicken livers
2 slices of bread, crumbed
1 green pepper, about 175 g (6 oz), seeded and cut into cubes
1 medium onion, skinned and cut into cubes
275 g (10 oz) beansprouts
1 small bunch of chives, snipped
salt and freshly ground pepper

1 Finely grate the rind of one of the oranges. Place in a saucepan with the orange juice and tarragon and simmer for 2-3 minutes until reduced by half.

2 Cut the tops and bottoms off both oranges, then remove the skin by working around the oranges in a spiral, using a sharp serrated knife and a sawing action.

3 Divide the oranges into segments by cutting through the membranes on either side of each segment with a sharp knife.

4 Cut the chicken livers in half; toss lightly in the breadcrumbs. Place in a lightly greased grill pan and grill for 2 minutes on each side or until just firm.

5 Thread the pepper and onion on to four oiled kebab skewers alternately with the livers.

6 Place the skewers in the grill pan and spoon over a little of the reduced orange juice. Grill for 2-3 minutes on each side, turning and basting occasionally.

7 Meanwhile, steam the beansprouts for 2-3 minutes. Warm the orange segments in a pan with the remaining reduced orange juice.

8 Mix the beansprouts with the chives and seasoning to taste, and arrange on a warmed serving dish. Top with the skewers and spoon over the orange and juices. Serve immediately.

PASTA WITH PESTO

SERVES 4

350-450 g (12-16 oz) pasta
100 ml (4 fl oz) olive oil
2 garlic cloves, skinned
50 g (2 oz) fresh basil leaves
50 g (2 oz) pine kernels
salt and freshly ground pepper
milk, to blend
50 g (2 oz) Parmesan cheese, grated
fresh basil, to garnish

1 Cook the pasta in a large saucepan of boiling water until just tender.

2 Meanwhile, make the pesto. Put the oil, garlic, basil, pine kernels and salt and pepper in a blender or food processor. Add a little milk to moisten the mixture and process to a thick purée. Transfer the purée to a bowl and stir in the cheese. Taste and adjust the seasoning, if necessary.

3 Drain the pasta, return to the pan and stir in the pesto. Cook, stirring, for 1-2 minutes over a very low heat. Serve garnished with basil.

Aubergine Cannelloni

SERVES 8

4 aubergines, about 250 g (9 oz) each
about 150 ml (¼ pint) olive oil
450 g (1 lb) ricotta cheese
100 g (4 oz) Parmesan cheese, freshly grated
30 ml (2 tbsp) finely shredded fresh basil leaves
salt and freshly ground pepper
SAUCE
30 ml (2 tbsp) olive oil
2 shallots or ¼ large Spanish onion, skinned and finely chopped
900 g (2 lb) ripe fresh tomatoes, skinned, seeded and chopped
2 garlic cloves, skinned and crushed
about 300 ml (½ pint) vegetable stock or water
15 ml (1 tbsp) tomato purée
2.5 ml (½ tsp) caster sugar, or to taste
30 ml (2 tbsp) dry white wine
freshly grated Parmesan cheese and sprigs of basil, to serve

1 Make the sauce first. Heat the olive oil in a heavy saucepan, add the shallots and cook gently, stirring frequently, for 5-7 minutes until softened. Add the tomatoes and garlic, cover with a lid and sweat over gentle heat, stirring occasionally, for 10 minutes. Add the stock, tomato purée, sugar and salt and pepper to taste, half cover the pan and simmer for 30 minutes, stirring frequently.

2 Remove the pan from the heat, then work the tomato mixture through a fine sieve into a clean saucepan. Bring to the boil, stirring, then add the white wine and set aside while preparing the cannelloni.

3 Cut the aubergines lengthways into thin slices, discarding the ends and rounded pieces from the sides. Heat 30-45 ml (2-3 tbsp) olive oil in a large non-stick frying pan. Add a single layer of aubergine slices and fry over moderate heat until light golden on both sides. Remove from the pan, drain, then place on absorbent kitchen paper. Repeat with more oil and the remaining aubergine slices.

4 Put the ricotta and Parmesan cheeses in a bowl with the shredded basil and salt and pepper to taste. Beat well to mix.

5 Place the aubergine slices on a flat surface; if the slices are small or broken, overlap two slices so that they will roll up as one (you will need 24 cannelloni altogether). Spoon or pipe the cheese mixture along the length of the aubergines, then roll the slices up around it.

6 Place the rolls, seam-side down, in a single layer in an ovenproof dish. Bake in the oven at 160°C Circotherm for 15 minutes until hot. Meanwhile, reheat the tomato sauce until bubbling, taste and adjust the seasoning, and add more stock if necessary.

7 To serve, arrange three cannelloni on each warmed plate. Drizzle over the tomato sauce, then sprinkle lightly with Parmesan and garnish with fresh basil sprigs. Serve hot, with extra Parmesan handed separately for those who like it.

MICROWAVE

Aubergine Cannelloni
To cook the sauce in the microwave, put the oil and shallots in a large bowl, cover and cook on HIGH for about 3-4 minutes, stirring, until soft. Stir in the remaining sauce ingredients adding only 150 ml (¼ pint) vegetable stock or water. Re-cover and cook on HIGH for 10 minutes, stirring several times. Work the tomato mixture through a sieve into a saucepan and set aside. Complete steps 3, 4 and 5. Arrange the rolls in two dishes, cover and cook one at a time on HIGH for 4 minutes until piping hot. Leave to stand, still covered, while reheating the sauce, covered, on HIGH for 2 minutes.

COOK'S TIP

To skin tomatoes, put them in a heatproof bowl and pour in boiling water to cover. Leave to stand for 2 minutes, then drain and plunge into a bowl of cold water. Remove from the water one at a time, then peel off the skin with your fingers.

MICROWAVE

Spaghetti with Ratatouille Sauce
To cook the sauce in the microwave, place all the vegetables in a bowl, substituting the tomatoes with two 397 g (14 oz) cans chopped tomatoes. Cover and cook on HIGH for 30 minutes until all the vegetables are tender, stirring several times during the cooking time.

SPAGHETTI WITH RATATOUILLE SAUCE

———— SERVES 4 ————

1 aubergine
salt and freshly ground pepper
1 green pepper, halved and seeded
1 red pepper, halved, cored and seeded
3 medium courgettes, topped and tailed
1 onion, skinned and finely chopped
1 garlic clove, skinned
350 g (12 oz) tomatoes, skinned and chopped (see Cook's Tip)
30 ml (2 tbsp) chopped fresh basil
15 ml (1 tbsp) tomato purée
350-450 g (12-16 oz) spaghetti
freshly grated Parmesan cheese, to serve

1 Dice the aubergine, then spread out on a plate and sprinkle with salt. Leave to dégorge for 30 minutes.
2 Meanwhile, slice the pepper flesh into thin strips. Slice the courgettes into very thin strips, leaving the skin on.
3 Tip the diced aubergine into sieve and rinse under cold running water. Put into a large, heavy-based pan with the prepared vegetables, basil and purée and season to taste with salt and pepper. Cover and cook over moderate heat for 30 minutes. Shake the pan and stir the vegetables frequently during this time, to encourage the juices to flow.
4 Meanwhile, cook the spaghetti in a separate large saucepan of boiling salted water until it is just tender.

5 Drain the spaghetti and turn into a warmed serving dish. Pour the ratatouille sauce over the spaghetti and serve immediately with the Parmesan cheese handed separately.

TAGLIATELLE WITH GORGONZOLA SAUCE

———— SERVES 4 ————

25 g (1 oz) butter
175 g (6 oz) Gorgonzola cheese
150 ml (¼ pint) whipping cream
30 ml (2 tbsp) dry white wine
15 ml (1 tbsp) chopped fresh sage
salt and freshly ground pepper
350-450 g (12-16 oz) tagliatelle

1 Make the sauce. Melt the butter in a heavy-based saucepan. Crumble in the Gorgonzola cheese, then stir over gentle heat for 2-3 minutes until melted.
2 Pour in the cream and wine, whisking vigorously. Stir in the sage, season to taste with salt and pepper and cook, stirring, until the sauce thickens. Remove the pan from the heat.
3 Cook the tagliatelle in a large saucepan of boiling salted water until just tender. Drain thoroughly.
4 Gently reheat the sauce, whisking vigorously. Taste and adjust the seasoning.
5 Divide the tagliatelle equally between four warmed serving plates. Top each portion with sauce and serve immediately.

SALMON AND DILL CAKES
——— SERVES 4 ———

225 g (8 oz) potatoes, scrubbed

15 g (½ oz) butter or margarine

30 ml (2 tbsp) natural yogurt

two 200 g (7 oz) cans pink salmon,
drained and flaked

40 ml (2½ tbsp) chopped fresh dill or
15 ml (1 tbsp) dried dill weed

15 ml (1 tbsp) grated onion

grated rind of 1 lemon

freshly ground pepper

15 ml (1 level tbsp) plain wholemeal flour

2 egg whites, beaten

75 g (3 oz) dried breadcrumbs or rolled oats

melted butter for brushing

45 ml (3 tbsp) mayonnaise

lemon wedges and fresh dill, to garnish

1 Cook the potatoes in a saucepan of boiling water for 20 minutes or until tender. Drain and peel. Add the butter and 15 ml (1 tbsp) of the yogurt. Mash until smooth. Turn into a bowl. Cool.

2 Add the salmon, 25 ml (1½ tbsp) of the fresh dill or 10 ml (2 tsp) dried dill, the onion, lemon rind and pepper. Mix well. Cover and chill for about 15 minutes until firm enough to handle.

3 Dust a work surface with the flour, then shape the salmon and potato mixture into eight even-sized cakes. Dip into the egg white, then coat in the breadcrumbs. Brush with melted butter. Place the fish cakes on a baking sheet. Cook in the oven at 170°C Circotherm for 25-30 minutes until hot and crisp.

4 Meanwhile, mix the remaining yogurt and dill with the mayonnaise. Serve this sauce in a separate bowl with the cooked fish cakes. Garnish with lemon wedges and fresh dill.

PRAWN PILAFF
——— SERVES 4 ———

1 medium onion, skinned and thinly sliced

1 garlic clove, skinned and crushed

1 litre (1¾ pints) chicken stock

225 g (8 oz) long-grain brown rice

50 g (2 oz) small button mushrooms

½ sachet saffron threads

salt and freshly ground pepper

225 g (8 oz) peeled prawns

50 g (2 oz) frozen petits pois

12 whole prawns, to garnish

1 Place the onion, garlic, stock, rice, mushrooms and saffron in a large saucepan or flameproof casserole. Add seasoning to taste. Bring to the boil and simmer, uncovered, for 35 minutes, stirring occasionally.

2 Stir in the prawns and petits pois. Cook over high heat for about 5 minutes, stirring occasionally until most of the liquid has been absorbed.

3 Taste and adjust the seasoning, then turn into a warmed serving dish. Garnish with the whole prawns and serve immediately.

COOK'S TIP

The *Salmon and Dill Cakes* are a low fat version of fish cakes. However, if preferred, they can be fried until browned instead of baking them in the oven.

Prawn Pilaff

SERVING IDEA

Serve *Prawn Pilaff* with a tomato, onion and basil salad.

99

Vegetables & Salads

MICROWAVE

Sweet Carrot Ribbons with Ginger
Put the honey, mustard, butter and ginger in a large bowl and cook on HIGH for 3 minutes, stirring once. Add the carrots and cook on HIGH for 1-2 minutes or until just hot, stirring once. Serve immediately.

COOK'S TIP

Fresh water chestnuts are sometimes available in oriental specialist shops, but canned water chestnuts can be bought from most large supermarkets and delicatessens. Water chestnuts are not actually chestnuts, but the sweet root-bulb of an Asian marsh plant. The canned variety are ready peeled and have a good crunchy texture. They are bland tasting, so need to be combined with strong-tasting foods.

Previous page: Salad of Baked Goat's Cheese and Hazelnuts (see page 122); Roasted Peppers with Yogurt and Pistachio Nuts (see page 110); Red Kidney Bean Hot Pot (see page 112)

Right: Chinese Vegetable Stir fry

SWEET CARROT RIBBONS WITH GINGER

SERVES 4-6

700 g (1 ½ lb) large carrots, peeled

25 g (1 oz) butter or margarine

1 cm (½ inch) piece of fresh root ginger, peeled and grated

30 ml (2 tbsp) clear honey

2.5 ml (½ level tsp) Dijon mustard

1 Using a potato peeler, slice the carrots lengthways into wafer thin strips.
2 Melt the butter in a very large frying pan or wok, add the ginger and carrots and stir fry over high heat for 3-5 minutes until the carrots are just tender but still crisp. Stir in the honey and mustard.

FRENCH BEANS WITH WATER CHESTNUTS

SERVES 2

225 g (8 oz) French beans

salt and freshly ground pepper

6 canned water chestnuts, drained (see Cook's Tip)

50 g (2 oz) butter or margarine

1 Top and tail the French beans. Cook in boiling salted water for about 3 minutes. Drain the beans and plunge into a bowl of cold water to set the colour and prevent any further cooking.
2 Meanwhile, slice the water chestnuts and set aside. Drain the beans. Melt the butter in a frying pan, add the French beans and cook, stirring, for 1-2 minutes. Stir in the water chestnuts and cook for a further minute, tossing the vegetables continuously. Season with salt and pepper and serve immediately.

CHINESE VEGETABLE STIR FRY

SERVES 4

350 g (12 oz) mange tout

2 large red peppers

1 bunch of spring onions

225 g (8 oz) can water chestnuts

5 cm (2 inch) piece of fresh root ginger, peeled

1-2 garlic cloves, skinned and crushed

30 ml (2 tbsp) vegetable oil

15 ml (1 tbsp) sesame oil (optional)

30 ml (2 tbsp) dry sherry

30 ml (2 tbsp) soy sauce

10 ml (2 tsp) honey or soft brown sugar

10 ml (2 tsp) tomato purée

salt and freshly ground pepper

1 First prepare the vegetables. Top and tail the mange tout. Cut the tops off the peppers, remove the cores and seeds and wash thoroughly inside and out.

2 Pat the peppers dry with absorbent kitchen paper, then shred the flesh finely. Trim and shred the spring onions.

3 Drain the water chestnuts, rinse under cold running water, then shred finely.

4 Cut the root ginger into matchstick lengths.

5 Heat the oils in a wok or deep, heavy-based frying pan. Add the spring onions, ginger and garlic and stir fry for 2-3 minutes. Add the remaining prepared vegetables and stir fry to mix them together.

6 In a bowl, or jug, mix together the remaining ingredients, with salt and pepper to taste. Pour over the vegetables, moisten with about 60 ml (4 tbsp) water and mix well. Cook for about 5 minutes, stirring constantly, until the mange tout and red peppers are tender but still crunchy. Transfer the vegetables to a warmed serving bowl and serve immediately.

SAUTÉED COURGETTES WITH CHIVES

SERVES 4

450 g (1 lb) courgettes

25 g (1 oz) butter

15 ml (1 tbsp) vegetable oil

grated rind and juice of ½ lemon

salt and freshly ground pepper

15 ml (1 tbsp) snipped fresh chives

1 Wash the courgettes and pat dry. Top and tail them and thinly slice.

2 Heat the butter and oil in a pan, add the courgettes and cook over medium heat, uncovered, for 5-8 minutes. When tender but still slightly crisp, add the lemon rind and juice and season to taste with salt and pepper.

3 Turn into a heated serving dish. Garnish with chives and serve immediately.

STIR-FRIED VEGETABLES

SERVES 4

15 ml (1 tbsp) vegetable oil

2.5 cm (1 inch) piece of fresh root ginger, peeled and grated

1 garlic clove, skinned and finely chopped

2 medium carrots, sliced into matchstick strips

1 red pepper, seeded and thinly sliced

100 g (4 oz) mange tout, trimmed

4 spring onions, trimmed and chopped

½ head of Chinese leaves, thinly sliced

50 g (2 oz) bean sprouts

15 ml (1 tbsp) soy sauce

30 ml (2 tbsp) dry sherry

1 Heat the oil in a large frying pan or wok, add the ginger and garlic and stir fry for 30 seconds.

2 Add the carrots and stir fry for 1 minute, add the pepper and stir fry for a further 1 minute.

3 Add the mange tout and spring onions and stir fry for 30 seconds. Add the Chinese leaves and bean sprouts and stir fry for 30 seconds.

4 Add the soy sauce and sherry and bring to the boil, stirring.

SERVING IDEA

Serve colourful *Chinese Vegetable Stir Fry* with pork, beef or duck, or with steamed or fried fish. Chinese egg noodles can be stir fried with the vegetables, or served separately.

MICROWAVE

Stir-Fried Vegetables
Put the oil, soy sauce, sherry, garlic, ginger and carrots in a large bowl. Mix well together and cook on HIGH for 5 minutes or until the carrot is tender, stirring occasionally. Add the remaining vegetables and mix together. Cook on HIGH for 5 minutes or until the vegetables are just tender, stirring frequently. Serve hot.

SERVING IDEA

For a nutritious vegetarian main course, serve *Vegetable Kebabs with Tofu Sauce* on a bed of brown or white and wild rice. Serve a crisp mixed salad separately. On their own, the kebabs also make a good starter for a vegetarian meal, in which case they will serve four people.

COOK'S TIP

Silken tofu is available from chilling cabinets in health food shops. It is a kind of bean curd made from soya beans, used extensively in oriental cooking for its nutritive value. Weight for weight it contains as much protein as meat, yet it is very low in fat, and much cheaper.

Opposite: Vegetable Kebabs with Tofu Sauce

VEGETABLE KEBABS WITH TOFU SAUCE

——— SERVES 2 ———

297 g (10½ oz) carton silken tofu
30 ml (2 tbsp) olive or vegetable oil
20 ml (4 tsp) soy sauce
about 30 ml (2 tbsp) lemon juice
1-2 garlic cloves, skinned and crushed
15 ml (1 tbsp) sesame oil (optional)
salt and freshly ground pepper
4 small courgettes
6 baby sweetcorns, halved crossways
16 button mushrooms, wiped
12 cherry tomatoes, or 3 medium tomatoes, quartered
12 bay leaves
30 ml (2 tbsp) sesame seeds

1 First prepare the tofu sauce. Put the tofu in a blender or food processor with half of the oil and soy sauce, the lemon juice, garlic and sesame oil (if using). Work until the ingredients are evenly combined, then add salt and pepper to taste and more lemon juice, if liked. Pour into a jug and chill while making the kebabs.
2 Trim the ends off the courgettes, then cut each courgette into three chunky pieces. Blanch in boiling salted water for 1 minute, then drain.
3 Thread the vegetables and bay leaves on to four oiled kebab skewers, alternating the different ingredients as much as possible.
4 Place the kebabs on the rack of the grill pan. Mix the remaining oil and soy sauce with the sesame seeds. Brush over the kebabs. Cook under a preheated grill for about 10 minutes, turning frequently and brushing with more of the oil and soy sauce mixture.
5 Serve the vegetable kebabs hot, with the chilled tofu sauce handed separately in a jug.

SUMMER VEGETABLES WITH WARM BASIL DRESSING

——— SERVES 4 ———

3 peppers, yellow, green and red
450 g (1 lb) broad beans, shelled
100 g (4 oz) tiny button mushrooms
1 or 2 beefsteak tomatoes, sliced
4 crisp lettuce hearts, halved or quartered
75 ml (5 tbsp) vegetable stock
75 ml (5 tbsp) dry white wine
45 ml (3 tbsp) fromage frais
salt and freshly ground pepper
12 small basil leaves

1 Cook the peppers under a hot grill until the skins are charred, turning them frequently. Wrap in damp absorbent kitchen paper, cool slightly, then peel off the skins. Cut off the tops and remove the seeds, then slice into strips.
2 Blanch the broad beans in a saucepan of boiling water for 2 minutes. Drain. Arrange all the vegetables in groups on a large serving plate.
3 To make the dressing, place the stock and wine in a small saucepan and bring to the boil. Boil rapidly to reduce it by half. Cool slightly, then stir in the fromage frais, seasoning and basil. Whisk until smooth, then pour over the vegetables and serve immediately.

MICROWAVE

Okra with Baby Onions and Coriander

Put the oil, coriander and garlic in a serving bowl. Cook on HIGH for 2 minutes, stirring once. Add the onions, okra and stock and mix well together. Cover and cook on HIGH for 5-7 minutes or until the onions and okra are tender, stirring occasionally. Season to taste with salt and pepper and serve hot.

SUMMER VEGETABLE FRICASSÉE
SERVES 4-6

4 courgettes, washed and trimmed
225 g (8 oz) French beans, topped and tailed and cut into 5 cm (2 inch) lengths
salt and freshly ground pepper
45 ml (3 tbsp) olive oil
1 medium onion, skinned and sliced
2 garlic cloves, skinned and crushed
5 ml (1 tsp) crushed coriander seeds
3 peppers (red, yellow, green), cored, seeded and sliced
150 ml (¼ pint) dry white wine
10 ml (2 tsp) tomato purée
2.5 ml (½ tsp) sugar

1 Cut the courgettes crossways into thirds, then cut them lengthways into slices about 0.5cm (¼ inch) thick.

2 Blanch the courgettes and beans in boiling salted water for 5 minutes only. Drain and set aside until required.

3 Heat the oil in a flameproof casserole, add the onion, garlic and coriander seeds and fry gently for 5 minutes until the onion is soft.

4 Add the pepper slices and fry gently for a further 5 minutes, stirring constantly. Stir in the wine, tomato purée and sugar and season to taste with salt and pepper. Bring to the boil, then simmer for a few minutes, stirring all the time until the liquid begins to reduce.

5 Add the courgettes and beans to the pan and stir gently to combine with the sauce. Heat through, taking care not to over-cook the vegetables. Taste and adjust the seasoning. Serve hot.

OKRA WITH BABY ONIONS AND CORIANDER
SERVES 4-6

30 ml (2 tbsp) olive oil
15 ml (1 tbsp) coriander seeds, crushed
1 garlic clove, skinned and crushed
225 g (8 oz) baby onions, skinned and halved
450 g (1 lb) okra, trimmed
300 ml (½ pint) vegetable stock
salt and freshly ground pepper

1 Heat the oil in a large frying pan, add the coriander seeds and garlic and fry for 1 minute.

2 Add the onions and fry gently for 2 minutes. Add the okra and stock, bring to the boil, cover and simmer for 10-15 minutes until the onions and okra are tender. Season to taste.

3 Boil rapidly to reduce the sauce to a glaze.

FRENCH BEANS IN SOURED CREAM WITH PAPRIKA
SERVES 4

700 g (1½ lb) French beans
25 g (1 oz) butter or margarine
1 small onion, skinned and chopped
5 ml (1 level tsp) paprika
salt and freshly ground pepper
150 ml (¼ pint) chicken or vegetable stock
150 ml (¼ pint) soured cream

1 Using kitchen scissors, top and tail the French beans and cut them into 2.5 cm (1 inch) lengths. Melt the butter in a pan, add the onion

and cook gently for 5 minutes until soft and golden, but do not brown.

2 Stir in 2.5 ml (½ level tsp) paprika, the beans, seasoning and stock. Bring to the boil, cover and simmer for 5-10 minutes until the beans are tender.

3 Stir the soured cream into the pan and reheat without boiling. Turn into a heated serving dish and dust the top with the remaining paprika.

BRAISED MIXED VEGETABLES

──── SERVES 8 ────

10 dried Chinese mushrooms, such as shiitake
45 ml (3 tbsp) peanut oil
1 garlic clove, skinned and crushed
1 Chinese cabbage, cut crossways into 2.5 cm (1 inch) strips
2 medium onions, skinned and cut into eighths and separated into layers
2 carrots, peeled and thinly sliced
16 baby sweetcorns
225 g (8 oz) broccoli, cut into very small florets
2.5 cm (1 inch) piece of fresh root ginger, peeled and grated
175 ml (6 fl oz) chicken or vegetable stock
15 ml (1 level tbsp) cornflour
30 ml (2 tbsp) light soy sauce
5-10 ml (1-2 tsp) caster sugar

1 Soak the mushrooms in hot water for 20 minutes. Squeeze out as much water as possible. Discard the stalks and thinly slice the caps.

2 Heat the oil in a wok or large frying pan. Add the garlic, cabbage, carrots, onions, baby sweetcorn, broccoli and ginger and stir fry for 2

minutes. Stir in the stock, cover with foil and cook for 2-3 minutes.

3 Blend the cornflour with the soy sauce to a smooth paste. Remove vegetables from the wok or pan, using a slotted spoon, and keep on one side. Stir the cornflour mixture into the wok and bring to the boil, stirring all the time. Boil for 1 minute, then add the sugar.

4 Return the vegetables to the pan and toss lightly to heat through. Serve at once.

Braised Mixed Vegetables

107

Right: Vegetable Jalousie

VEGETABLE JALOUSIE
SERVES 4

3 medium leeks, total weight about 450 g (1 lb), trimmed
4 medium new carrots, peeled
600 g (1¼ lb) fresh broad beans, shelled, or 350 g (12 oz) frozen
salt and freshly ground pepper
25 g (1 oz) butter or margarine
25 g (1 oz) plain flour
300 ml (½ pint) milk
100 g (4 oz) Caerphilly or Wensleydale cheese, grated
45ml (3 tbsp) grated Parmesan cheese
1.25 ml (¼ level tsp) ground mace
10 ml (2 tsp) chopped fresh herbs
500 g (1 lb 2 oz) ready prepared puff pastry, thawed if frozen
a little beaten egg, to glaze

SERVING IDEA

Vegetable Jalousie is rich and filling. Serve with a tomato and onion salad, or a salad of crisp chicory, orange and walnuts tossed in a dressing of walnut oil and cider vinegar.

1 Slice the leeks thickly, then wash well under cold running water to remove any grit. Scrub the carrots and slice thinly.

2 Parboil the broad beans in boiling salted water for 4 minutes. Remove with a slotted spoon and set aside. Add the carrots to the water and parboil for 2 minutes only. Remove with a slotted spoon and set aside with the carrots. Parboil the leeks for 1 minute and reserve the blanching water.

3 Melt the butter in a clean pan, add the flour and cook gently, stirring, for 1-2 minutes. Remove from the heat and gradually blend in the milk. Bring to the boil, stirring constantly, then simmer for 3 minutes until very thick and smooth. Add the cheese, mace and salt and pepper to taste.

4 Remove the cheese sauce from the heat and fold in the vegetables. Cover the surface of the sauce closely with cling film, then leave until the mixture is cold.

5 Meanwhile, roll out half of the pastry thinly on a lightly floured surface to a 30.5 × 23 cm (12 × 9 inch) rectangle. Place on a buttered baking sheet.

6 Stir 30 ml (2 tbsp) of the reserved blanching water and the herbs into the cold filling, then spread over the pastry on the baking sheet to within about 1 cm (½ inch) of the edges. Brush the edges with water.

7 Roll out the remaining pastry to a slightly larger rectangle than the first rectangle. Fold in half lengthways.

8 With kitchen scissors, cut through the double thickness of the pastry six times at 5 cm (2 inch) intervals along the folded edge.

9 Unfold the pastry and place over the top of the filling. Press the edges firmly to seal, then flute or crimp.

10 Brush the pastry with beaten egg, then bake in the oven at 190°C Circotherm for about 30 minutes until golden brown. Serve hot.

PETITS POIS WITH PARMA HAM

SERVES 4

50 g (2 oz) Parma ham
50 g (2 oz) butter or margarine
900 g (2 lb) fresh young peas, shelled
12 spring onions, washed, trimmed and sliced
1 firm-hearted lettuce, washed and shredded
5 ml (1 tsp) sugar
salt and freshly ground pepper
150 ml (¼ pint) chicken stock
sprig of mint, to garnish

1 Using a sharp knife, cut the ham into small strips. Melt the butter in a large saucepan, add the peas, ham and all the remaining ingredients, except the garnish.

2 Bring to the boil, cover and simmer gently for 15-20 minutes. Serve the vegetables and ham in a warm serving dish with the cooking liquid. Garnish with a sprig of mint.

ASPARAGUS MALTAISE

SERVES 6

450 g (1 lb) asparagus, washed and trimmed
3 egg yolks
grated rind and juice of 1 orange
salt and freshly ground pepper
100 g (4 oz) unsalted butter, softened
15 ml (1 tbsp) lemon juice
30-45 ml (2-3 tbsp) double cream
orange twists, to garnish

1 Tie the asparagus in bundles of six to eight stalks. Stand them upright in a saucepan of boiling water and cook for 10-15 minutes until they are just tender.

2 Meanwhile, make the sauce. Beat together the egg yolks, orange rind and seasoning in a bowl with a knob of the softened butter.

3 Place the bowl over a pan of hot water and whisk in the orange and lemon juice. Cook over a gently heat and gradually beat in remaining butter, a little at a time.

4 Once the sauce begins to thicken, remove from the heat and continue beating for 1 minute. Adjust the seasoning to taste. Stir in the cream.

5 Remove the asparagus from the pan and drain well. To serve, remove the string, garnish and serve immediately with the orange butter sauce handed separately.

COOK'S TIP

The sauce for *Asparagus Maltaise* is a variation of hollandaise sauce – grated orange rind and juice is added to make the sauce a delicate shade of pink. Hollandaise sauce is not difficult to make, but it does require patience – if you want to make a perfect sauce there is no cutting corners! From the same family of sauces as mayonnaise – it is in fact a cooked emulsion of egg yolks and butter as opposed to the uncooked emulsion of egg yolks and oil – the skill lies in the whisking in of the butter. This should be added a little at a time: if you rush this stage and whisk in more butter before the first amount has emulsified, the resulting sauce will be curdled.

SERVING IDEA

Herby Courgette Fingers with Cream goes especially well with lamb and chicken dishes.

COOK'S TIP

It is a good idea to dégorge courgettes before cooking. They are a watery vegetable, and can dilute sauces such as this creamy one if they are not dégorged beforehand. Older courgettes can also be bitter, another reason for extracting the juice before cooking. Always rinse them thoroughly after dégorging or the finished dish may be salty.

HERBY COURGETTE FINGERS WITH CREAM

SERVES 6-8

900 g (2 lb) small or medium courgettes

salt and freshly ground pepper

50 g (2 oz) butter

1-2 garlic cloves, skinned and crushed

150 ml (¼ pint) vegetable stock or water

20 ml (4 tsp) chopped fresh basil or
10 ml (2 tsp) dried

150 ml (¼ pint) double cream

1 Trim the courgettes, then cut them into neat strips about 5 cm (2 inches) long and 0.5 cm (¼ inch) wide.

2 Put the courgette strips in a colander, sprinkling each layer with salt. Cover with a plate, place heavy weights on top and leave to dégorge for 1 hour.

3 Rinse the courgette strips thoroughly under cold running water, then pat dry in a clean tea towel or with absorbent kitchen paper.

4 Melt half of the butter in a heavy-based saucepan, add the courgettes and garlic and toss over moderate heat for a few minutes.

5 Pour in the stock, then add half of the basil with salt and pepper to taste. Cover the pan and simmer gently for 5 minutes or until the courgettes are tender but still with some crunch. Transfer the courgettes to a warmed serving dish with a slotted spoon, cover and keep hot.

6 Increase the heat and boil the liquid to reduce slightly. Add the cream and the remaining butter and basil. Simmer until the sauce is of a coating consistency. Taste and adjust the seasoning, then pour over the courgettes. Serve immediately.

ROASTED PEPPERS WITH YOGURT AND PISTACHIO NUTS

SERVES 8

8 large peppers

60 ml (4 tbsp) virgin olive oil

salt and freshly ground pepper

60 ml (4 tbsp) chopped fresh marjoram or oregano

few salad leaves

450 ml (¾ pint) Greek natural yogurt

100 g (4 oz) shelled pistachio nuts,
roughly chopped

fresh herb sprigs, to garnish

1 Place the peppers in a grill pan and cook under a hot grill until the skin is blackened. Turn the peppers over and cook until the other side is blackened. This will take at least 10-15 minutes.

2 Wrap in damp absorbent kitchen paper, cool slightly, then peel off the skins. Cut off the tops and remove the seeds. Cut the peppers into chunky strips and place in a shallow dish. Pour over the olive oil and season generously with salt and pepper. Sprinkle with the marjoram. Leave to marinate until ready to serve.

3 To serve, arrange the peppers on eight plates with a few salad leaves. Place a large spoonful of yogurt on each plate and sprinkle with the pistachio nuts. Generously grind black pepper over the top and garnish with herb sprigs.

MUSHROOMS IN RED WINE
SERVES 4

350 g (12 oz) small button mushrooms
300 ml (½ pint) red wine
15 ml (1 tbsp) crushed coriander seeds
salt and freshly ground pepper
30 ml (2 tbsp) olive oil
1 small onion, skinned and finely chopped
1 garlic clove, skinned and crushed
15 ml (1 tbsp) tomato purée
30 ml (2 tbsp) chopped fresh coriander or parsley
8 lettuce leaves, to serve

1 Wipe the mushrooms with a damp cloth; leave them whole if they are very small, otherwise halve them or cut them into even slices.
2 Put the mushrooms in a bowl with the red wine, coriander seeds and season to taste with salt and pepper. Cover and leave to marinate for about 4 hours.
3 Heat the oil in a heavy-based frying pan. Add the onion and fry gently for 5 minutes until soft but not coloured. Add the garlic and tomato purée and fry for 2 minutes more.
4 Drain the marinade from the mushrooms and reserve. Add the mushrooms to the frying pan, increase the heat and fry, stirring, for 2 minutes until the juices run.
5 Pour the reserved marinade into the pan and bring to boiling point. Remove from the heat, turn into a bowl and leave until cold. Cover with cling film and chill in the refrigerator.
6 To serve, stir the coriander into the mushrooms. Leave to stand at room temperature for about 30 minutes, then taste and adjust the seasoning. Place two lettuce leaves in each of four individual dishes and spoon the mushrooms on to them. Serve immediately.

SOUFFLÉED CAULIFLOWER
SERVES 2-4

350 g (12 oz) cauliflower florets
salt and freshly ground pepper
15 g (½ oz) butter
150 ml (¼ pint) thick mayonnaise
10 ml (2 tsp) Dijon mustard
finely grated rind of ½ lemon (optional)
4 eggs, separated
100 g (4 oz) Cheddar cheese, grated
sprigs of parsley, to garnish

1 Cook the cauliflower florets in boiling salted water for about 5 minutes – they should retain their crispness. Drain well.
2 Butter a shallow ovenproof dish and place the cauliflower in the bottom.
3 Put the mayonnaise, mustard and lemon rind, if using, in a medium bowl, stir in the egg yolks and 25 g (1 oz) of the grated cheese. Season with salt and pepper to taste.
4 Put the egg whites in a separate bowl and whisk until stiff. Fold the egg whites carefully into the mayonnaise mixture.
5 Spoon this mixture over the cauliflower, sprinkle with the remaining cheese and bake in the oven at 160°C Circotherm for about 25 minutes or until risen and golden. Serve immediately, garnished with a sprigs of parsley.

SERVING IDEA

Serve *Souffléed Cauliflower* as an accompaniment to a grilled chop, chicken portion or steak. It would also make a good light lunch or supper dish, with wholemeal French-style bread. It would serve two people as a main course.

COOK'S TIP

It is best to use Dijon mustard for *Souffléed Cauliflower* as its smooth, mild flavour will not override the other delicate flavours of this dish. Made in the town of Dijon in the region of Burgundy, *moutarde à la Dijonnaise* is unique in that it is made from mustard grains mixed with verjuice (the juice of sour Burgundy grapes), plus herbs and flavourings. Most other mustards are made with vinegar, which is why they are sharper in flavour than Dijon.

SERVING IDEA

Serve *Red Kidney Beans Hot Pot* for a nutritious vegetarian main course, with nutty brown rice or wholemeal bread, and a crisp green salad.

RED KIDNEY BEAN HOT POT

SERVES 2

100 g (4 oz) dried red kidney beans, soaked in cold water overnight
1 medium onion
100 g (4 oz) celery, trimmed
100 g (4 oz) carrots, peeled
100 g (4 oz) courgettes, trimmed
25 g (1 oz) butter or margarine
15 ml (1 level tbsp) plain flour
300 ml (½ pint) vegetable or chicken stock
salt and freshly ground pepper
100 g (4 oz) French beans, topped and tailed
25 g (1 oz) wholemeal breadcrumbs
75 g (3 oz) Cheddar cheese, grated

1 Drain the soaked kidney beans and rinse well under cold running water. Put in a large saucepan, cover with plenty of fresh cold water and bring slowly to the boil.

2 Skim off any scum with a slotted spoon, then boil rapidly for 10 minutes. Half cover the pan with a lid and simmer for about 1½ hours until the beans are tender.

3 Skin the onion and chop roughly. Slice the celery, carrots and courgettes.

4 Melt the butter in a large saucepan, add the onion and fry gently for about 5 minutes until softened. Add the celery and carrots. Cover and cook gently for 5 minutes.

5 Add the flour and cook gently, stirring, for 1-2 minutes. Remove from the heat and gradually blend in the stock. Bring to the boil, stirring, then simmer for 5 minutes. Season to taste.

6 Add the French beans and simmer for a further 5 minutes, then add the courgettes. Cook for a further 5-10 minutes until the vegetables are tender but still with a bite to them.

7 Drain the kidney beans, add to the vegetables and heat for about 5 minutes. Adjust seasoning, then turn into a deep flameproof dish.

8 Mix the breadcrumbs and cheese together. Sprinkle on top of the bean mixture and brown under a preheated grill until crusty. Serve hot.

SWISS CHALET POTATOES WITH CREAM AND CHEESE

SERVES 6-8

1.4 kg (3 lb) even-sized small potatoes, scrubbed
salt and freshly ground pepper
300 ml (½ pint) double cream
1-2 garlic cloves, skinned and crushed
good pinch of freshly grated nutmeg
75 g (3 oz) Gruyère or Emmental cheese, grated
75 g (3 oz) Parmesan cheese, freshly grated

1 Cook the potatoes in a large saucepan of boiling salted water for 10 minutes. Drain well.

2 Stand the potatoes upright in a buttered baking dish. Mix the cream with the garlic, nutmeg and salt and pepper to taste, then pour over the potatoes.

3 Mix the two cheeses together and sprinkle over the potatoes to cover them completely. Bake, uncovered, in the oven at 160°C Circotherm for 40-45 minutes or until the potatoes feel tender when pierced with a skewer. Serve hot, straight from the dish.

SERVING IDEA

Swiss Chalet Potatoes with Cream and Cheese is a rich dish that goes particularly well with a plain roast joint.

CHAKCHOUKA

——— SERVES 2 ———

1 small aubergine
salt and freshly ground pepper
1 red pepper
1 green pepper
225 g (8 oz) tomatoes
1 fresh green chilli or
2.5 ml (½ level tsp) chilli powder
60 ml (4 tbsp) olive oil
1 medium onion, skinned and thinly sliced
1 garlic clove, skinned and crushed
sprigs of parsley or coriander, to garnish

1 Slice the aubergine thinly, then place in a colander, sprinkling each layer with salt. Cover with a plate, put heavy weights on top and leave to dégorge for 20-30 minutes.

2 Put the peppers under a preheated moderate grill and cook until the skins char on all sides, turning them frequently.

3 Remove the peppers from the grill and wrap in damp absorbent kitchen paper. Cool.

4 Skin the tomatoes. Plunge them into boiling water, then into cold. Peel off the skins and chop the flesh roughly. Halve the chilli, if using, remove the seeds under cold running water, then chop the flesh finely.

5 Rinse the aubergine slices under cold running water, then pat dry with a absorbent kitchen paper. Heat the oil in a heavy-based saucepan, add the sliced onion, crushed garlic and fresh chilli, if using, and fry gently for about 5 minutes until soft but not coloured.

6 Add the aubergines slices, the tomatoes, chilli powder, if using, and salt and pepper. Cook for 20 minutes, stirring frequently.

7 Meanwhile, unwrap the peppers and peel off the skins by rubbing with your fingers under cold running water. Discard the cores and seeds, then pat the flesh dry with absorbent kitchen paper. Cut into thin strips.

8 Add the pepper strips to the pan and heat through for about 5 minutes. Taste and adjust the seasoning, then garnish and serve.

Chakchouka

SERVING IDEA

Chakchouka is a spicy, Moroccan version of the well-known French vegetable dish, ratatouille. Serve it as an alternative to ratatouille, with roast or grilled steak and chops. In Morocco, *Chakchouka* is often served as a lunch or supper dish with eggs, which are either dropped into the vegetables and cooked whole for the last few minutes of the cooking time, or stirred in until creamy. In this recipe, it is served hot as a vegetable accompaniment, but it tastes just as good served chilled as a starter, with crusty French bread and butter and a bottle of chilled dry white wine.

COOK'S TIPS

Salting the aubergine flesh draws out the bitter juices; if these are not extracted the finished dish may be spoilt.

Grilling peppers until charred, then wrapping them in kitchen paper until cold, and then peeling them, gives them a wonderful smoky flavour and soft, juicy texture. It is a favourite way of preparing peppers on the continent and in the Middle East and Africa.

113

POTATO, CARROT AND ONION CASSEROLE

SERVES 4

25 g (1 oz) butter or margarine

15 ml (1 tbsp) vegetable oil

15 ml (1 tbsp) demerara sugar

225 g (8 oz) carrots, peeled and thickly sliced

225 g (8 oz) small onions, skinned

450 g (1 lb) small new potatoes,
scrubbed and cut in half

100 g (4 oz) button mushrooms

15 ml (1 level tbsp) plain flour

150 ml (¼ pint) red wine

10 ml (2 tsp) tomato purée

150 ml (¼ pint) vegetable stock

1 bay leaf

salt and freshly ground pepper

parsley, to garnish

1 Heat the butter and oil together in a flame-proof casserole. Add the sugar, carrots, onions and potatoes. Cook, stirring, over high heat for 5 minutes until the vegetables colour.

2 Add the mushrooms and cook for a further minute. Stir in the flour, scraping any sediment from the bottom of the pan, then add the red wine, tomato purée, stock, bay leaf and salt and pepper to taste.

3 Cover the casserole tightly, then bake in the oven at 160°C Circotherm for about 1 hour or until the vegetables are tender, adding more liquid if necessary.

4 Remove the bay leaf. Taste and adjust the seasoning, then garnish with parsley and serve.

SERVING IDEA

Potato, Carrot and Onion Casserole is the perfect dish to cook in the oven while you are roasting meat or cooking a meat or poultry casserole for a main course.

JERUSALEM ARTICHOKE GRATIN

SERVES 4

900 g (2 lb) Jerusalem artichokes

salt and freshly ground pepper

225 g (8 oz) small button or pickling onions

3 medium leeks, trimmed

75 g (3 oz) butter or margarine

15 ml (1 tbsp) olive oil

2 garlic cloves, skinned and crushed

150 ml (¼ pint) dry white wine or vegetable stock,
or a mixture of both

1.25 ml (¼ level tsp) freshly grated nutmeg

225 g (8 oz) fresh or frozen peas

150 ml (¼ pint) double cream

75 g (3 oz) Gruyère cheese, grated

75 g (3 oz) Cheddar cheese, grated

50 g (2 oz) dried wholemeal breadcrumbs

114   *Potato, Carrot and Onion Casserole*

1 Parboil the Jerusalem artichokes in salted water for 5-10 minutes, depending on the size. Remove and leave until cool.

2 Peel the skins off the Jerusalem artichokes and slice the flesh thickly. Set aside.

3 Add the button onions to the water and boil for 2 minutes, then remove with a slotted spoon. Peel off the skins, leaving the root ends intact so that the onions remain whole.

4 Slice the leeks thickly, then wash well under cold running water to remove any grit.

5 Heat 50 g (2 oz) of the butter with the oil in a heavy-based saucepan, add the onions and garlic and toss over moderate heat until the onions are well coated in the butter and oil.

6 Pour in the wine and 150 ml (¼ pint) water and bring to the boil. Add the nutmeg, cover and simmer for 10 minutes.

7 Add the artichokes, leeks and peas and continue simmering for 5 minutes or until all the vegetables are tender. With a slotted spoon, transfer them to a flameproof gratin dish.

8 Boil the cooking liquid rapidly until reduced to about half of its original volume. Lower the heat and stir in the cream.

9 Mix the two cheeses together. Stir half of this mixture into the sauce. Add salt and pepper to taste and stir until the cheeses have melted.

10 Pour the cheese sauce over the vegetables in the dish. Mix the remaining cheese with the breadcrumbs, then sprinkle evenly over the top.

11 Dot the remaining butter over the gratin, then bake in the oven at 180°C Circotherm for 10-15 minutes until the topping is golden brown. Serve hot, straight from the dish.

LENTIL HOT POT

SERVES 2

175 g (6 oz) green lentils
salt and freshly ground pepper
25 g (1 oz) butter or margarine
1 medium onion, skinned and chopped
2.5 ml (½ level tsp) curry powder
100 g (4 oz) celery, trimmed and sliced
100 g (4 oz) carrots, peeled and sliced
15 ml (1 tbsp) plain flour
300 ml (½ pint) chicken or vegetable stock
100 g (4 oz) French beans, topped and tailed
100 g (4 oz) courgettes, sliced
25 g (1 oz) fresh breadcrumbs
75 g (3 oz) Cheddar cheese, grated

1 Cook the lentils in boiling salted water for 20 minutes or until tender. Drain well.

2 Meanwhile, melt the butter in a large saucepan, add the onion and fry for about 5 minutes until soft. Add curry powder, celery and carrots, cover and cook gently for 5 minutes.

3 Stir in the flour and cook for 1 minute, then stir in the stock. Bring to the boil, stirring. Season to taste and simmer for 5 minutes.

4 Add the French beans and simmer for a further 5 minutes, then add the courgettes. Cook for about 10 minutes until tender.

5 Drain the lentils and add to the vegetables. Heat through for 2-3 minutes. Taste and adjust seasoning, then turn into a flameproof dish.

6 Mix the breadcrumbs and cheese together and sprinkle on top. Put under a preheated hot grill until crisp and golden brown. Serve hot.

SERVING IDEA

Lentil Hot Pot goes especially well with smoked or spicy sausages. It can also be served as a vegetarian dish, in which case substitute vegetable stock for the chicken stock and serve with wholemeal bread to make a more nutritious meal.

COOK'S TIP

This warming winter hot pot calls for green lentils, which you will find in health food shops, Indian stores and continental delicatessens. They have quite a pronounced 'earthy' flavour. The beauty of this type of lentil is that it keeps its shape during cooking, unlike the split red and yellow varieties, which quickly disintegrate to a mush. Lentils do not need to be soaked like other pulses. They are also extremely nutritious as they are high in protein and fibre, yet low in fat.

115

Spinach Roulade

To cook the spinach in the microwave, put half on a plate or in a bowl, cover and cook on HIGH for 9 minutes, stirring halfway through. Repeat with second half, then drain. If using frozen spinach, cook on HIGH, covered, for 6-7 minutes, stirring halfway through. Drain.

Serve *Spinach Roulade* for a weekend lunch dish with new potatoes tossed in butter, or jacket-baked potatoes topped with soured cream and snipped chives.

Opposite: Spinach Roulade; Crispy Potato Galette (see page 118)

SPINACH ROULADE

SERVES 3-4

900 g (2 lb) spinach, trimmed, or 450 g (1 lb) packet frozen spinach
4 eggs, size 2, separated
pinch of freshly grated nutmeg
salt and freshly ground pepper
25 g (1 oz) butter or margarine
1 medium onion, skinned and finely chopped
100 g (4 oz) curd cheese
50 g (2 oz) Gruyère cheese, grated
30 ml (2 tbsp) soured cream
TOMATO SAUCE
397 g (14 oz) can tomatoes
5 ml (1 tsp) tomato purée
1 small onion, skinned and chopped
1 garlic clove, skinned and crushed (optional)
pinch of dried basil
pinch of sugar
freshly ground pepper
15 ml (1 tbsp) vegetable oil

1 Grease a 35 × 25.5 cm (14 × 10 inch) Swiss roll tin and line with non-stick baking parchment. Set aside.

2 Wash the fresh spinach in several changes of cold water. Place in a saucepan with only the water that clings to the leaves. Cook gently, covered, for about 5 minutes until wilted or for about 7-10 minutes until it is thawed, if using a packet of frozen spinach.

3 Drain the spinach well and chop finely. Turn into a bowl and allow to cool slightly for about 5 minutes, then beat in the egg yolks, nutmeg and salt and pepper to taste.

4 Whisk the egg whites until they form stiff peaks, then fold into the spinach mixture with a large metal spoon until they are evenly incorporated.

5 Spread the mixture in the prepared tin. Bake in the oven at 170°C Circotherm for 12-15 minutes until firm.

6 Meanwhile, prepare the filling. Melt the butter in a saucepan. Add the onion and fry gently for about 5 minutes until soft and lightly coloured. Remove from the heat and stir in the cheeses, soured cream and season to taste with salt and pepper.

7 Make the sauce. Put all the ingredients in a blender or food processor and process until smooth. Heat in a saucepan for 10-15 minutes until slightly thickened.

8 Turn the roulade out on to greaseproof paper, peel off the lining paper and spread the roulade immediately and quickly with the cheese and onion mixture.

9 Roll the roulade up by gently lifting the greaseproof paper. Serve hot, cut into thick slices, with the tomato sauce.

COOK'S TIP

You will need a non-stick frying pan with an ovenproof handle and lid to make this galette – the French cast iron type is ideal. If your pan handle and lid knob are not ovenproof, cover them with several thicknesses of foil for protection, or bake the galette in a sandwich tin.

Baked Peppers with Wild Rice Filling

BAKED PEPPERS WITH WILD RICE FILLING

SERVES 8

175 g (6 oz) mixed long-grain and wild rice

salt and freshly ground pepper

2 red peppers

2 green peppers

a little oil for brushing

50 g (2 oz) butter

1 medium onion, skinned and chopped

175 g (6 oz) button mushrooms, sliced

good pinch of cayenne pepper

1 Cook the rice in a large saucepan of boiling water for about 15 minutes or until tender. Drain well and rinse with boiling water, then drain well again.

2 Cut the peppers in half lengthways. Leave the stalks in place but discard the seeds and pith. Blanch the peppers in boiling water for 5 minutes. Drain, then plunge into cold water and leave until cold. Drain and pat dry, then brush with oil.

3 Melt the butter in a saucepan and fry the onion and mushrooms until lightly golden. Stir in the rice, salt and pepper and cayenne. Remove from the heat and spoon the mixture into the prepared peppers and arrange in a greased, shallow ovenproof dish. Cover with lightly greased foil.

4 Bake in the oven at 160°C Circotherm for 30-35 minutes or until the peppers are tender and the filling is heated through. Uncover, then fluff up the rice with a fork. Serve hot.

CRISPY POTATO GALETTE

SERVES 4-6

900 g (2 lb) old potatoes, peeled

50 g (2 oz) butter

15 ml (1 tbsp) olive oil

salt and freshly ground pepper

1 Cut the potatoes into very thin rings and dry thoroughly on a clean tea towel.

2 Melt the butter with the oil in a 20 cm (8 inch) non-stick frying pan with a lid (see Cook's Tip). Heat until foaming, then remove the pan from the heat and add the potato rings, overlapping them in a circular pattern. Season well with salt and pepper, then press the potatoes down firmly with a metal spatula.

3 Cover the potatoes with a sheet of buttered greaseproof paper, then with the pan lid. Cook over moderate heat for 10-15 minutes until potatoes are golden brown on the underside.

4 Transfer the covered pan to the oven. Bake at 170°C Circotherm for 30 minutes, or until the potatoes feel tender when pierced with a skewer. Remove from the oven and leave to rest, covered, for 10 minutes.

5 Uncover the potatoes and place a warmed flat serving plate on top. Invert the potato galatte on to the plate. Serve hot, cut into wedges.

ITALIAN COURGETTE, PARMESAN AND TOMATO BAKE

SERVES 4

700 g (1½ lb) courgettes

salt and freshly ground pepper

about 150 ml (¼ pint) vegetable oil

1 medium onion, skinned and finely chopped

450 g (1 lb) tomatoes, skinned and crushed

1 large garlic clove, skinned and crushed

30 ml (2 tbsp) tomato purée

15 ml (1 tbsp) chopped fresh marjoram

350 g (12 oz) Mozzarella cheese, thinly sliced

75 g (3 oz) freshly grated Parmesan cheese

1 Cut the courgettes into 0.5 cm (¼ inch) thick slices. Sprinkle with salt and leave to dégorge for at least 20 minutes.

2 Heat 30 ml (2 tbsp) of the oil in a saucepan, add the onion and fry for about 5 minutes until just beginning to brown.

3 Stir in the tomatoes, garlic and tomato purée and season to taste with salt and pepper. Simmer for about 10 minutes, stirring. Stir in the marjoram and remove from the heat.

4 Rinse the courgettes and pat dry with absorbent kitchen paper. Heat half of the remaining oil in a frying pan, add half of the courgettes and fry until golden brown. Drain while frying the remaining courgettes in the remaining oil.

5 Layer the courgettes, tomato sauce and Mozzarella cheese in a shallow ovenproof dish. Sprinkle with the Parmesan cheese.

6 Bake in the oven at 160°C Circotherm for about 40 minutes or until brown and bubbling.

RISOTTO ALLA MILANESE

SERVES 4

1.1 litres (2 pints) chicken stock

75 g (3 oz) butter or margarine

1 small onion, skinned and finely chopped

350 g (12 oz) Arborio (Italian risotto) rice

few saffron strands

salt and freshly ground pepper

50 g (2 oz) Parmesan cheese, freshly grated

1 Bring the stock to the boil in a large saucepan and keep at barely simmering point.

2 Meanwhile, in a large, heavy-based saucepan, melt 25 g (1 oz) butter, add the onion and fry gently for about 5 minutes until it is soft but not coloured.

3 Add the rice to the pan and stir with a fork for 2-3 minutes until the rice is well coated with the butter.

4 Add a ladleful of stock to the pan, cook gently, stirring frequently, until the stock is absorbed. Add more stock as soon as each ladleful is absorbed, stirring frequently.

5 When the rice becomes creamy, sprinkle in the saffron with salt and pepper to taste. Continue adding stock and stirring until the risotto is thick, creamy and tender but not sticky. The process should take about 20-25 minutes to complete; it must not be hurried.

6 Just before serving, stir in the remaining butter and the Parmesan, then taste and adjust the seasoning. Serve hot.

SERVING IDEA

Italian Courgette, Parmesan and Tomato Bake makes a rich and filling main course served with crusty French bread and a mixed side salad.

119

Serve rich individual *Broccoli Gougères* for a lunch dish with a crisp salad of curly endive and radicchio tossed in a dressing of olive oil, lemon juice and chopped fresh herbs.

Broccoli Gougères

BROCCOLI GOUGÈRES

— SERVES 4 —

2 egg quantity Choux Pastry (see page 190) with 25 g (1 oz) Cheddar cheese added to the mixture after the eggs

700 g (1½ lb) broccoli

25 g (1 oz) butter or margarine

25 g (1 oz) plain flour

300 ml (½ pint) milk

30 ml (2 tbsp) chopped fresh parsley

salt and freshly ground pepper

15 g (½ oz) flaked almonds (optional)

1 Pipe or spoon the choux mixture around the edge of four scallop shells or shallow ovenproof dishes. Bake in the oven at 170°C Circotherm for 30 minutes or until well risen and brown.

2 Meanwhile, cut the broccoli into small florets. Cook in boiling salted water for 3-4 minutes until nearly tender. Drain well.

3 Melt the butter in a saucepan, add the flour and cook gently, stirring, for 1-2 minutes. Remove from the heat and gradually blend in the milk. Bring to boil, stirring, then simmer for 3 minutes. Stir in the parsley, season and remove from heat. Fold in broccoli.

4 Spoon into the centre of the shells, sprinkle with the almonds, if using, and bake at 170°C Circotherm until the broccoli is piping hot.

MIXED VEGETABLE CURRY

— SERVES 8 —

100 ml (4 fl oz) ghee or vegetable oil

2 large onions, skinned and finely chopped

3-4 green chillies, seeded and finely chopped

10 ml (2 level tsp) chilli powder

2.5 ml (½ level tsp) turmeric

120 ml (8 tbsp) tomato purée

300 ml (½ pint) natural yogurt

450 g (1 lb) young turnips, peeled and sliced

450 g (1 lb) small carrots, diced

450 g (1 lb) cauliflower florets

1.1 litres (2 pints) coconut milk (see page 47)

salt

450 g (1 lb) frozen peas

16 whole cloves

16 black peppercorns

seeds of 16 green cardamoms

20 ml (4 level tsp) fennel seeds

2.5 ml (½ level tsp) freshly grated nutmeg

1 Heat the ghee in a heavy-based saucepan or flameproof casserole, add the onions and fry gently for about 5 minutes or until soft and lightly coloured.

2 Add the chillies and stir to mix with the onions, then add the chilli powder and turmeric and fry, stirring, for 2 minutes.

3 Add the tomato purée and stir for a further 2 minutes, then add the yogurt, 15 ml (1 tbsp) at a time. Cook each addition over high heat, stirring constantly, until the yogurt is absorbed.

4 Add the turnips and carrots and fry, stirring frequently, for 5 minutes, then add the cauliflower and fry for 5 minutes.

5 Gradually stir in the coconut milk and 600 ml (1 pint) water. Add salt to taste and bring to the boil. Lower the heat, cover and simmer for about 40 minutes or until the vegetables are very tender, adding the peas for the last 10 minutes.

6 Meanwhile, dry fry the whole spices in a heavy-based frying pan for a few minutes, then grind to a fine powder with a pestle and mortar.

7 Remove the pan from the heat, sprinkle the ground spices and nutmeg over the vegetables and fold to mix. Cover the pan tightly with a lid, and remove from the heat. Leave to stand for 5 minutes, for the flavours to develop. Taste and adjust the seasoning, then turn into a warmed serving dish.

CURRIED SPINACH AND POTATOES

SERVES 4-6

two 225 g (8 oz) packets frozen leaf spinach, thawed and drained
50 g (2 oz) ghee or 30 ml (2 tbsp) vegetable oil
1 onion, skinned and thinly sliced
2 garlic cloves, skinned and crushed
10 ml (2 level tsp) ground coriander
5 ml (1 tsp) mustard seeds
2.5 ml (½ level tsp) turmeric
1.25-2.5 ml (¼-½ level tsp) chilli powder, according to taste
salt
450 g (1 lb) potatoes, peeled and cut roughly into cubes

1 Put the spinach in a heavy-based saucepan and place over very gentle heat for about 5 minutes to drive off as much liquid as possible.

2 Meanwhile, melt the ghee in a separate heavy-based pan. Add the onion, garlic, spices and salt to taste and fry gently for about 5 minutes, stirring frequently.

3 Add the potatoes and fold gently into the spice mixture, then pour in 150 ml (¼ pint) water. Bring to the boil, then lower the heat and simmer uncovered, for 10 minutes, stirring occasionally and adding a few more spoonfuls of water if necessary.

4 Fold the spinach gently into the potato mixture. Simmer for a further 5-10 minutes until the potatoes are just tender. To serve, taste and adjust the seasoning, then turn into a warmed serving dish. Serve hot.

MICROWAVE

Curried Spinach and Potatoes
Put the ghee or oil, onion, garlic and spices in a bowl and cook, uncovered, on HIGH for 3-4 minutes. Add the spinach (thawed but not drained), potatoes and 75 ml (5 tbsp) water. Cover and cook on HIGH for 20-25 minutes.

SERVING IDEA

Curried Spinach and Potatoes is an Indian vegetable accompaniment known as Sag Aloo (sag meaning spinach and aloo potatoes). It goes particularly well with Indian dishes such as Raan (see page 50) or curries.

COOK'S TIP

Different goat's cheeses take very different times to cook, so the time given for *Salad of Baked Goat's Cheese and Hazelnuts* is a rough guide.

SERVING IDEA

Serve *Vegetable Lasagne* as a vegetarian main course with bread and a mixed green salad.

VEGETABLE LASAGNE

SERVES 4-6

175 g (6 oz) dried lasagne verde
salt and freshly ground pepper
30 ml (2 tbsp) vegetable oil
2 medium onions, skinned and thinly sliced
1 garlic clove, skinned and crushed
350 g (12 oz) tomatoes, skinned and thinly sliced
350 g (12 oz) courgettes, trimmed and thinly sliced
15 ml (1 tbsp) tomato purée
5 ml (1 tsp) chopped fresh basil or 2.5 ml (½ tsp) dried
25 g (1 oz) butter or margarine
25 g (1 oz) plain flour
600 ml (1 pint) milk
150 g (5 oz) Cheddar cheese, grated
50 g (2 oz) walnut pieces, chopped

1 Cook the lasagne in a large saucepan of boiling salted water with 15 ml (1 tbsp) oil for 15 minutes. Drain on absorbent kitchen paper.

2 Heat the remaining oil in a pan, add the onions, garlic, tomatoes and 300 g (10 oz) of the courgettes and fry gently until the tomatoes begin to break down. Stir in the tomato purée, basil and plenty of seasoning.

3 Put the butter, flour, milk and salt and pepper to taste in a saucepan. Heat, whisking continuously, until the sauce thickens. Cook for 1-2 minutes, then remove from the heat and stir in 50 g (2 oz) of the cheese.

4 Grease a deep-sided 2 litre (3½ pint) ovenproof dish. Layer the vegetables, lasagne and nuts in the dish, ending with a layer of lasagne.

Pour over the sauce, then sprinkle with the remaining cheese.

5 Bake the lasagne in the oven at 170°C Circotherm for about 40 minutes or until set. Serve hot, straight from the dish.

SALAD OF BAKED GOAT'S CHEESE AND HAZELNUTS

SERVES 6

25 g (1 oz) hazelnuts
12 thin slices French bread
12 thin slices of goat's cheese
salad leaves
10 ml (2 tsp) hazelnut oil
45 ml (3 tbsp) vinaigrette
freshly ground pepper

1 Place the hazelnuts on a baking sheet and toast in the oven at 170°C Circotherm for 10-12 minutes until thoroughly browned. Tip the nuts on to a clean tea towel and rub off the loose skins. Roughly chop the nuts, then return to the oven for 2-3 minutes or until evenly browned.

2 Increase the oven temperature on 180°C Circotherm. Arrange the slices of French bread on a baking sheet. Top each with a slice of cheese and bake for about 10 minutes until bread is crisp and the cheese hot but not melted.

3 Arrange the salad leaves on six plates. Whisk the hazelnut oil into the vinaigrette.

4 When the cheese and bread are ready, arrange on top of the salad leaves. Sprinkle each with a little of the dressing and the hazelnuts. Grind a little pepper over the top and serve.

SALADE TIÈDE AUX LARDONS
——— SERVES 4 ———

135 ml (9 tbsp) olive oil
30 ml (2 tbsp) wine vinegar
2 garlic cloves, skinned and crushed
5 ml (1 tsp) French mustard
salt and freshly ground pepper
8 streaky bacon rashers, rinded
4 thick slices of white bread, crusts removed
30 ml (2 tbsp) single or double cream
1 small head of curly endive, leaves separated

1 Put 90 ml (6 tbsp) of the oil in a large salad bowl with the wine vinegar, garlic, mustard and salt and pepper to taste. Whisk with a fork until thick.

2 Cut the bacon and bread into small dice. Heat the remaining oil in a frying pan, add the bacon and bread and fry over brisk heat until crisp and golden brown on all sides. Remove with a slotted spoon and drain on absorbent kitchen paper.
3 Stir the cream into the dressing, then add the endive and warm bacon and croûtons. Toss quickly to combine and serve immediately.

FLAGEOLET AND TOMATO SALAD WITH HERBY DRESSING
——— SERVES 4 ———

135 ml (9 tbsp) olive oil
45 ml (3 tbsp) lemon juice
30 ml (2 tbsp) mayonnaise
45 ml (3 tbsp) mixed chopped fresh herbs (parsley, chervil, chives, marjoram, basil)
salt and freshly ground pepper
397 g (14 oz) can green flageolet beans
4 tomatoes, skinned and chopped
1 small onion, skinned and finely chopped
2 garlic cloves, skinned and finely chopped
lettuce leaves, snipped chives and lemon twists, to serve

1 Put the olive oil, lemon juice, mayonnaise, herbs and seasoning in a bowl and whisk until thick.
2 Rinse the beans under cold running water. Drain and add to the dressing with the chopped tomatoes, onion and garlic.
3 Toss well, cover and chill for 30 minutes. Serve on lettuce leaves, garnished with snipped chives and lemon twists.

MENU SUGGESTION

Salade Tiède aux Lardons is a very popular first course in France, served with crusty French bread and red or white wine. Follow with a substantial main course such as *Filet de Boeuf en Croûte* (see page 58) or *Boeuf à la Bourguignonne* (see page 57), then finish the meal with a French *Tarte Tatin* (see page 148).

Left: Salade Tiède aux Lardons

123

COOK'S TIP

Do not make *Salad Elona* in advance as the strawberries will discolour the cucumber.

Salad Elona

SALAD ELONA

SERVES 4

½ medium cucumber

salt

225 g (8 oz) fresh ripe strawberries

10 ml (2 tsp) green peppercorns in brine

45 ml (3 tbsp) sunflower or corn oil

15 ml (1 tbsp) wine or balsamic vinegar

few lettuce leaves, to serve

1 Score the skin of the cucumber lengthways with a cannelle knife or the prongs of a fork. Slice the cucumber very thinly, then place on a plate and sprinkle with salt. Leave to stand for about 30 minutes to draw out the excess moisture.

2 Meanwhile, prepare the strawberries. Reserve a few whole fruit (the smallest possible) for the garnish. Hull the remaining strawberries, and slice in half lengthways.

3 Drain the peppercorns and pat dry with absorbent kitchen paper. Crush them with the back of a metal spoon in a small bowl. Add the oil and vinegar and whisk with a fork until they are well combined.

4 Drain the cucumber and pat dry with absorbent kitchen paper. Shred the lettuce, then arrange on a round serving platter. Arrange the cucumber slices and halved strawberries on the lettuce, alternating rings of each. Sprinkle over the dressing, then garnish the centre of the salad with the reserved whole strawberries. Serve the salad immediately.

FENNEL AND TOMATO SALAD

SERVES 6

90 ml (6 tbsp) vegetable oil or half vegetable, half walnut oil

45 ml (3 tbsp) lemon juice

salt and freshly ground pepper

12 black olives, halved and stoned

450 g (1 lb) Florence fennel

450 g (1 lb) ripe tomatoes

1 In a medium mixing bowl, whisk the oil(s), lemon juice and salt and pepper together. Add the olives to the dressing.

2 Snip off the feathery ends of the fennel.

3 Halve each bulb of fennel lengthways, then slice thinly crossways, discarding the roots. Blanch in boiling salted water for 2-3 minutes, then drain. While it is still warm, stir the fennel into the dressing.

4 Leave to cool, cover tightly with cling film and chill. Meanwhile, skin and slice the tomatoes and refrigerate covered.

5 Just before serving, arrange the tomatoes and fennel mixture on individual serving plates and snip the fennel tops over them.

AVOCADO AND ORANGE SALAD WITH LIME AND CHILLI

SERVES 8

7 small juicy blood oranges
3 ripe avocados
finely grated rind and juice of 1 lime
60 ml (4 tbsp) olive oil
salt and freshly ground pepper
2 pickled chillies (or to taste)

1 Squeeze the juice from one orange. Halve the avocados, remove the stone from each, then carefully peel off the skin. Thinly slice the avocados. Sprinkle generously with the juice from the orange.

2 Peel the remaining oranges, removing as much of the bitter white pith as you can. Using a very sharp knife, thinly slice the oranges and

arrange on the plate with the avocados.

3 Mix the lime rind and juice with the oil and season to taste with salt and pepper. Pour the dressing over the salad.

4 Chop the chillies and sprinkle over the salad.

FRESH SPINACH AND BABY CORN SALAD

SERVES 8

350 g (12 oz) fresh young spinach
175 g (6 oz) fresh baby sweetcorn
50 ml (2 fl oz) olive oil
1 garlic clove, skinned and crushed
15 ml (1 tbsp) white wine vinegar
10 ml (2 tsp) Dijon mustard
5 ml (1 tsp) caster sugar
salt and freshly ground pepper
100 g (4 oz) alfalfa sprouts
1 head of chicory, trimmed and shredded

1 Wash the spinach well in several changes of cold water. Remove any coarse stalks. Drain well and pat dry on absorbent kitchen paper.

2 Halve the sweetcorn cobs lengthways. Cook in boiling water for about 10 minutes or until the cobs are just tender. Drain and refresh under cold running water.

3 Whisk together the olive oil, crushed garlic, vinegar, Dijon mustard and sugar. Season with salt and pepper to taste.

4 Mix together the spinach, sweetcorn, alfalfa sprouts and chicory, toss in the dressing and serve immediately.

COOK'S TIPS

The best avocados for *Avocado and Orange Salad with Lime and Chilli* are the small brown, knobbly skinned Hass avocados.

Pickled chillies are relatively mild and are sold in jars in supermarkets.

COURGETTE AND TOASTED PINE KERNEL SALAD

——— SERVES 8 ———

450 g (1 lb) courgettes, trimmed and thinly sliced
½ head of endive
2 oranges
60 ml (4 tbsp) vinaigrette
15 ml (1 tbsp) chopped fresh parsley (optional)
salt and freshly ground pepper
30 ml (2 tbsp) toasted pine kernels or slivered, blanched almonds
2 tart green eating apples

1 Blanch the courgettes in boiling water for 1 minute. Drain and refresh under cold running water. Leave to cool completely, then pat dry with absorbent kitchen paper. Cover and refrigerate. Wash the endive, dry and place in a polythene bag. Chill in the refrigerator.
2 With a serrated knife and holding the fruit over a bowl to catch the juice, cut all the peel and pith away from the oranges. Cut down between the membranes to release the segments into the bowl.
3 Whisk together the vinaigrette, parsley, if using, and salt and pepper to taste. Add to the orange segments with the pine kernels.
4 Just before serving, halve, core and thinly slice the apples into the dressing mixture. Add the courgettes and endive. Stir well. Adjust the seasoning and serve immediately.

WINTER CABBAGE AND CAULIFLOWER SALAD

——— SERVES 4 ———

225 g (8 oz) hard white cabbage
225 g (8 oz) cauliflower florets
2 large carrots, peeled
75 g (3 oz) mixed shelled nuts, roughly chopped
50 g (2 oz) raisins
60 ml (4 tbsp) chopped fresh parsley or coriander
90 ml (6 tbsp) mayonnaise
90 ml (6 tbsp) soured cream or natural yogurt
10 ml (2 tsp) French mustard
30 ml (2 tbsp) olive or vegetable oil
juice of ½ lemon
salt and freshly ground pepper
3 red-skinned eating apples

1 Shred the cabbage finely with a sharp knife and place in a large bowl. Divide the cauliflower florets into small sprigs and add to the cabbage. Mix the vegetables gently with your hands.
2 Grate the carrots into the bowl, then add the nuts, raisins and parsley. Mix the vegetables together again until evenly combined.
3 Put the remaining ingredients except the apples in a jug. Whisk well to combine, then pour over the vegetables in the bowl and toss well.
4 Core and chop the apples, but do not peel them. Add to the salad and toss again to combine with the other ingredients. Cover the bowl and chill the salad in the refrigerator for about 1 hour before serving.

SERVING IDEA

Crunchy *Winter Cabbage and Cauliflower Salad* can be served as an accompaniment to a selection of cold meats for a quick and nutritious lunch. For a vegetarian meal, serve the salad with cheese and wholemeal or granary bread.

ORIENTAL SALAD

SERVES 8

1 large cucumber
salt and freshly ground pepper
1 small head Chinese leaves
1 red pepper
100 g (4 oz) button mushrooms
225 g (8 oz) bean sprouts
30 ml (2 tbsp) soy sauce
15 ml (1 tbsp) peanut butter
30 ml (2 tbsp) sesame oil
30 ml (2 tbsp) rice or wine vinegar
50 g (2 oz) shelled unsalted peanuts

1 Cut the cucumber in half lengthways and scoop out the seeds. Cut the halves into 5 cm (2 inch) sticks, leaving the skin on.

2 Shred the Chinese leaves, wash and drain well. Cut the red pepper in half and remove the core and seeds. Cut the flesh into thin strips.

Wipe and slice the mushrooms. Rinse the bean sprouts and drain well.

3 Just before serving, mix the soy sauce in a large bowl with the peanut butter, oil, vinegar and salt and pepper to taste. Add the salad ingredients and the peanuts and toss together. Transfer to a serving bowl.

THREE BEAN SALAD

SERVES 4-6

75 g (3 oz) dried red kidney beans, soaked in cold water overnight
75 g (3 oz) dried black-eye beans, soaked overnight
75 g (3 oz) dried pinto or borlotti beans, soaked overnight
100 ml (4 fl oz) vinaigrette
15 ml (1 tbsp) chopped fresh coriander
1 small onion, skinned and sliced into rings
salt and freshly ground pepper

1 Drain the beans and rinse well under cold running water. Put in a large saucepan, cover with plenty of fresh cold water and bring slowly to the boil.

2 Skin off any scum with a slotted spoon, then boil rapidly for 10 minutes. Half cover the pan with a lid and simmer for about 1½ hours until the beans are tender. Drain the cooked beans thoroughly and place them in a large salad bowl.

3 Combine the vinaigrette and coriander, and pour over the beans while they are still warm.

4 Toss thoroughly and leave to cool for 30 minutes. Mix the onion into the beans, season well and chill for 2-3 hours before serving.

COOK'S TIPS

Use dark soy sauce for *Oriental Salad* as it is fairly mild; light soy sauce can be very salty.

Sesame oil is made from sesame seeds, and has a rich, golden-brown colour and a nutty aroma and flavour. In Chinese cooking, it is used as a seasoning rather than for cooking, because it burns easily.

Left: Oriental Salad

Desserts & Puddings

SUMMER PUDDING

SERVES 8

175 g (6 oz) redcurrants, stalks removed

350 g (12 oz) blackcurrants, stalks removed

225-275 g (8-10 oz) granulated sugar

thinly pared rind of 1 large orange,
in one continous spiral if possible

225 g (8 oz) raspberries, hulled

225 g (8 oz) loganberries, hulled

12 thick slices of white bread, about 2 days old,
crusts removed

Crème Chantilly (see right), to serve

MICROWAVE

Summer Pudding
Put the currants, sugar and orange rind in a bowl, cover and cook on HIGH for 5-7 minutes until softened, stirring occasionally. Continue from step 2.

Autumn Pudding
Put the fruit, water and sugar in a bowl, cover and cook on HIGH for 4-8 minutes, stirring occasionally. Continue from step 2.

1 Put the currants, sugar and orange rind in a large saucepan. Cover and cook gently until the juices flow and the sugar has dissolved. Add the raspberries and loganberries, and continue cooking for about 5 minutes until they are softened. Remove from the heat and leave to cool.

2 Cut a round from one of the slices of bread, large enough to fit in the base of a 1.7 litre (3 pint) pudding basin. Place the round in the basin, then line the sides of the basin with slightly overlapping slices of bread; reserve the rest for the centre and top.

3 Remove the orange rind from the fruit. Spoon half of the fruit and juice into the lined basin, then place a layer of bread on top. Add the remaining fruit and juice, then cover completely with the remaining bread.

4 Cover the top of the pudding with cling film, then place a small, flat plate on the top. Stand the basin on a plate to catch any juices that overflow. Place some heavy weights on top of the plate. Chill overnight.

5 To serve, gently loosen the pudding from the sides of the basin with a palette knife, then turn out on to a flat plate. Serve with Crème Chantilly.

VARIATIONS

Autumn Pudding
Use 900 g (2 lb) mixed autumn fruit such as apples, blackberries, plums. Put the fruit, 90 ml (6 tbsp) water and 50 g (2 oz) sugar in a saucepan. Cover and cook as above. Finish as above.

CRÈME CHANTILLY

MAKES 300 ML (½ PINT)

300 ml (½ pint) double cream, well chilled

15 ml (1 tbsp) icing sugar, sifted

2.5-5 ml (½-1 tsp) vanilla essence

1 Put the cream, sugar and vanilla essence to taste into a well chilled bowl.

2 Whip until the cream forms soft peaks, or a little thicker if required for piping. Take care not to overwhip the cream or it will turn buttery and be unusable.

Previous page: Minted Strawberry Custards (see page 136); Chocolate Roulade (see page 153); Summer Fruit Tart (see page 146)

EXOTIC FRUIT SALAD

SERVES 6

900 g (2 lb) ripe pineapple
1 mango or small papaya
1 guava or banana, peeled and sliced
1 passion fruit or pomegranate
4 lychees or rambutans
1 kiwi fruit

1 Cut the pineapple in half lengthways, with the leaves attached. Remove the core in a wedge from each half and discard. Cut out the flesh, cut into small chunks and place in a bowl. Scrape out the remaining flesh and juice with a spoon and add to the bowl. Reserve the empty halves of skin.

2 Peel the mango or papaya and discard the stone or seeds. Cut the flesh into cubes and add to the pineapple with the guava or banana.

3 Cut the passion fruit or pomegranate in half, and scoop out the seeds with a teaspoon. Add the seeds to the pineapple.

4 Peel the lychees or rambutans and cut in half. Remove the stones and add to the bowl of fruit.

5 Peel the kiwi fruit and cut the flesh into round slices. Add to the bowl of fruit and stir.

6 Spoon the fruit salad into the pineapple halves. Cover and chill until required.

VARIATIONS

If any of these tropical fruits are unavailable, you can substitute other fruits of your choice.

BLACK FRUIT SALAD

SERVES 4-6

350 g (12 oz) blueberries or blackcurrants, stalks removed
350 g (12 oz) black cherries, stoned
350 g (12 oz) black grapes, seeded
finely grated rind and juice of 1 large orange
50-75 g (2-3 oz) light brown soft sugar
Frozen Yogurt (see page 160), to serve

1 Mix the fruits together in a bowl with the orange rind and juice and the sugar.

2 Leave to stand for 3-4 hours or overnight, stirring occasionally. Serve the salad with Frozen Yogurt.

Exotic Fruit Salad

COOK'S TIP

Serve *Black Fruit Salad* in a plain white or glass bowl for the most stunning effect.

MICROWAVE

Poires Belle Hélène

To make the chocolate sauce in the microwave, break the chocolate into small pieces and place in a heatproof bowl with the liqueur, then cook on LOW for 7-8 minutes or until melted, stirring occasionally.

COOK'S TIP

The Alpine strawberry is a version of the rare wild strawberry, that is now cultivated in France. Also known as frais du bois, these deliciously flavoured baby strawberries do not need to be hulled before they are eaten.

MICROWAVE

Wild Strawberry and Champagne Jelly

Put the sugar, lemon rind and water in a bowl and cook on HIGH for 3 minutes or until dissolved, stirring occasionally. In step 2, instead of placing the bowl over a pan of simmering water, cook on HIGH for 30 seconds or until the gelatine has dissolved; do not boil.

POIRES BELLE HÉLÈNE

SERVES 6

100 g (4 oz) sugar
thinly pared rind and juice of 2 oranges
6 cooking pears (preferably Conference)
225 g (8 oz) plain chocolate
60 ml (4 tbsp) orange-flavoured liqueur
orange slices, to decorate

1 Put the sugar, 900 ml (1½ pints) water and half the orange rind in a large heavy-based saucepan and heat gently, without stirring, until the sugar has dissolved.

2 Meanwhile, peel the pears quickly (to prevent discoloration), leaving the stalks on. Cut out the cores from the bottom and level them so that the pears will stand upright.

3 Stand the pears in the syrup, cover the pan and simmer gently for 20 minutes or until tender. Remove from the heat and leave to cool, covered tightly. Spoon the syrup over the pears occasionally during cooling.

4 Cut the remaining orange rind into thin matchstick (julienne) strips. Blanch in boiling water for 2 minutes, then drain and immediately refresh under cold running water. Leave to drain on absorbent kitchen paper.

5 To make the chocolate sauce, break the chocolate into small pieces. Place in a heatproof bowl with the liqueur. Stand the bowl over a pan of simmering water and heat gently until the chocolate melts.

6 Remove the pears from the syrup and stand them on a serving dish and chill for 2 hours.

7 Discard the orange rind from the syrup. Stir the melted chocolate into 150 ml (¼ pint) of the syrup with the orange juice, then slowly bring to the boil, stirring constantly. Simmer, stirring, until the sauce is thick and syrupy.

8 To serve, pour the hot chocolate sauce over the cold pears and sprinkle with the orange julienne. Decorate with orange slices and serve.

WILD STRAWBERRY AND CHAMPAGNE JELLY

SERVES 6

100 g (4 oz) caster sugar
pared rind and juice of 1 lemon
20 ml (4 level tsp) powdered gelatine
450 ml (¾ pint) pink champagne
175 g (6 oz) Alpine strawberries or frais du bois
edible flowers or sprigs of mint, to decorate

1 Put the sugar, lemon rind and 300 ml (½ pint) water in a saucepan. Heat gently until the sugar has dissolved. Leave to cool.

2 Sprinkle the gelatine over the lemon juice in a small bowl and leave to soak for 2-3 minutes. Place the bowl over a pan of simmering water and stir until dissolved.

3 Mix the sugar syrup with the dissolved gelatine and the champagne. Divide most of the strawberries between six champagne flutes. Carefully pour over a little of the jelly and chill until set. When the jelly has set, pour over the remaining jelly. Chill until set.

4 Decorate with the reserved strawberries and edible flowers or mint sprigs.

PEARS POACHED IN GINGER SYRUP

SERVES 4

150 ml (¼ pint) dry white wine

75 ml (5 tbsp) ginger wine

75 g (3 oz) light brown soft sugar

1 strip lemon rind

1 cinnamon stick

4 firm pears

1-2 pieces preserved ginger in syrup, thinly sliced, plus a little of the syrup

cream, to serve

1 Pour the white wine into a large heavy-based pan. Add 300 ml (½ pint) water, the ginger wine, sugar, lemon rind and cinnamon. Heat gently until sugar has dissolved, then remove from the heat.

2 Using a vegetable peeler or canelle knife, peel the pears from top to bottom in a spiral pattern.

3 Put the pears in the wine and simmer gently for 30 minutes. Transfer to a serving bowl.

4 Boil the liquid in the pan until reduced by half, then strain and stir in the preserved ginger and syrup. Pour over the pears in the bowl.

5 Leave the pears for 1-2 hours until cold, then chill overnight, spooning the syrup over them occasionally. Serve chilled, with cream.

SUMMER CURRANT COMPOTE

SERVES 6

50-75 g (2-3 oz) granulated sugar

225 g (8 oz) blackcurrants, stalks removed

450 g (1 lb) redcurrants, stalks removed

pared rind and juice of 1 medium orange

30 ml (2 tbsp) honey

350 g (12 oz) strawberries, hulled and sliced

1 Dissolve the sugar in 150 ml (¼ pint) water in a saucepan. Boil for 1 minute.

2 Add the currants and orange rind and simmer until the fruits are just beginning to soften – about 1 minute only.

3 Carefully transfer the fruits and syrup to a serving bowl, stir in the honey and leave to cool.

4 Mix in the orange juice, cover and chill well.

5 Just before serving, stir in the strawberries.

COOK'S TIP

Use firm Conference or slightly underripe Comice pears for *Pears Poached in Ginger Syrup.*

MICROWAVE

Pears Poached in Ginger Syrup
In step 1, put the ingredients in a bowl and cook on HIGH for 3-4 minutes until boiling, stirring occasionally. In step 3, add the pears to the syrup and cook on HIGH for 8-10 minutes or until the pears are tender. Transfer the pears to a serving bowl and continue cooking the liquid on HIGH for 10 minutes or until reduced by half. Stir in the ginger and pour over the pears.

COOK'S TIP

For *Summer Currant Compote*, add sugar to taste – with 50 g (2 oz) the compote will be quite tart.

MICROWAVE

Summer Currant Compote
In step 1, cook the sugar and water on HIGH for 3 minutes, stirring frequently, then cook on HIGH for a further 1 minutes. Add the currants and orange rind and cook on HIGH for 1-2 minutes or until beginning to soften.

Left: Pears Poached in Ginger Syrup

AMARETTI-STUFFED PEACHES

SERVES 4

4 firm yellow peaches, skinned
50 g (2 oz) Amaretti
1 egg yolk
25 g (1 oz) butter
25 g (1 oz) sugar
150 ml (¼ pint) dry white wine

1 Lightly grease an ovenproof dish.
2 Cut the peaches in half and carefully ease out the stones. Make the hollows in the peaches a little deeper with a sharp-edged teaspoon and reserve the removed flesh.
3 Crush the Amaretti and mix them with the reserved peach flesh, the egg yolk, butter and 15 g (½ oz) of the sugar.

4 Use this mixture to stuff the hollows of the peach halves, mounding the filling slightly. Place the peaches in the prepared ovenproof dish and sprinkle with the rest of the sugar. Pour the white wine over and around the peaches.
5 Bake in the oven at 160°C Circotherm for 20 minutes or until tender. Serve hot or cold.

STUFFED FIGS

SERVES 8

225 g (8 oz) ricotta cheese, at room temperature
150 ml (¼ pint) double or whipping cream
few drops of almond extract or rose water
16 ripe, fresh figs
fig or vine leaves and rose petals, to serve

1 Beat the ricotta cheese in a bowl until softened. Whip the cream in another bowl until just standing in soft peaks, then fold into the ricotta, with almond extract or rose water according to taste.
2 With a sharp knife, cut a cross in each fig at the top (stem end). Continue cutting down almost to the base of the fig, but keeping the fruit whole. With your fingers, gently prise the four 'petals' of each fig apart.
3 Spoon the ricotta mixture into a piping bag fitted with a large rosette nozzle and pipe into the centre of each fig. Chill in the refrigerator until serving time.
4 To serve, arrange fig or vine leaves decoratively over a flat serving platter, place the stuffed figs on top and scatter rose petals around. Serve chilled.

COOK'S TIP

Amaretti are almond macaroons made in Italy. They are available at Italian delicatessens, both in boxes and individually wrapped in tissue paper. Amaretti are delicious served with coffee and liqueurs at the end of a meal. If you cannot find them, use shop bought or home-made macaroons instead.

MICROWAVE

Amaretti-stuffed Peaches
In step 5, arrange the peaches around the edge of a large shallow dish, cover and cook on HIGH for 3-5 minutes or until tender. Leave to stand, covered, for 5 minutes.

Amaretti-stuffed Peaches

ALMOND BAKED APPLES

SERVES 4

75 g (3 oz) dried figs, rinsed and chopped

grated rind of 1 lime or ½ lemon

15 ml (1 tbsp) golden syrup

15 g (½ oz) flaked almonds

few drops of almond essence

4 cooking apples, about 225 g (8 oz) each

50 g (2 oz) ground almonds

30 ml (2 tbsp) light brown soft sugar

15 g (½ oz) butter or margarine, melted

1 Put the figs in a bowl, cover with boiling water and leave to soak for 5 minutes. Drain, then mix in the grated lime rind, golden syrup, flaked almonds and almond essence.
2 Peel and core the apples. Fill with the fig mixture, packing down firmly.
3 Mix the ground almonds and sugar together. Brush each apple with the melted butter, then roll the apples in the ground almond mixture. Place the apples in a shallow 1.1 litre (2 pint) ovenproof dish.
4 Bake in the oven at 160°C Circotherm for about 40 minutes or until the apples are cooked through and tender when pricked with a skewer. Serve hot.

ORANGES IN CARAMEL

SERVES 6

225 g (8 oz) granulated sugar

6 large oranges

30-45 ml (2-3 tbsp) orange-flavoured liqueur

Crème Chantilly (see page 130), to serve

1 Put the sugar and 50 ml (2 fl oz) water in a saucepan and heat gently until the sugar has dissolved, brushing down the sides of the pan with hot water. Bring to the boil, then boil until the syrup turns a golden caramel colour.
2 Immediately, dip the base of the pan into cold water to prevent the caramel darkening further. Carefully, pour 300 ml (½ pint) boiling water into the pan. Return the caramel to the heat and heat gently until it has completely dissolved into the water.
3 Meanwhile, thinly pare the rind from two of the oranges, taking care not to remove the white pith. Cut the rind into very fine shreds and set aside. Using a very sharp knife, remove the skin and white pith from all the oranges.
4 Put the oranges and shredded rinds into the caramel, cover and cook them very gently for 25-30 minutes until the oranges are tender, but do not allow to overcook – they must retain a good shape. Turn the oranges frequently during cooking.
5 Transfer the oranges and syrup to a large serving dish. Add the liqueur and leave to cool. Cover and chill. Serve with Crème Chantilly.

SERVING IDEA

For a sweet, crunchy topping to *Oranges in Caramel* make caramel chips: dissolve 75 g (3 oz) granulated sugar very gently in 75 ml (3 fl oz) water. Increase the heat and boil rapidly without stirring until the syrup turns a rich brown caramel colour. Pour at once into a greased shallow tin (a Swiss roll tin is ideal), then leave until cold and set. Crush with a rolling pin or mallet into fine pieces and sprinkle over the oranges just before serving (not earlier or the caramel will soften).

MICROWAVE

Oranges in Caramel
To make caramel chips (see Serving Idea) in the microwave, put the sugar and water in a bowl and cook, uncovered, on HIGH for 10 minutes until a golden caramel colour. Pour at once into the tin.

135

Strawberry Yogurt Mould
To dissolve the gelatine in the microwave instead of over a pan of simmering water, cook the gelatine and water on HIGH for 30 seconds or until dissolved; do not boil.

Minted Strawberry Custards
To dissolve the gelatine in the microwave instead of over a pan of simmering water, cook the gelatine and water on HIGH for 30 seconds or until dissolved; do not boil.

Opposite: Strawberry Yogurt Mould; Gooseberry Charlotte (see page 138)

STRAWBERRY YOGURT MOULD

SERVES 6

3 eggs
50 g (2 oz) caster sugar
finely grated rind and juice of 1 large lemon
450 g (1 lb) strawberries
20 ml (4 level tsp) powdered gelatine
150 ml (¼ pint) natural yogurt, plus extra for serving
150 ml (¼ pint) strawberry yogurt

1 Whisk the eggs, sugar and lemon rind together in a large bowl, using an electric mixer, until the mixture is pale, thick and creamy and leaves a trail when the whisk is lifted.

2 Hull 225 g (8 oz) of the strawberries and place in a blender or food processor with half of the lemon juice. Process to a smooth purée.

3 Gradually whisk the purée into the mousse mixture, whisking well to keep the bulk.

4 Sprinkle the gelatine over the remaining lemon juice in a small bowl and leave to soak for 2-3 minutes. Place the bowl over a pan of simmering water and stir until dissolved. Leave until cool.

5 Gradually add the dissolved gelatine to the mousse mixture with the natural and strawberry yogurts. Stir carefully but thoroughly to mix. Pour into a greased 1.7 litre (3 pint) ring mould and chill for 4-5 hours or until set.

6 To serve, dip the mould briefly in hot water, then invert on to a serving plate. Hull most of the remaining strawberries. Fill the centre of the ring with all the fruit. Serve with yogurt.

MINTED STRAWBERRY CUSTARDS

SERVES 6

450 ml (¾ pint) milk
4 large sprigs of mint
1 egg
2 egg yolks
45 ml (3 tbsp) caster sugar
20 ml (4 level tsp) powdered gelatine
700 g (1½ lb) strawberries, hulled
15 ml (1 level tbsp) icing sugar
strawberries, to decorate

1 Oil six 150 ml (¼ pint) ramekin dishes.

2 Place the milk and mint sprigs in a saucepan. Bring slowly to the boil, cover and leave to infuse for about 30 minutes.

3 Whisk the egg and yolks with the caster sugar in a bowl. Strain over the milk. Return to the pan and cook gently, stirring, until the custard just coats the back of the spoon. Do not boil. Leave to cool.

4 Sprinkle the gelatine over 45 ml (3 tbsp) water in a small bowl and leave to soak for 2-3 minutes. Place the bowl over a pan of simmering water and stir until dissolved. Stir the gelatine into the custard.

5 Purée and sieve the strawberries. Whisk about two-thirds into the cold, but not set, custard. Pour the custard into the dishes and chill for about 3 hours until set.

6 Meanwhile, whisk the icing sugar into the remaining strawberry purée. Chill.

7 To serve, turn out the custards. Surround with sauce, then decorate with strawberries.

GOOSEBERRY CHARLOTTE

— SERVES 6 —

450 g (1 lb) gooseberries, topped and tailed

75 g (3 oz) caster sugar

10 ml (2 level tsp) powdered gelatine

2 egg yolks

300 ml (½ pint) milk

300 ml (½ pint) double cream

angelica, to decorate

20 langue de chat biscuits

MICROWAVE

Gooseberry Charlotte

In step 2, cook the gooseberries and water in a bowl, covered, on HIGH for 6 minutes until soft. To dissolve the gelatine in the microwave instead of over a pan of simmering water, cook the gelatine and water on HIGH for 30 seconds or until dissolved; do not boil.

1 Oil a 15 cm (6 inch) soufflé or non-metal straight sided dish and line the base with grease-proof paper.

2 Place the gooseberries in a small saucepan with 60 ml (4 tbsp) water. Cover and simmer for about 10 minutes until the fruit softens to a pulpy consistency.

3 Purée the gooseberries in a blender or food processor, then sieve to remove the pips. Stir in 50 g (2 oz) of the sugar.

4 Sprinkle the gelatine over 30 ml (2 tbsp) water in a small bowl and leave to soak for 2-3 minutes. Place the bowl over a pan of simmering water and stir until dissolved.

5 Meanwhile, make the custard. Beat the egg yolks and remaining sugar together in a bowl until light in colour. In a small saucepan, warm the milk, and pour over the eggs and sugar, stirring until blended.

6 Return to the pan and cook over a low heat, stirring all the time, until the custard thickens sufficiently to lightly coat the back of the spoon – do not boil.

7 Remove from the heat and add the dissolved gelatine. Pour the custard out into a large bowl and mix in the gooseberry purée. Leave to cool for 45 minutes.

8 Lightly whip the cream. When the gooseberry mixture is cold, but not set, stir in half the cream until evenly blended. Pour the gooseberry mixture into the prepared dish. Chill for 1-2 hours to set. When firm, turn out on to a flat serving plate.

9 Spread a thin covering of the remaining cream around the edge of the charlotte.

10 Spoon the rest of the cream into a piping bag fitted with a 1 cm (½ inch) large star nozzle. Pipe the cream around the top edge of the charlotte. Decorate with angelica. Just before serving, arrange the biscuits carefully around the outside, trimming them to fit as necessary.

FRUDITÉS

— SERVES 6 —

2 crisp eating apples

2 bananas

225 g (8 oz) apricots, stoned

175 g (6 oz) black or green grapes, seeded

225 g (8 oz) strawberries

juice of 1 lemon

DIP

150 ml (¼ pint) double cream

150 ml (¼ pint) soured cream

30 ml (2 tbsp) icing sugar, sifted

1 To make the dip, whip the two creams and icing sugar together in a bowl until standing in soft peaks. Pipe into six individual dishes.

2 Quarter and core the apples, but do not peel them. Peel the bananas and cut into 4 cm (1½ inch) chunks.

3 Arrange the fruit on individual serving plates and sprinkle immediately with lemon juice.

4 Place the dishes of cream dip next to the fruit and serve immediately. Use fingers or small fondue forks to dunk the fruit into the dip.

PETITS POTS AU CHOCOLAT

SERVES 6-8

15 ml (1 tbsp) coffee beans
3 egg yolks
1 egg
75 g (3 oz) caster sugar
750 ml (1¼ pints) milk and double cream mixed
75 g (3 oz) plain chocolate
DECORATION
150 ml (¼ pint) whipping cream
Chocolate Shapes (see page 188) or coffee dragées

1 Toast the coffee beans under a moderate grill for a few minutes, then set aside.

2 Beat the egg yolks, egg and sugar together in a bowl until very pale.

3 Place the milk and cream and the coffee beans in a saucepan and bring to the boil. Strain the hot milk on to the egg mixture, stirring all the time. Discard the coffee beans. Return the mixture to the saucepan.

4 Break up the chocolate and add to the pan. Stir over gently heat (do not boil) for about 5 minutes until the chocolate has almost melted and the mixture is slightly thickened. Whisk lightly until the mixture is evenly blended. Leave to stand for a few minutes to allow the bubbles to rise to the surface.

5 Stand six or eight individual 150 ml (¼ pint) ramekin dishes or custard pots in a roasting tin, then pour in enough hot water to come halfway up the sides of the dishes. Pour the custard mixture slowly into the dishes, dividing it equally between them. Cover.

6 Bake in the oven at 140°C Circotherm for 1¼ hours or until the custard is lightly set. Leave to cool completely.

7 To serve, whip the cream and spoon into a piping bag fitted with a large star nozzle. Pipe a whirl on top of each dessert. Decorate with Chocolate Shapes or coffee dragées.

COOK'S TIP

Petits Pots au Chocolat rely heavily on the flavour of the chocolate used, so it is essential to use a good quality chocolate – don't use chocolate flavoured cake covering.

Petits Pots au Chocolat

CRÈME CARAMEL

SERVES 8

CARAMEL
175 g (6 oz) granulated sugar

CUSTARD
1 vanilla pod or a few drops of vanilla essence

600 ml (1 pint) milk

4 eggs

4 egg yolks

**60 ml (4 tbsp) caster sugar
or more to taste**

1 To make the caramel, slightly warm eight 150 ml (¼ pint) ramekin dishes. Put the granulated sugar in a small heavy saucepan with 100 ml (4 fl oz) water to moisten. Place over a low heat and heat without boiling until the sugar has dissolved. (If boiled before it has dissolved, the sugar will crystallize and never form a caramel.) Prod the sugar occasionally to help it dissolve.

2 Bring to the boil and boil rapidly for a few minutes until the sugar begins to turn pale brown. Watch it carefully as it will turn brown very quickly and could easily catch and burn. Gently swirl the caramel to ensure even browning.

3 Quickly pour a little caramel into each of the warm ramekins and rotate each one to coat the bottom and part way up the sides with caramel. Leave to cool.

4 To make the custard, split the vanilla pod to expose the seeds. Place in a pan with the milk and heat until almost boiling (if using vanilla essence, add after heating the milk first). Meanwhile, beat the eggs, yolks and caster sugar until well mixed. Strain on to the milk. Stir well and strain again into the ramekins.

5 Place the ramekins in a roasting tin and fill the tin with hot water to come two thirds up the sides of the dishes.

6 Bake in the oven at 150°C Circotherm for 20 minutes or until just set. To test, insert the tip of a small sharp knife into the centre of a custard – if cooked it should come out clean. Also, if sufficiently set, when gently tapped the custard will wobble slightly like a jelly. Remove from the water bath. Leave to cool, then chill overnight.

7 To turn out, allow the custards to come to room temperature for 15 minutes. Free the edges by pressing with fingertips, then loosen the sides with a thin-bladed, blunt-edged knife. Place a serving dish over the top and invert. Lift off the ramekin.

VARIATIONS

This light silken, baked custard can be made with most types of milk. For richer results, however, use single cream.

Different flavourings such as vanilla or cardamom pods, orange rind, or even scented geranium leaves may be infused in the milk.

SERVING IDEA

Crown *Crème Caramel* with a froth of spun sugar, if liked. To make spun sugar, lightly oil a rolling pin. Cover the work surface with newspaper, and also cover the floor immediately below. Cover the newspaper on the work surface with greaseproof paper. Put 100 g (4 oz) granulated sugar, 45 ml (3 tbsp) water and 7.5 ml (1½ tsp) liquid glucose into a heavy-based saucepan and heat gently until every granule of sugar dissolves, brushing down the sides of the pan with a little hot water. Boil the sugar syrup to a temperature of 160°C (320°F). Immediately plunge the base of the pan into cold water to prevent further cooking. Dip two forks, held together, into the syrup, then hold them up high until a fine thread starts to fall. Gently spin the sugar threads around the rolling pin until a good quantity accumulate. Remove from the rolling pin and set aside. Repeat until all the syrup has been used.

INDIVIDUAL APPLE SOUFFLÉS

──────── SERVES 6-8 ────────

icing sugar for dusting
350 g (12 oz) cooking apples
50 g (2 oz) butter or margarine
25 g (1 oz) caster sugar
30 ml (2 level tbsp) plain flour
150 ml (¼ pint) milk
3 eggs, separated
30 ml (2 tbsp) apple brandy
apple slices, to decorate (optional)
single cream, to serve

1 Lightly grease six to eight 150 ml (¼ pint) ramekin dishes. Dust them out with icing sugar.
2 Peel, quarter, core and roughly chop the apples. Place in a small saucepan with 25 g (1 oz) of the butter and the sugar. Cover tightly and cook gently until the apples are very soft. Uncover and cook over a moderate heat, stirring frequently until all excess moisture evaporates. Mash or beat until smooth; cool slightly.

3 Melt the remaining butter in a pan, add the flour and cook for 2 minutes. Remove from the heat and stir in the milk. Cook, stirring, for 2-3 minutes.
4 Remove from the heat, cool slightly, then stir in the apple purée and egg yolks. Gently mix in the apple brandy. Whisk the egg whites until stiff but not dry. Stir one large spoonful into the apple mixture, then gently fold in the remaining egg whites. Divide between the prepared ramekin dishes so that each is three-quarters full.
5 Bake in the oven at 170°C Circotherm for about 20 minutes or until the soufflés are just set and golden brown. Dust them quickly with icing sugar and decorate with apple slices, if using. Serve straight away with single cream handed separately.

ZABAGLIONE

──────── SERVES 6 ────────

4 egg yolks
65 g (2½ oz) caster sugar
100 ml (4 fl oz) Marsala
sponge fingers, to serve

1 Beat the egg yolks and sugar together in a large bowl. Add the Marsala and beat until mixed.
2 Place the bowl over a saucepan of simmering water and heat gently, whisking the mixture until it is very thick and creamy.
3 To serve, pour the zabaglione into six glasses and serve immediately, with sponge fingers.

Left: Individual Apple Soufflés

MICROWAVE

Individual Apple Soufflés
Put the chopped apples, butter and sugar in a bowl, cover and cook on HIGH for 5 minutes, or until really soft, stirring several times. In step 3, put the butter, flour and milk in a bowl and cook on HIGH for 3-4 minutes or until boiling and thickened, whisking several times.

SERVING IDEA

Zabaglione is a classic, rich Italian dish, ideal for serving after a light main course. It should be served as soon as it is made so that it remains light, fluffy and slightly warm.

141

COOK'S TIP

It really is worth making the effort to prepare your own fresh tasting lemon curd for *Lemon Curd Creams* but if time is at a premium a good quality bought variety will do!

MICROWAVE

Lemon Curd Creams
To make the lemon curd in the microwave, put all the ingredients in a bowl and cook, uncovered, on HIGH for 1 minute and then on LOW for 8 minutes, whisking after every minute.

SERVING IDEA

Individual, golden-tinted *Baked Saffron Yogurts* make an attractive finale to an Indian meal. They are also excellent for children at tea-time, served with different fruits.

LEMON CURD CREAMS

SERVES 6

LEMON CURD

finely grated rind and juice of 2 lemons

2 eggs, whisked

50 g (2 oz) butter, cut into pieces

100 g (4 oz) caster sugar

CUSTARD

3 eggs, whisked

45 ml (3 tbsp) caster sugar

300 ml (½ pint) single cream

150 ml (¼ pint) milk

150 ml (¼ pint) double cream, lightly whipped, to decorate

1 To make the lemon curd, place the lemon rind, strained lemon juice, eggs, butter and sugar into a medium heatproof bowl. Place the bowl over a saucepan of simmering water and cook gently, whisking occasionally, until the curd thickens slightly – it should just coat the back of a spoon.

2 Strain the curd into a cold bowl, place a piece of damp greaseproof paper on the surface of the curd and leave to cool.

3 Spoon about 30 ml (2 tbsp) lemon curd into the base of six 150 ml (¼ pint) ramekin dishes.

4 To make the custard, whisk the eggs, sugar, cream and milk together. Strain, then gently pour into the ramekins.

5 Stand the ramekins in a roasting tin and pour in hot water to come halfway up the sides. Cover the top of the roasting tin with foil.

6 Bake in the oven at 150°C Circotherm for about 55 minutes or until the custards are just set. Do not overcook or the mixture will curdle.

7 Take the ramekins out of the roasting tin and cool. When cold, cover and chill well before serving decorated with lightly whipped cream.

BAKED SAFFRON YOGURTS

SERVES 8

300 ml (½ pint) milk

pinch of saffron threads

6 green cardamom pods

2 eggs and 2 egg yolks

383 g (13.5 oz) can condensed milk

300 ml (½ pint) natural yogurt

1 large ripe mango, to decorate

1 Bring the milk, saffron and cardamoms to the boil in a pan. Remove from the heat, cover and infuse for 10-15 minutes.

2 Beat the eggs, egg yolks, condensed milk and yogurt together in a bowl.

3 Strain in the milk, stirring gently to mix. Divide between eight 150 ml (¼ pint) ramekin dishes in a roasting tin. Add hot water to come halfway up the sides.

4 Bake in the oven at 150°C Circotherm for about 25 minutes until firm to the touch.

5 Cool the baked yogurt desserts completely. Chill for at least 2 hours before serving.

6 To serve, run a blunt-edged knife around the edge of each yogurt, then turn out on to individual dishes. Peel and slice the mango. Serve with the yogurts.

LEMON MERINGUE PIE

SERVES 6-8

1 quantity of Pâte Sucrée (see page 190)
FILLING
pared rind and juice of 4 large lemons
65 g (2½ oz) cornflour
50-75 g (2-3 oz) caster sugar
3 egg yolks
MERINGUE
3 egg whites
175 g (6 oz) caster sugar

1 First, prepare the filling. Put the lemon rind in a saucepan with 600 ml (1 pint) water, bring to the boil, then remove from the heat, cover and leave to stand for at least 30 minutes.

2 Meanwhile, roll out the pastry on a lightly floured surface to a round 2.5 cm (1 inch) larger than a 23 cm (9 inch) fluted flan tin. Line the dish with the pastry, pressing it well into the flutes.

3 Trim the edge, then prick the pastry well, all over, with a fork. Chill for 30 minutes, then bake blind at 170°C Circotherm for 15 minutes with the paper and beans and 5 minutes without. Allow to cool.

4 Remove all the lemon rind from the pan, then stir in the lemon juice. Blend the cornflour with a little of the lemon liquid to form a smooth paste, pour it into the pan and stir well. Bring the lemon mixture to the boil, stirring continuously. Reduce the heat and continue cooking until every trace of raw cornflour disappears, and the mixture has thickened.

5 Stir in the sugar to taste, adding a little more if liked, then beat in the egg yolks. Pour the lemon filling into the pastry case.

6 To make the meringue, whisk the egg whites until stiff, but not dry, then gradually whisk in the sugar, adding a little at a time and whisking well between each addition, until the meringue is very stiff and shiny. Put the meringue into a large piping bag fitted with a large star nozzle, then pipe it attractively on top of the lemon filling. Alternatively, spoon the meringue on to the filling and shape it into swirls with a palette knife.

7 Bake in the oven at 180°C Circotherm for 10 minutes until the meringue is very lightly browned. Remove the pie from the oven and allow to cool. Serve at room temperature.

Lemon Meringue Pie

143

PEACH PIE

— SERVES 6 —

PASTRY

225 g (8 oz) plain flour

50 g (2 oz) walnuts, finely chopped

100 g (4 oz) softened butter or margarine, cut into pieces

75 g (3 oz) caster sugar

2 egg yolks

FILLING

900 g (2 lb) peaches

15 g (½ oz) semolina

50 g (2 oz) caster sugar

1 egg white for glazing

caster sugar for dredging

1 To make the pastry, place the flour on a work surface and sprinkle the walnuts over the top. Make a well in the centre and add the butter, sugar, egg yolks and 30 ml (2 tbsp) water.

2 Using the fingertips of one hand only, work the well ingredients together until evenly blended. Using a palette knife, gradually draw in the flour, then knead lightly until just smooth.

3 Roll out two-thirds of the pastry on a floured work surface and use to line a 23 cm (9 inch) loose-bottomed fluted flan tin. Chill the pastry for 30 minutes.

4 To make the filling, quarter the peaches and easy away from the stone. Peel off the skins carefully and divide each quarter in two lengthways.

5 Sprinkle the pastry with semolina. Arrange the peaches in the pastry case and sprinkle with the sugar. Roll out the remaining pastry and use

to cover the pie, sealing well. Make a small hole in the centre to let steam escape.

6 Bake in the oven at 170°C Circotherm for about 20-25 minutes or until just beginning to brown.

7 Brush the top of the pie with lightly beaten egg white and dredge with caster sugar. Return to the oven for a further 10 minutes or until well browned and crisp. Cool for 15 minutes in the tin before removing. Serve while still slightly warm.

VARIATION

Nectarines work equally well. Choose firm, but ripe fruit.

OLD ENGLISH APPLE PIE

— SERVES 6 —

350 g (12 oz) Shortcrust Pastry, made with 350 g (12 oz) flour (see page 189)

FILLING

700 g (1½ lb) cooking apples

finely grated rind and juice of ½ lemon

50 g (2 oz) granulated sugar

50 g (2 oz) dark muscovado or molasses sugar

15 ml (1 level tbsp) plain flour

pinch of grated nutmeg

1.25 ml (¼ tsp) ground cinnamon

finely grated rind and juice of ½ orange

50 g (2 oz) sultanas

15-25 g (½-1 oz) butter or margarine

caster sugar for dredging

1 Roll out two-thirds of the pastry on a floured work surface and use to line a 1.1 litre (2 pint) capacity pie dish. Chill for 30 minutes with the remaining dough, wrapped in cling film.

2 Meanwhile to make the filling, peel and core the apples, then slice them thickly into a bowl of cold water to which the lemon juice has been added.

3 Mix the sugars, flour, nutmeg, cinnamon, lemon and orange rinds together and sprinkle a little of this on to the pastry lining.

4 Cover the base of the pastry lining with half of the sliced apples, then sprinkle with 25 g (1 oz) of the sultanas and half of the remaining sugar mixture. Repeat, using all the apples, sultanas and sugar. Sprinkle the fruit with the orange juice and dot with the butter.

5 Roll out the remaining pastry and use to cover the pie, sealing the edges well. Slash the top twice to let steam escape.

6 Use the pastry trimmings to make decorations for the pie. Brush the top of the pie with water and place on the decorations. Dredge with caster sugar.

7 Bake in the oven at 170°C Circotherm for 45 minutes, then reduce the temperature to 160°C Circotherm for about 25 minutes until the apple is soft when tested with a skewer. Serve warm.

BAKLAVA

MAKES 20 SQUARES OR DIAMONDS

225 g (8 oz) walnuts, finely chopped
50 g (2 oz) light muscovado sugar
2.5 ml (½ level tsp) ground cinnamon
450 g (1 lb) packet filo pastry, thawed if frozen
150 g (5 oz) butter, melted
175 g (6 oz) clear honey, warmed

1 Grease a 24 x 18 cm (9½ x 7 inch) roasting tin.

2 Mix the walnuts, sugar and cinnamon together in a bowl. Halve each sheet of pastry to measure a 25.5 cm (10 inch) square.

3 Separate the pastry sheets into four piles. Set aside three, covered with a damp cloth to prevent them drying out.

4 Take one sheet from the uncovered pile and fit it into the prepared tin, allowing it to come up the sides (use two sheets, if necessary). Brush with melted butter, cover with a second sheet and brush with butter. Repeat until the first pile is used up. Sprinkle with a third of nuts.

5 Repeat step 4 twice more to produce three layers of walnut mixture. Top with the remaining pastry and trim the sheets to fit the tin. Mark the surface of the pastry into 20 squares or diamonds with the tip of a sharp knife.

6 Bake in the oven at 180°C Circotherm for 15 minutes. Reduce the oven to 160°C Circotherm and bake for 10 minutes or until golden brown.

7 Warm the honey over a low heat. Spoon over the baklava and leave to cool in the tin for 1-2 hours. Cut out the marked squares or diamonds.

Baklava

145

MICROWAVE

Sponge Pudding

Halve the ingredients but use 100 g (4 oz) flour. Mix to a very soft consistency with 45-60 ml (3-4 tbsp) milk. Cover and cook on HIGH for 5-7 minutes or until just moist on the surface. Stand for 5 minutes.

COOK'S TIP

Steamed puddings are made by a very gentle method of cooking. Follow the rules below and the result will always be soft and moist.

● Half-fill the steamer with water and heat so that it is boiling by the time the pudding is made. If you have no steamer, fill a large saucepan with water to come halfway up the pudding basin. Cover and bring to the boil.

● Cut double greaseproof paper or a piece of foil to cover the pudding basin and grease well. Put a pleat in the paper or foil to allow the pudding to rise.

● Cover the basin tightly with paper or foil to prevent steam or water entering.

● Keep the water in the steamer boiling rapidly all the time and top it up regularly, or the steamer will boil dry. If using a saucepan, put an old saucer or metal pastry cutter in the base to keep the basin off the bottom.

STEAMED FRUIT PUDDING

———— SERVES 4 ————

450 g (1 lb) fruit, prepared and stewed, or drained canned fruit
100 g (4 oz) butter or margarine
100 g (4 oz) caster sugar
2 eggs, beaten
few drops of vanilla essence
175 g (6 oz) self-raising flour
a little milk, to mix
custard, to serve

1 Half-fill a steamer or large saucepan with water and put it on to boil. Grease a 900 ml (1½ pint) pudding basin and spoon the fruit into the bottom.

2 Cream the butter and sugar together in a bowl until pale and fluffy. Gradually add the eggs and vanilla, beating well after each addition.

3 Using a metal spoon, fold in half the flour, then fold in the rest, with enough milk to give a dropping consistency.

4 Pour the mixture into the prepared pudding basin. Cover with greased greaseproof paper or foil (see Cook's Tip) and secure with string. Steam for 1½ hours. Serve with custard.

VARIATION

Mincemeat Pudding
Line the bottom and sides of the basin with a thin layer of mincemeat and fill with the sponge mixture. Turn it out carefully so that the outside remains covered with mincemeat.

SUMMER FRUIT TART

———— MAKES 6 SLICES ————

100 g (4 oz) plain wholemeal flour
100 g (4 oz) plain white flour
100 g (4 oz) butter or margarine
150 ml (¼ pint) Greek natural yogurt or fromage frais
225 g (8 oz) strawberries, hulled
2 peaches, halved, stoned and sliced
2 kiwi fruit, peeled and sliced
60 ml (4 tbsp) apricot jam
15 ml (1 tbsp) lemon juice

1 Mix the flours together in a bowl and rub in the margarine until the mixture resembles fine breadcrumbs. Add 45 ml (3 tbsp) chilled water and mix to a soft dough. Roll out and use to line a 10 x 30 cm (4 x 12 inch) rectangular loose-bottomed tin. Chill for 15 minutes.

2 Line the pastry case with greaseproof paper and baking beans. Bake blind at 160°C Circotherm for 15 minutes. Remove the paper and beans and bake for a further 5-10 minutes. Allow to cool, then remove the flan tin and place the pastry case on a serving plate or board.

3 Spread the yogurt over the base of the pastry case and arrange the fruit in an attractive pattern. Mix together the jam and lemon juice and brush evenly over the fruits. Serve immediately, cut into slices.

Apfel Strüdel

SERVES 6-8

4 large sheets filo pastry, measuring 45 x 30 cm (18 x 12 inches), thawed if frozen

FILLING

900 g (2 lb) cooking apples, peeled, cored and roughly chopped

finely grated rind and juice of 1 lemon

50 g (2 oz) sultanas

50 g (2 oz) almonds, chopped

75 g (3 oz) caster sugar

5 ml (1 level tsp) ground cinnamon

40 g (½ oz) butter, melted

100 g (4 oz) ground almonds

icing sugar, for dredging

1 Grease a baking sheet. Rest in a warm place for 1 hour.

2 To make the filling, mix the apples, lemon rind and juice, sultanas, chopped almonds, sugar and cinnamon together.

3 Spread a clean cotton cloth on a large surface and sprinkle lightly with flour. Place the pastry on the cloth, overlapping the sheets to make them into a square 50 x 50 cm (20 x 20 inches).

4 Brush the pastry with half the melted butter and sprinkle with the ground almonds. Spread the apple mixture along one side, leaving a 5 cm (2 inch) border all round the edge.

5 Fold the pastry edges over the apple mixture, towards the centre. Lift the corners of the cloth nearest to you over the pastry, causing the strüdel to roll up, but stop after each turn in order to pat it into shape and to keep the roll

even. Form the roll into a horseshoe shape. Brush with the rest of the melted butter and slide it on to the prepared baking sheet.

6 Bake in the oven at 160°C Circotherm for 45-50 minutes or until golden brown. Dredge thickly with icing sugar. Serve warm.

Apfel Strüdel

VARIATION

Although an apple filling has become synonymous with strüdel, it is equally good filled with fresh cherries or pears.

LAVENDER-SCENTED TARTLETS

SERVES 4

PASTRY

50 g (2 oz) butter

100 g (4 oz) plain flour

5 ml (1 tsp) lavender sugar (see Cook's Tip)

1 egg

FILLING

30 ml (2 tbsp) plus 20 ml (4 tsp) lavender sugar

2 eggs

150 ml (5 fl oz) single cream

selection of seasonal fruits

50 ml (2 fl oz) dry vermouth

10 ml (2 level tsp) powdered gelatine

1 Make the pastry as for Rich Shortcrust Pastry (see page 190), adding the egg and a little water if necessary. Chill for 10 minutes.
2 Roll out the pastry thinly on a lightly floured work surface and use to line four shallow, fluted flan dishes, about 9 cm (3½ inch) in diameter. Chill for 20 minutes.
3 Bake blind in the oven at 170°C Circotherm for about 20 minutes. Reduce the oven temperature to 140°C Circotherm.
4 To make the filling, whisk 15 ml (1 tbsp) of the sugar, the eggs and cream together. Pour into the pastry cases and bake for 20 minutes or until lightly set. Leave to cool completely.
5 Arrange a selection of fruits, some whole, some sliced, over the surface of the tartlets.
6 In a small bowl, stir the remaining sugar into the vermouth and 50 ml (2 fl oz) water. Sprinkle the gelatine over the liquid and leave to soak for 2-3 minutes. Place the bowl over a saucepan of simmering water and stir until dissolved. Cool slightly, then spoon evenly over the fruits to cover. Chill until set, about 5 minutes.

TARTE TATIN

SERVES 8

PASTRY

100 g (4 oz) butter or margarine

175 g (6 oz) plain flour

15 g (½ oz) caster sugar

1 egg yolk

FILLING

25 g (1 oz) butter or margarine

50 g (2 oz) caster sugar

450 g (1 lb) crisp eating apples

crème fraîche or soured cream, to serve

1 Make the pastry as for Rich Shortcrust Pastry (see page 190). Chill while making the filling.
2 To make the filling, melt the butter in a saucepan and add the sugar. Heat until caramelized and golden brown. Pour into a 20.5 cm (8 inch) round sandwich tin.
3 Peel, core and halve the apples. Slice into 1 cm (½ inch) pieces. Pack tightly in tin.
4 Roll out the pastry on a floured work surface to a round slightly larger than the tin. Place on top of apples and tuck in around edges of tin. Chill for 30 minutes. Place on a baking sheet.
5 Bake in the oven at 170°C Circotherm for 30-35 minutes until the pastry is golden. Turn out, apple side uppermost, on to a warmed serving dish. Serve warm, with crème fraîche.

COOK'S TIP

Lavender sugar gives the pastry a delicious flavour and it is really simple to make. Place 10 ml (2 tsp) dried lavender blossom in a screw-top jar with 30 ml (2 tbsp) caster sugar. Shake well and leave overnight. Sieve and discard the lavender.

Lavender-scented Tartlets;
Tarte Tatin

If you do not wish to use a piping bag to fill the buns with cream, the choux buns can be split in half, then sandwiched with the cream.

MICROWAVE

Profiteroles

To make the chocolate sauce in the microwave, place all the ingredients in a bowl, cover and cook on LOW for 4 minutes, stirring halfway through, then cook on HIGH for 30 seconds.

SERVING IDEA

Serve *Chocolate Cheesecake* hot with Greek yogurt or cold with vanilla ice cream.

MICROWAVE

Chocolate Cheesecake

To melt the chocolate for the filling, put the chocolate pieces in a bowl with the butter and cook on LOW for 4-5 minutes or until melted, stirring occasionally.

PROFITEROLES
SERVES 4

2 egg quantity of Choux pastry (see page 190)
CHOCOLATE SAUCE AND FILLING
100 g (4 oz) plain chocolate
15 g (½ oz) butter or margarine
30 ml (2 tbsp) golden syrup
2-3 drops of vanilla essence
300 ml (½ pint) double cream
icing sugar for dusting

1 Put the choux pastry in a piping bag fitted with a 1 cm (½ inch) plain nozzle. Pipe about 20 small bun shapes on two baking buttered sheets.
2 Bake in the oven at 180°C Circotherm for about 20-25 minutes until well risen and golden brown. Reduce the oven temperature to 160°C Circotherm. Remove the choux buns from the oven and make a hole in the side of each bun with a skewer or knife. Return to the oven for 5 minutes to dry out completely. Leave to cool on a wire rack.
3 For the chocolate sauce, melt the chocolate, butter, 30 ml (2 tbsp) water, the golden syrup and vanilla essence in a small saucepan over a very low heat. Stir well until smooth and well blended.
4 Whip the cream until it just holds its shape. Spoon into a piping bag, fitted with a medium plain nozzle and use to fill the choux buns through the hole in the sides.
5 Dust the profiteroles with icing sugar and serve with the chocolate sauce spooned over or served separately.

CHOCOLATE CHEESECAKE
SERVES 16

BASE
225 g (8 oz) chocolate chip cookies
50 g (2 oz) chocolate drops
75 g (3 oz) butter, melted
FILLING
100 g (4 oz) plain chocolate
150 g (5 oz) butter or margarine
150 g (5 oz) caster sugar
3 eggs
100 g (4 oz) plain flour
vanilla essence
150 g (5 oz) low fat soft cheese

1 Grease a 20.5 cm (8 inch) loose-based cake tin.
2 To make the base, roughly crush the chocolate chip cookies and mix with the chocolate chips and butter. Spoon into tin and pack down with back of a spoon. Chill.
3 To make the filling, break the chocolate into small pieces. Place in a large bowl with the butter. Stand the bowl over a pan of simmering water and heat gently until the chocolate melts.
4 Add half of the sugar, two of the eggs, the flour and a few drops of vanilla essence to the chocolate and beat together. Pour into tin.
5 Beat the cheese, remaining sugar and egg and a few drops of vanilla essence together. Spoon on top of the chocolate mixture and stir gently.
6 Bake in the oven at 160°C Circotherm for 1 hour 10-1 hour 20 minutes or until firm to the touch. Leave to cool in the tin for 5 minutes.

RASPBERRY RIPPLE CHEESECAKE

SERVES 12

BASE

25 g (1 oz) blanched almonds

225 g (8 oz) almond butter biscuits, crushed

100 g (4 oz) butter or margarine, melted

few drops of almond flavouring

FILLING

450 g (1lb) raspberries

300 ml (½ pint) Greek yogurt

150 g (5 oz) low fat soft cheese

15 ml (1 level tbsp) powdered gelatine

2 egg whites

50 g (2 oz) icing sugar

mint leaves, to decorate

1 Grease a 2.3 litre (4 pint) loose-based cake tin or spring-release cake tin.

2 To make the base, lightly toast the almonds, then finely chop. Mix with the biscuits and butter. Add a few drops of almond flavouring. Spoon the mixture into the base of the prepared tin and pack down with the back of a metal spoon. Chill while making the filling.

3 To make the filling, purée 225 g (8 oz) of the raspberries in a blender or food processor, then press through a sieve. Pour three-quarters of the purée into a bowl and reserve. Add the yogurt and cheese to the purée remaining in the blender and process until well blended.

4 Sprinkle the gelatine over 30 ml (2 tbsp) water in a small bowl and leave to soak for 2-3 minutes. Place the bowl over a pan of simmering water and stir until dissolved. Leave gelatine to cool, then add to the cheese mixture.

5 Whisk the egg whites with the icing sugar until very thick. Fold into the cheese mixture.

6 Arrange 100 g (4 oz) of the reserved raspberries over the biscuit base. Pour the cheese mixture into the tin. Sprinkle with the remaining raspberries. Spoon in the reserved purée and mark in a swirl with a knife to make a marbled pattern. Chill for 3-4 hours or until set.

7 To serve, unmould and decorate with mint leaves.

Raspberry Ripple Cheesecake

MICROWAVE

Raspberry Ripple Cheesecake
To dissolve the gelatine in the microwave instead of over a pan of simmering water, cook the gelatine and water on HIGH for 30 seconds or until dissolved; do not boil.

151

Mississippi Mud Pie

SERVING IDEA

Rich, sticky *Mississippi Mud Pie* originated in the United States, where it is served warm with hot fudge sauce or cold topped with whipped cream and grated chocolate.

MICROWAVE

Mississippi Mud Pie
To make the filling, put the butter, chocolate and syrup in a bowl and cook on LOW for 4-6 minutes or until melted, stirring frequently. Cool; beat in eggs and nuts.

MISSISSIPPI MUD PIE

SERVES 10-12

BASE
100 g (4 oz) ginger biscuits, crushed
100 g (4 oz) digestive biscuits, crushed
75 g (3 oz) butter, melted
25 g (1 oz) light muscovado sugar
FILLING
225 g (8 oz) butter or margarine
175 g (6 oz) plain chocolate
100 ml (4 fl oz) golden syrup
4 eggs, beaten
50 g (2 oz) pecan nuts, chopped

1 Grease a 23 cm (9 inch) loose-based cake tin.
2 To make the base, mix the biscuits with the butter and sugar. Press into the bottom and 4 cm (1½ inches) up the sides of the prepared tin. Chill while making the filling.
3 To make the filling, put the butter, chocolate and syrup in a saucepan and heat very gently until melted, stirring all the time. Cool, then beat in the eggs and pecans. Pour the mixture into the biscuit crust.
4 Bake in the oven at 160°C Circotherm for about 35 minutes or until just firm to the touch but still soft in the centre. Serve warm or cold.

TROPICAL CHEESECAKE

SERVES 8

BASE
75 g (3 oz) butter, melted
175 g (6 oz) plain chocolate digestive biscuits, finely crushed
50 g (2 oz) desiccated coconut
FILLING
2 medium mangoes
30 ml (2 level tbsp) powdered gelatine
150 ml (¼ pint) orange juice
350 g (12 oz) full fat soft cheese
100 g (4 oz) caster sugar
2 eggs, separated
30 ml (2 tbsp) lemon juice
300 ml (½ pint) double cream
3 kiwi fruit, peeled and sliced, to decorate

1 Lightly oil a 22 cm (8½ inch) spring-release cake tin. Line the base with greaseproof and grease the paper.
2 To make the base, stir the melted butter into the biscuit crumbs and coconut. Mix well together. Press into the prepared tin. Chill for 30 minutes.
3 To make the filling, peel the mangoes and cut the flesh from the stone. Discard the stone. Roughly chop or mash the flesh.
4 Sprinkle the gelatine over the orange juice in a bowl and leave to soak for 2-3 minutes. Place the bowl over a pan of simmering water and stir until dissolved. Leave the gelatine to cool for 5 minutes.
5 Beat the soft cheese and sugar together in a

bowl until smooth, then beat in the egg yolks and lemon juice. Stir in the mango flesh and dissolved gelatine. Lightly whip the cream and fold into the mixture.

6 Whisk the egg whites until stiff, then carefully fold into the cheese mixture. Pour on to the biscuit base. Chill for 3-4 hours until firm. Carefully remove the cheesecake from the tin. Decorate with the kiwi fruit.

CHOCOLATE ROULADE

——— SERVES 8-10 ———

ROULADE
100 g (4 oz) plain chocolate
4 eggs, separated
100 g (4 oz) caster sugar
FILLING
150 ml (¼ pint) double cream
15 ml (1 level tbsp) icing sugar
150 ml (¼ pint) Greek yogurt
few drops of rose water (optional)
225 g (8 oz) raspberries
DECORATION
icing sugar for dusting
150 ml (¼ pint) double cream
100 g (4 oz) raspberries, hulled
few small rose, geranium or mint leaves

1 Grease a 23 x 33 cm (9 x 13 inch) Swiss roll tin, line with greaseproof paper and grease the paper.

2 To make the roulade, break the chocolate into small pieces. Place in a heatproof bowl

standing over a pan of simmering water and heat gently until the chocolate melts.

3 Whisk the egg yolks and sugar together in a bowl until very thick and pale in colour. Beat in the chocolate. Whisk the egg whites until stiff, then fold carefully into the chocolate mixture. Pour the mixture into the prepared tin and spread out evenly.

4 Bake in the oven at 160°C Circotherm for 15-20 minutes until well risen and firm to the touch.

5 While the roulade is cooking, lay a piece of greaseproof paper on a flat work surface and sprinkle generously with caster sugar. When the roulade is cooked, turn it out on to the paper. Carefully peel off the lining paper. Cover the roulade with a warm, damp tea towel and leave to cool.

6 To make the filling, whip the cream with the icing sugar until it forms soft peaks. Fold in the yogurt with a few drops of rose water. Spread the cream over the roulade. Sprinkle with the raspberries. Starting from one of the narrow ends, carefully roll it up, using the paper to help. Transfer the roulade to a serving plate and dust generously with icing sugar.

7 To make the decoration, whip the remaining cream until it forms soft peaks and spoon into a piping bag fitted with a star nozzle. Pipe the cream down the centre of the roulade and the sides. Decorate with raspberries and rose, geranium or mint leaves.

MICROWAVE

Tropical Cheesecake
To dissolve the gelatine in the microwave instead of over a pan of simmering water, cook the gelatine and water on HIGH for 30 seconds or until dissolved; do not boil.

COOK'S TIP

Do not worry if the *Chocolate Roulade* cracks as you roll it, the cracks are part of its charm.

MICROWAVE

Chocolate Roulade
To melt the chocolate in the microwave, break into small pieces, put in a bowl and cook on LOW for 4-5 minutes or until melted, stirring occasionally.

CHOCOLATE BOX GÂTEAU

SERVES 9

SPONGE

3 eggs

100 g (4 oz) caster sugar

75 g (3 oz) plain flour

30 ml (2 tbsp) cocoa powder

FILLING AND DECORATION

150 g (5 oz) plain chocolate

300 ml (½ pint) double cream

700 g (1½ lb) mandarin oranges or tangerines, peeled and segmented

APRICOT GLAZE

350 g (12 oz) jar apricot conserve

15-30 ml (1-2 tbsp) kirsch, brandy, orange or almond-flavoured liqueur (optional)

Chocolate Box Gâteau

1 Grease and flour an 18 cm (7 inch) square cake tin, then line the base of the tin with greaseproof paper.

2 To make the sponge, using an electric whisk, whisk the eggs and sugar together in a bowl until very thick and pale, and the mixture leaves a trail when the whisk is lifted. Sift the flour and cocoa powder over the mixture, then fold in using a large metal spoon. Transfer to the prepared tin.

3 Bake in the oven at 160°C Circotherm for about 35 minutes or until firm to the touch and shrunken from the sides of the tin. Turn out and cool on a wire rack.

4 Break the chocolate into small pieces. Place in a heatproof bowl standing over a pan of simmering water and heat gently until the chocolate melts.

5 Meanwhile, spread a sheet of foil on a baking sheet and mark a 22 cm (8½ inch) square. Spread the chocolate evenly over the square marked on the foil. Leave until set. When set, trim the edges and cut into 24 squares measuring about 5 cm (2 inches).

6 Make the apricot glaze. Put the conserve into a small saucepan and heat gently, stirring all the time, until melted. Press through a nylon sieve into another small, clean saucepan. Add the liqueur, or a little water, then bring to the boil, stirring. Keep warm.

7 Whip the cream until it just holds its shape. Cut the cake in half horizontally, then sandwich together with a little of the cream and a few of the mandarins.

8 Arrange the rest of the fruit evenly all over

the top of the cake and brush gently with the warm apricot glaze.

9 Spread a little of the remaining cream round the sides of the cake. Press on the chocolate squares, over-lapping each one slighly. Spoon the remaining cream into a piping bag fitted with a star nozzle and pipe around the top of the cake.

CHOCOLATE AND CHESTNUT MERINGUE GÂTEAU

MAKES 10-12

CAKE
175 g (6 oz) shelled hazelnuts
6 egg whites
350 g (12 oz) caster sugar
FILLING AND DECORATION
225 g (8 oz) dark or bitter chocolate
15-30 ml (1-2 tbsp) dark rum
350 g (12 oz) sweetened chestnut purée
600 ml (1 pint) double or whipping cream
Chocolate Caraque (see page 188) or grated chocolate, to decorate

1 Grease three 20.5 cm (8 inch) round sandwich tins and line the base of each tin with non-stick baking paper.

2 Toast the hazelnuts lightly under the grill, shaking the pan frequently. Transfer the nuts to a clean tea towel and rub gently while still hot to remove the skins. Grind until very fine.

3 Put the egg whites in a large bowl and whisk until very stiff and standing in peaks. Whisk in half of the sugar until the meringue is glossy.

Fold in the remaining sugar with the hazelnuts.

4 Spoon the meringue into the prepared sandwich tins. Level the tops and bake in the oven at 160°C Circotherm for 40 minutes until the meringue is crisp.

5 Invert the tins on to a wire rack and turn out the meringues. Peel off the lining papers carefully. (Don't worry if the meringues are cracked.) Leave to cool.

6 To make the filling, break the chocolate in pieces into a heatproof bowl standing over a saucepan of gently simmering water. Add the rum and heat gently until the chocolate has melted, stirring only once or twice after the chocolate has started to melt. Remove from the heat and gradually blend in 225 g (8 oz) of the chestnut purée.

7 Put one meringue round, soft side uppermost, on a serving plate. Spread with half of the chocolate and chestnut mixture, then top with the second meringue round, crisp side uppermost. Spread the remaining mixture then top with the last round.

8 Whip the cream until it holds its shape. Reserve 30 ml (2 tbsp) of the cream and swirl the remainder all over the gâteau to cover the top and sides completely. Blend the remaining chestnut purée into the reserved cream, then pipe around the edge. Decorate with Chocolate Caraque or grated chocolate. Chill in the refrigerator before serving.

COOK'S TIP

The Meringues for *Chocolate and Chestnut Meringue Gâteau* can be made in advance and stored in an airtight container. Do not sandwich them with the filling more than 2 hours before serving.

MERINGUE BASKET

SERVES 6-8

MERINGUE

4 egg whites

225 g (8 oz) icing sugar

FILLING

450 ml (¾ pint) whipping cream

30 ml (2 tbsp) kirsch

**about 450 g (1 lb) prepared fresh fruit in season,
such as strawberries, raspberries,
blackberries, starfruit**

1 Line three baking sheets with non-stick baking paper (turn rimmed baking sheets upside down and use the bases) and draw a 19 cm (7½ inch) circle on each. Turn the paper over so that the pencilled circle is visible but does not come into contact with the meringues.

2 To make the meringue, place three of the egg whites in a large bowl standing over a pan of simmering water. Sift in 175 g (6 oz) of the icing sugar. Whisk the egg whites and sugar until the mixture stands in very stiff peaks. Do not allow the bowl to get too hot or the meringue will crust around edges.

3 Spoon a scant half of the meringue mixture into a piping bag fitted with a large star nozzle. Secure the paper to the baking sheets with a little meringue. Pipe rings of meringue, about 1 cm (½ inch) thick, inside two of the circles on the paper. Fill the bag with the remaining meringue and, starting from the centre, pipe a continuous coil of meringue on the third sheet of paper to make the base of the basket.

4 Bake all the meringues in the oven at 100°C Circotherm for 2½-3 hours or until dry.

5 Use the remaining egg white and sugar to make meringue as before and put into the piping bag. Remove the cooked meringue rings from the paper and layer up on the base, piping a ring of fresh meringue between each. Return to the oven for a further 2 hours.

6 Leave to cool, then slide on to a wire rack and peel off the base paper. Just before serving, stand the meringue shell on a flat serving plate.

7 To make the filling, lightly whip the cream and fold in the kirsch. Spoon half into the base of the meringue basket and top with fruit. Whirl the remaining cream over the top and decorate with more fruit.

VARIATION

Mini Meringue Baskets
Prepare the baking sheets as above, but draw sixteen 5 cm (2 inch) circles or eight 10 cm (4 inch) circles on the paper. Make the meringue as above, using 3 egg whites and 175 g (6 oz) icing sugar. Pipe a continuous coil of meringue on each circle to make the bases, then pipe a ring on top of each circle. Bake as step 4 above for 2½ hours to dry out.

COOK'S TIP

The unfilled basket for *Meringue Basket* will keep well for several days in an airtight container. Alternatively, the unfilled meringue can be frozen. Thaw overnight at cool room temperature, then finish as before.

Opposite: Mini Meringue Baskets; Meringue Basket

MICROWAVE

Iced Raspberry Mousse
To dissolve the gelatine in the microwave instead of over a pan of simmering water, cook the gelatine and water on HIGH for 30 seconds or until dissolved; do not boil.

COOK'S TIP

Freezing ice cream by hand:
● Set the freezer to maximum or fast freeze about 1 hour before you intend to freeze the mixture.
● Make the ice cream as directed in the recipe.
● Pour the mixture into a shallow non-metal, freezer container. Cover and freeze for about 3 hours or until just frozen all over. It will have a mushy consistency.
● Spoon into a bowl and mash with a fork or flat whisk to break down the ice crystals. Work quickly so that the ice cream does not melt completely.
● Return the mixture to the shallow container and freeze again for about 2 hours or until mushy, then mash again.
● Return to the freezer and freeze for 3 hours or until firm.

ICED RASPBERRY MOUSSE
SERVES 6-8

225 g (8 oz) raspberries, hulled
2 egg yolks
50 g (2 oz) caster sugar
7.5 ml (1½ level tsp) powdered gelatine
150 ml (¼ pint) whipping cream
1 egg white
15 ml (1 tbsp) orange-flavoured liqueur
DECORATION
mint leaves
raspberries, hulled

1 To purée the raspberries, press through a sieve.
2 Using an electric mixer, whisk the egg yolks and caster sugar together in a bowl until very thick. Slowly add the raspberry purée and continue whisking until the mixture is very thick again.
3 Sprinkle the gelatine over 30 ml (2 tbsp) water in a small bowl and leave to soak for 2-3 minutes. Place the bowl over a saucepan of simmering water and stir until dissolved.
4 Lightly whip the cream. Whisk the egg white. Stir the dissolved gelatine, cream, egg white and liqueur into the raspberry mixture.
5 Divide between six to eight small freezerproof serving dishes and freeze for at least 5 hours until the mixture is firm.
6 Transfer the mousses to the refrigerator for 30-45 minutes to soften slightly before serving. Decorate with a few mint leaves and surround them with raspberries.

VANILLA ICE CREAM
SERVES 4-6

1 vanilla pod or vanilla essence
300 ml (½ pint) milk
3 egg yolks
50-75 g (2-3 oz) caster sugar
300 ml (½ pint) double cream

1 Split the vanilla pod to reveal the seeds. Put the milk and vanilla pod into a heavy-based saucepan and bring almost to the boil. Remove from the heat, cover and leave to infuse for about 20 minutes. (If using vanilla essence, add during step 3 below.)
2 Beat the egg yolks and sugar together in a bowl until well blended. Stir in the milk and strain back into the pan. Cook the custard over a gentle heat, stirring all the time, until it thickens very slightly. It is very important not to let the custard boil or it will curdle. Pour out into a bowl and leave to cool.
3 Whisk the cream into the cold custard mixture, with about 1.25 ml (¼ tsp) vanilla essence, if using (omit if vanilla pod used).
4 Freeze the ice cream mixture by hand (see Cook's Tip) or in an ice cream machine. An ice cream machine will freeze an ice cream or sorbet mixture and churn it at the same time, thus eliminating the physical effort. The results will be smooth and even textured. There are several types of ice cream machine available, some use a salt solution and others a disc which needs to be frozen before use. Always follow manufacturer's instructions.

VARIATIONS

Fruit Ice Cream

Add 300 ml (½ pint) fruit purée sweetened to taste, to the cooled custard. Complete as before. Serves 4-6.

Chocolate and Orange Liqueur Ice Cream

Prepare Vanilla Ice Cream to the end of step 3, omitting the vanilla. Break up 100 g (4 oz) plain chocolate. Place in a bowl with 30 ml (2 tbsp) orange-flavoured liqueur and melt over a pan of simmering water. Stir occasionally until smooth. Cool slightly. Add the chocolate to the custard mixture and complete as before. Serves 4-6.

Avocado and Pistachio Ice Cream

Prepare Vanilla Ice Cream to the end of step 3. Purée 1 medium ripe avocado with the finely grated rind and juice of 1 lime, 45 ml (3 tbsp) icing sugar and the cream. Stir into the cooled custard. Fold in 50 g (2 oz) chopped pistachio nuts, if freezing in an ice cream machine. If freezing by hand, fold in the nuts after the second mashing. Freeze as before. Serves 6.

Peanut and Toffee Ice Cream

Put the milk in a saucepan with 75 ml (5 tbsp) golden syrup and 30 ml (2 tbsp) soft dark brown sugar. Heat gently until sugar has dissolved, stirring occasionally. Complete the custard as before, then stir in 75 ml (5 tbsp) crunchy peanut butter. Serves 4-6.

Mango Ice Cream

Cut the flesh from 2 medium ripe mangoes, discarding the skin and stone. Purée in a blender or food processor until smooth with the juice of 1 large lime, then press through a nylon sieve. Chill. Prepare Vanilla Ice Cream to the end of step 3, omitting the vanilla. Add the mango purée and complete as before. Serves 8.

Chocolate Flake Ice Cream

Crumble 2 large chocolate flakes. Stir half into the cooled custard with the cream. Complete as before. Stir in the remaining flake just before the ice cream is completely frozen. Serves 4-6.

Mango Ice Cream

MICROWAVE

Vanilla Ice Cream

In step 1, put the vanilla pod and milk in a large bowl and cook on HIGH for 3 minutes or until almost boiling. In step 2, beat the egg yolks and sugar together in a bowl until well blended. Stir in the milk and strain into another bowl. Cook on LOW for 12-15 minutes or until slightly thickened, stirring frequently.

SNOWCAP ICED PUDDING

SERVES 6-8

150 ml (¼ pint) kirsch
about 15 sponge fingers
¾ quantity Chocolate Flake Ice Cream (see page 159)
225 g (8 oz) ripe cherries, stoned and roughly chopped
¾ quantity Vanilla Ice Cream (see page 158)
150 ml (¼ pint) double cream

1 Cut a circle of greaseproof paper and use to line base of 1.2 litre (2½ pint) pudding basin.

2 Mix the kirsch with 60 ml (4 tbsp) water and dip the sponge fingers one at a time into the mixture. Use to line the sides of the pudding basin, trimming them to fit so that there are no gaps in between. Fill the base with leftover pieces of sponge. Refrigerate for 15 minutes.

3 Stir any remaining kirsch liquid into the chocolate ice cream and mash the ice cream well with a fork to soften it slightly and make it smooth without any ice crystals.

4 Spoon the chocolate ice cream into the basin and work it up the sides of the sponge fingers to the top of the basin so that it forms an even layer. Freeze for about 2 hours until firm.

5 Mix the cherries into the vanilla ice cream and mash well with a fork as in step 3.

6 Spoon the vanilla ice cream into the centre of the basin and smooth it over the top so that it covers the chocolate ice cream and sponge fingers. Cover with foil and freeze overnight.

7 To serve, whip the cream until it will just hold its shape. Run a knife around the inside of the basin, then turn the ice cream out on to a well chilled serving plate.

8 Spoon the cream over the top and let it just start to run down the sides, then freeze immediately for about 15 minutes or until the cream has frozen solid. Serve straight from the freezer.

FROZEN YOGURT

SERVES 4-6

2 egg whites
25-50 g (1-2 oz) caster sugar
600 ml (1 pint) Greek natural yogurt
30 ml (2 tbsp) milk
5 ml (1 tsp) vanilla essence

1 Whisk the egg whites and sugar together until stiff.

2 Mix the yogurt, milk and vanilla essence together in a bowl, then fold in the egg whites.

3 Freeze in an ice cream machine or by hand as for ice cream (see pages 158 and 159).

VARIATIONS

Frozen Fruit Yogurt
Add 300 ml (½ pint) fruit purée to the yogurt mixture, then finish as above.

Frozen Muesli Yogurt
Blend 100 g (4 oz) muesli, 30 ml (2 tbsp) milk and 30 ml (2 tbsp) clear honey with the yogurt, then finish as above.

COOK'S TIP

Frozen Yogurt will be more granular if made by hand rather than in an ice cream machine.

ORANGES EN SURPRISE

— SERVES 6 —

6 large oranges

300 ml (½ pint) double cream

50 g (2 oz) icing sugar

90 ml (6 tbsp) orange-flavoured liqueur

90 ml (6 tbsp) chunky orange marmalade

fresh bay leaves or Chocolate Rose Leaves
(see page 188), to decorate

1 Cut a slice off the top of each orange and reserve. Scoop out all the flesh, pips and juice from the oranges and discard (the juice can be used for drinking or in other recipes). Wash, then dry thoroughly. Set aside.
2 Whip the cream and icing sugar together in a bowl until standing in stiff peaks. Mix the liqueur and marmalade together, then fold into the cream until evenly distributed.
3 Spoon the cream mixture into the orange shells, mounding it up over the top. Freeze for at least 4 hours, or preferably overnight to allow the flavours to develop.
4 Serve straight from the freezer, decorate with reserved orange lids, bay leaves or Chocolate Rose Leaves.

KIWI FRUIT SORBET

— SERVES 6 —

100 g (4 oz) sugar

6 kiwi fruit, peeled

2 egg whites

1 Put the sugar in a heavy-based saucepan. Add 300 ml (½ pint) water and heat gently until the sugar dissolves. Do not stir, but occasionally loosen the sugar from the base of the pan to help it dissolve. Bring to the boil and boil for 2 minutes. Leave to cool.
2 Put the kiwi fruit in a blender or food processor with the cooled syrup and process until puréed. Press through a sieve to remove the pips.
3 Pour into a shallow freezer container. Cover and freeze for about 3 hours until mushy.
4 Whisk the egg whites until stiff. Turn the sorbet into a bowl and beat gently to break down the ice crystals. Fold in the egg white. Return to the freezer container, cover and freeze for 4 hours or until firm.
5 Leave in the refrigerator for about 40 minutes to soften slightly before serving.

Left: Oranges en Surprise

SERVING IDEA

Serve *Kiwi Fruit Sorbet* decorated with slices of kiwi fruit.

Breads, Cakes & Biscuits

COOK'S TIP

If preferred, you can use easy blend dried yeast for making bread. Unlike ordinary dried yeasts, easy blend yeast does not require sugar or pre-mixing with warm water. Simply add the salt to the flour and blend in the yeast. Mix in the liquid and start to knead immediately. For *Basic Bread and Rolls* you need 1 sachet (6 g).

Previous page: Cherry and Coconut Cake (see page 174); Orange and Caraway Castles (see page 182); Orange Teabread (see page 169)

BASIC BREAD AND ROLLS

MAKES 1 LARGE LOAF OR 8 ROLLS

**15 g (½ oz) fresh yeast or
7.5 ml (1½ level tsp) dried yeast and
a pinch of sugar (see Cook's Tip)**

about 350 ml (12 fl oz) tepid milk

**450 g (1 lb) strong wholemeal flour or
strong white flour**

5 ml (1 level tsp) salt

beaten egg, to glaze

poppy, caraway, fennel or sesame seeds

1 Dissolve the fresh yeast in 300 ml (½ pint) of the milk. If using dried yeast, sprinkle it into the milk with the sugar and leave in a warm place for 15 minutes or until frothy.

2 Mix the flour and salt in a bowl. Make a well in the centre, then pour in the yeast liquid. Beat well together until the dough leaves the sides of the bowl clean, adding extra milk, if necessary.

3 Turn on to a floured surface and knead for 10 minutes until smooth and elastic. Place in an oiled bowl. Cover with oiled cling film; leave in a warm place for 1 hour until doubled in size.

4 Turn the dough on to a floured surface and knead lightly. Shape into the desired shape. Cover with oiled cling film and leave in a warm place for 30 minutes or until doubled in size.

5 Brush with beaten egg to glaze and sprinkle with seeds. Bake in the oven at Bread Setting Circotherm for 10 minutes. Reduce temperature to 170°C Circotherm and bake loaf for a further 20 minutes or rolls for a further 10-15 minutes. Cool on a wire rack.

LOAF SHAPES

Loaf
For a perfect shape, fill a 1.1 litre (2 pint) loaf tin two-thirds full. Fold the dough in three, smooth over the top and tuck in the ends.

Baton
Divide the dough into two and shape each piece into a long roll with tapering ends, about 35.5 cm (14 inches) long.

Plait
Divide the dough into three and shape each into roll about 30.5 cm (12 inches) long. Pinch the ends together and plait loosely, then pinch the other ends together.

ROLL SHAPES

Rounds
Divide the dough into eight. Place the pieces on a very lightly floured surface and roll each into ball: hold the hand flat almost at table level and move it round in a circular motion, gradually lifting the palm to get a good round shape.

Floury Baps
Divide the dough into eight. Shape each piece into a ball, place on a baking sheet and flatten slightly. Cover with oiled cling film and leave in a warm place for about 30 minutes or until doubled in size. Dredge with flour before baking at 170°C Circotherm for 15-20 minutes.

OLIVE BREAD

MAKES 2 LOAVES

25 g (1 oz) fresh yeast or 1 sachet (6 g) easy blend yeast
400 g (14 oz) strong white flour
50 g (2 oz) buckwheat flour
2.5 ml (½ level tsp) salt
freshly ground black pepper
15 ml (1 tbsp) olive oil
225 g (8 oz) stoned black olives, roughly chopped

1 Blend the fresh yeast, if using, with 300 ml (½ pint) tepid water.

2 Put the flours, salt and pepper and easy blend yeast, if using, in a bowl then add the yeast liquid, if using fresh yeast, or 300 ml (½ pint) tepid water if using easy blend, and mix to a moist dough, adding more water if necessary.

3 On a lightly floured surface, knead the dough for 10-12 minutes or until smooth. Place in a large oiled bowl and cover with oiled cling film. Leave in a warm place for about 1 hour until doubled in size.

4 Turn out the dough on to a floured surface, punch down and press out until quite flat. Drizzle over the oil and knead until smooth.

5 Halve the dough, roll out each piece to a 30.5 x 20.5 cm (12 x 8 inch) rectangle. Spread with the olives. Roll up tightly from the longest edge and place on an oiled baking sheet. Brush with water and make three or four slashes across the top of each loaf. Leave to rise for about 15 minutes.

6 Bake in the oven at Bread Setting Circo-therm for 15 minutes. Reduce the temperature to 160°C Circotherm and continue to bake for a further 15 minutes or until the loaves sound hollow when tapped on the base. Cool on a wire rack.

VARIATIONS

For a less rich dough, use half the quantity of olives; chop them a little more finely and knead into the risen dough. Shape into an oblong and prove as before.

Olive Bread

BRIOCHE

MAKES 1 LOAF

15 g (½ oz) fresh yeast or 5 ml (1 level tsp) easy blend yeast
225 g (8 oz) strong white flour
a pinch of salt
15 ml (1 level tbsp) caster sugar
2 eggs, beaten
50 g (2 oz) butter or block margarine, melted
beaten egg, to glaze

SERVING IDEA

The French traditionally serve *Brioche* warm for breakfast, with a large cup of coffee or chocolate and homemade fruit preserves.

1 Brush a 1.1 litre (2 pint) fluted mould with oil.

2 Blend the fresh yeast, if using, with 25 ml (5 tsp) tepid water.

3 Mix together the flour, salt, sugar and the easy blend yeast, if using. Stir the yeast liquid, if using fresh yeast, or 25 ml (5 tsp) tepid water if using easy blend yeast into the flour, with the eggs and melted butter. Work to a soft dough, turn out on to a floured board and knead for about 5 minutes until smooth and elastic.

4 Put the dough in a large oiled bowl, cover with oiled cling film and leave in a warm place for about 1 hour until doubled in size.

5 Knead the dough well on a lightly floured surface. Shape three-quarters of it into a ball and place in the bottom of the mould. Press a hole in the centre as far as the tin base. Shape the remaining dough into a 'knob', put into the hole and press down lightly.

6 Cover with oiled cling film and leave in a warm place until the dough, is light and puffy and nearly reaches the top of the mould.

Opposite: Brioche and Individual Brioches

7 Brush lightly with beaten egg and bake in the oven at Bread Setting Circotherm for about 20 minutes until golden. Turn out and serve at once or cool on a wire rack.

VARIATIONS

Individual Brioches

For small brioches, divide the dough into 12 pieces, put into deep 7.5 cm (3 inch) oiled fluted patty tins, then cover with oiled cling film and leave in a warm place until the dough is light and puffy and nearly reaches the top of the tins. Bake as above for about 10-12 minutes. Serve hot or cool on wire racks.

ICED APRICOT BUNS

MAKES 10

20 g (¾ oz) fresh yeast or 1 sachet (6 g) easy blend yeast
200 ml (7 fl oz) tepid milk
450 g (1 lb) strong white flour
50 g (2 oz) caster sugar
2.5 ml (½ level tsp) salt
100 g (4 oz) butter or margarine, melted
1 egg, beaten
FILLING
225 g (8 oz) no-soak dried apricots
25 g (1 oz) caster sugar
1.25 ml (¼ level tsp) ground cinnamon
25 g (1 oz) ground almonds
25 g (1 oz) toasted flaked almonds
ICING
50 g (2 oz) icing sugar
15 ml (1 tbsp) Amaretto
25 g (1 oz) toasted flaked almonds, to decorate

1 To make the dough, blend the fresh yeast with the milk.

2 Put the flour, sugar, salt and the easy blend yeast, if using, in a bowl. Make a well in the centre, then pour in the yeast liquid, if using fresh yeast, or the milk if using easy blend yeast, with the butter and egg. Beat well to make a soft dough that leaves the sides of the bowl clean.

3 Turn the dough on to a floured surface and knead for about 10 minutes until smooth, elastic and no longer sticky. Put the dough in a large oiled bowl and cover with oiled cling film. Leave in a warm place until doubled in size.

4 To make the filling, put the apricots and 200 ml (7 fl oz) water in a saucepan and bring to the boil. Cover and simmer gently for about 20 minutes. Leave to cool. Blend the apricots and their cooking water with the sugar and cinnamon to make a smooth purée or rub through a sieve. Stir in the ground almonds and flaked almonds.

5 Turn the dough on to a floured surface and knead again lightly. Grease a 24 cm (9½ inch) spring-release cake tin. Roll out the dough on a floured surface to a 38 cm (15 inch) square. Spread the apricot mixture over the dough. Carefully roll the dough up like a Swiss roll and cut into 10 slices. Arrange in the prepared tin, cut side down.

6 Cover with oiled cling film and leave in a warm place for 30 minutes or until doubled in size.

7 Bake in the oven at 160°C Circotherm for 40-45 minutes, or until golden brown and firm to the touch. Turn out and cool on a wire rack for 20 minutes.

8 To make the icing, sieve the icing sugar into a bowl and blend with the Amaretto to make a thin icing. Drizzle over the buns and sprinkle with the almonds. Leave to cool completely.

Iced Apricot Buns

ORANGE TEABREAD

— MAKES 10 - 12 SLICES —

50 g (2 oz) butter or margarine
175 g (6 oz) caster sugar
1 egg, beaten
finely grated rind of 1 orange
30 ml (2 tbsp) orange juice
75 g (3 oz) sultanas
30 ml (2 tbsp) milk
225 g (8 oz) plain flour
12.5 ml (2½ level tsp) baking powder

1 Grease a 1.3 litre (1¼ pint) loaf tin and line with greaseproof paper.
2 Cream the butter and sugar together until pale and fluffy. Gradually beat in the egg. Slowly add the orange rind and juice: do not worry if the mixture curdles. Stir in the sultanas. Lightly beat in the milk alternately with the sifted flour and baking powder.
3 Turn into the prepared tin and bake in the oven at 160°C Circotherm for 40-50 minutes or until well risen and firm to the touch. Cover with foil if it starts to overbrown. Turn out and cool on a wire rack. Serve buttered.

VARIATIONS

When mandarins and tangerines are in season, take advantage of their strong sweet flavours and use them in this teabread in place of the oranges.

OVEN SCONES

— MAKES 10 - 12 —

225 g (8 oz) self-raising flour
2.5 ml (½ level tsp) salt
5 ml (1 level tsp) baking powder
50 g (2 oz) butter or margarine
25-50 g (1-2 oz) sugar
75-100 ml (3-4 fl oz) milk
beaten egg or milk, to glaze (optional)

1 Sift the flour, salt and baking powder together into a bowl, then rub in the fat until the mixture resembles fine breadcrumbs. Stir in the sugar.
2 Make a well in the centre and stir in enough milk to give a fairly soft dough. Turn it on to a lightly floured surface, knead very lightly if necessary to remove any cracks, then roll out lightly to about 2 cm (¾ inch) thick, or pat it out with the hand.
3 Cut into 10-12 rounds with a floured 5 cm (2 inch) cutter or cut into triangles with a sharp knife. Place on a baking sheet, brush if wished with beaten egg or milk and bake at 190°C Circotherm for 10-15 minutes until brown and well risen. Transfer to a wire rack to cool.

VARIATIONS

Rich Afternoon Tea Scones
Follow the basic recipe, adding 15-30 ml (1-2 level tbsp) caster sugar to the dry ingredients and using 1 beaten egg with 75 ml (5 tbsp) water or milk in place of 150 ml (¼ pint) milk; 50 g (2 oz) dried fruit may also be included.

COOK'S TIP

If plain flour and baking powder are used instead of self-raising flour, allow 15 ml (1 level tbsp) baking powder to 225 g (8 oz) flour and sift them together twice before using.

If you use cream of tartar and bicarbonate of soda in place of baking powder, allow 5 ml (1 level tsp) cream of tartar and 2.5 ml (½ level tsp) bicarbonate of soda to 225 g (8 oz) plain flour.

169

VICTORIA SANDWICH CAKE

MAKES ABOUT 8 SLICES

CAKE

175 g (6 oz) butter softened

175 g (6 oz) caster sugar

3 eggs, beaten

175 g (6 oz) self-raising flour

FILLING

45-60 ml (3-4 level tbsp) jam

300 ml (½ pint) whipping cream, whipped (optional)

caster sugar for dredging

1 Grease two 18 cm (7 inch) sandwich tins and line with greaseproof paper.

2 Beat the butter and sugar together until pale and fluffy. Add the eggs, a little at a time, beating well after each addition. Fold in half the flour using a metal spoon, then fold in the rest.

3 Divide the mixture evenly between the tins and level the surface. Bake in the oven at 160°C Circotherm for 20-25 minutes until they are well risen, firm to the touch and beginning to shrink away from the sides of the tins. Turn out and cool on a wire rack.

4 When the cakes are cool, sandwich them together with jam and cream, if using, and sprinkle the top with sugar.

COOK'S TIP

To make a quick all-in-one cake, add 5 ml (1 level tsp) baking powder to the ingredients for *Victoria Sandwich Cake*. Simply put all the ingredients in a large bowl and beat until smooth and glossy.

Opposite: Victoria Sandwich Cake; Almond Fingers (see page 186)

VARIATIONS

For a special occasion cake, increase the quantities to 225 g (8 oz) butter, 225 g (8 oz) sugar, 4 eggs and 225 g (8 oz) flour and divide the mixture between three sandwich tins. Sandwich the layers together with whipped cream and fresh fruit.

Chocolate Victoria Sandwich

Replace 45 ml (3 level tbsp) flour with 45 ml (3 level tbsp) cocoa powder. Sandwich the cakes with chocolate butter cream, made by dissolving 15 ml (1 level tbsp) cocoa powder in a little hot water and beating with 75 g (3 oz) butter, 175 g (6 oz) icing sugar and 15-30 ml (1-2 tbsp) milk.

Coffee Victoria Sandwich

Add 10 ml (2 level tsp) instant coffee powder, dissolved in a little warm water, to the creamed butter and sugar mixture with the eggs, or use 10 ml (2 tsp) coffee essence. Sandwich the cakes with coffee butter cream, made by dissolving 10 ml (2 level tsp) instant coffee in a little warm water and beating with 75 g (3 oz) butter and 175 g (6 oz) icing sugar.

Orange or Lemon Victoria Sandwich

Add the finely grated rind of an orange or lemon to the mixture. Sandwich the cakes together with orange or lemon butter cream, made by beating 75 g (3 oz) butter with 175 g (6 oz) icing sugar, the finely grated rind of 1 lemon or 1 orange and 15-30 ml (1-2 tbsp) juice.

GENOESE CAKE

MAKES ABOUT 8 SLICES

CAKE
40 g (1½ oz) butter
3 eggs, size 2
75 g (3 oz) caster sugar
65 g (2½ oz) plain flour
15 ml (1 level tbsp) cornflour
FILLING AND DECORATION
300 ml (½ pint) double cream, whipped
icing sugar for dredging

COOK'S TIP

When making *Genoese Cake*, it is important to add the butter slowly, carefully and lightly, in step 5, or the cake will have a heavy texture.

1 Grease two 18 cm (7 inch) sandwich tins or one 18 cm (7 inch) deep round cake tin and line with greaseproof paper.
2 Put the butter into a saucepan and heat gently until melted, then cool slightly.
3 Put the eggs and sugar in a bowl, place over a pan of hot water and whisk until pale and creamy and thick enough to leave a trail on the surface when the whisk is lifted. Remove from the heat and whisk until cool.
4 Sift the flours together into a bowl. Fold half into the egg mixture with a metal spoon.
5 Pour half the cooled butter around the edge of the mixture. Gradually fold in the remaining butter and flour alternately.
6 Pour the mixture into the tins. Bake sandwich cakes in the oven at 160°C Circotherm for 25 minutes or the deep cake for about 30 minutes, until well risen, firm to the touch and beginning to shrink away from the tin. Turn out and cool on a wire rack.
7 Sandwich the cakes together with the cream and dredge the top with icing sugar. The large cake may be cut in half horizontally and sandwiched with cream or left plain.

ORANGE MADEIRA CAKE

MAKES ABOUT 12 SLICES

175 g (6 oz) butter or margarine
175 g (6 oz) caster sugar
3 eggs, beaten
150 g (5 oz) self-raising flour
100 g (4 oz) plain flour
finely grated rind of 1 orange
30 ml (2 tbsp) orange juice
1 thin slice citron peel

1 Grease a 1.4 litre (2½ pint) loaf tin or 18 cm (7 inch) round tin and line the base with greaseproof paper.
2 Cream together the butter and sugar until pale and fluffy. Gradually beat in the eggs. Sift together the flours and fold into the mixture. Fold in the orange rind and juice.
3 Spoon into the tin and level the surface. Place the citron peel on top.
4 Bake in the oven at 150°C Circotherm for about 55-60 minutes or until firm to the touch. Turn out on to a wire rack to cool.

VARIATION

Plain Madeira Cake
Omit the orange rind and juice and replace with 30 ml (2 tbsp) milk. Add 2.5 ml (½ tsp) vanilla essence, or use vanilla sugar in place of caster.

WHISKED SPONGE

MAKES ABOUT 8 SLICES

| 3 eggs |
| 100 g (4 oz) caster sugar |
| 75 g (3 oz) plain flour |
| 45-60 ml (3-4 tbsp) strawberry or apricot jam, to fill |
| caster sugar for dredging |

1 Grease two 18 cm (7 inch) sandwich tins, line with greaseproof paper, then dust with a mixture of flour and caster sugar.
2 Put the eggs and sugar in a large bowl and stand over a saucepan of hot water. Whisk the eggs and sugar until doubled in volume and thick enough to leave a thin trail on the surface of the batter when the whisk is lifted.
3 Remove the bowl from the heat and continue whisking for a further 5 minutes until the mixture is cool.
4 Sift half the flour over the mixture and fold it in very lightly, using a large metal spoon. Sift and fold in the remaining flour in the same way.
5 Pour the mixture into the tins, tilting the tins to spread the mixture evenly. Do not use a palette knife or spatula to smooth the mixture as this will crush out the air bubbles.
6 Bake in the oven at 160°C Circotherm for about 25 minutes until well risen, firm to the touch and beginning to shrink away from the sides. Turn out and cool on a wire rack.
7 When the cakes are cold, sandwich them together with strawberry jam and dredge caster sugar over the top.

VARIATION

Plain Madeira Cake
Omit the orange rind and juice and replace with 30 ml (2 tbsp) milk. Add 2.5 ml (½ tsp) vanilla essence, or use vanilla sugar in place of caster.

1 Tilt the tin backwards and forwards to spread the mixture in an even layer. Bake in the oven at 170°C Circotherm for 10-12 minutes until golden brown, well risen and firm.
2 Meanwhile, place a sheet of greaseproof paper over a damp tea towel. Dredge the paper with caster sugar.
3 Quickly turn out the cake on to the paper, trim off the crusty edges and spread with jam. Roll up the cake with the aid of the paper. Make the first turn firmly so that the whole cake will roll evenly and have a good shape when finished, but roll more lightly after this turn.
4 Place seam-side down on a wire rack and dredge with sugar.

Chocolate Swiss Roll
Make the sponge as for Swiss roll, above, but replace 15 ml (1 level tbsp) flour with 15 ml (1 level tbsp) cocoa powder. Turn out the cooked sponge and trim as above, then cover with a sheet of greaseproof paper and roll with the paper inside. When cold, unroll and remove the paper. Spread with whipped cream and re-roll. Dust with icing sugar.

Swiss Roll

CHERRY AND COCONUT CAKE

MAKES ABOUT 10 SLICES

250 g (9 oz) self-raising white flour
1.25 ml (¼ level tsp) salt
100 g (4 oz) butter or margarine
75 g (3 oz) desiccated coconut
100 g (4 oz) caster sugar
100 g (4 oz) glacé cherries, finely chopped
2 eggs, size 6, beaten
225 ml (8 fl oz) milk
25 g (1 oz) shredded coconut

1 Grease a 1.3 litre (2¼ pint) loaf tin. Line the base with greaseproof paper, grease the paper and dust with flour.
2 Put the flour and salt into a bowl and rub in the fat until the mixture resembles fine bread-crumbs. Stir in the desiccated coconut, sugar and cherries.
3 Whisk together the eggs and milk and beat into the dry ingredients. Turn the mixture into the tin, level the surface and scatter over the shredded coconut.
4 Bake in oven at 160°C Circotherm for 1¼ hours until a fine warmed skewer inserted in the centre comes out clean. Check after 40 minutes and cover with greaseproof paper if overbrowning. Turn out on to a wire rack to cool.

COOK'S TIP

To prevent glacé cherries sinking to the bottom of a cake, wash off any excess syrup before use and dry thoroughly, then toss in a little flour.

CHOCOLATE FUDGE CAKE

MAKES 12 - 14 SLICES

CAKE
275 g (10 oz) plain flour
45 ml (3 tbsp) cocoa powder
6.25 ml (1¼ level tsp) baking powder
2.5 ml (½ tsp) bicarbonate of soda
large pinch of salt
100 g (4 oz) plain chocolate
150 g (5 oz) butter
225 g (8 oz) light brown soft sugar
2 eggs, size 2, beaten
150 ml (¼ pint) natural yogurt
2.5 ml (½ tsp) vanilla flavouring
FUDGE ICING
450 g (1 lb) icing sugar
100 g (4 oz) cocoa powder
100 g (4 oz) butter
90 ml (6 tbsp) milk

1 Grease three 18 cm (7 inch) sandwich tins, line with greaseproof paper and grease the paper.
2 Sift together the flour, cocoa powder, baking powder, bicarbonate of soda and salt.
3 Break the chocolate into a bowl. Place over a saucepan of simmering water and heat gently, stirring, until the chocolate has melted. Leave to cool for 30 minutes.
4 Cream the butter and the brown sugar together until light and fluffy. Beat in the eggs, then fold in the chocolate, the sifted ingredients, the yogurt and the vanilla flavouring.
5 Turn the mixture into the prepared tins and

level the surface. Bake in the oven at 160°C Circotherm for about 25 minutes until risen and firm to the touch. Turn out and leave to cool on a wire rack.

6 To make the fudge icing, sift the icing sugar and cocoa powder together, then put into heavy-based saucepan with the butter and the milk. Heat gently until the butter has melted, then beat until smooth. Remove from the heat.

7 Use some of the fudge icing to sandwich the three cakes together. Cover the sides and top of the cake with the remaining icing.

STRAWBERRY SHORTBREAD GÂTEAU

—— MAKES 8 SLICES ——

SHORTBREAD
150 g (5 oz) plain flour
25 g (1 oz) cornflour
50 g (2 oz) caster sugar
100 g (4 oz) butter, softened
SPONGE
2 eggs
50 g (2 oz) caster sugar
50 g (2 oz) plain flour
FILLING AND DECORATION
225 g (8 oz) strawberries
300 ml (½ pint) double cream
45 ml (3 tbsp) milk
icing sugar for dredging

1 Grease two 22 cm (8½ inch) sandwich tins and line with greaseproof paper.

2 To make the shortbread, sift together the flour, cornflour and sugar. Knead in the butter, using fingertips, to give a soft dough. Roll out on a lightly floured board and trim, using a pan lid as a guide, to give a 20.8 cm (8 inch) round. Transfer to a baking sheet and bake at 150°C Circotherm for about 30 minutes until pale and golden brown. Cut into eight sections while still warm. Leave to cool on a wire rack.

3 To make the sponge, put the eggs and sugar in a bowl, stand it over a pan of hot water and whisk until thick, creamy and pale in colour. The mixture should be stiff enough to leave a trail when the whisk is lifted. Remove from the heat and continue whisking until cool.

4 Sift in the flour and fold in with a large metal spoon.

5 Divide between the tins and bake in the oven at 160°C Circotherm for about 15 minutes until golden brown and firm to the touch. Cool on a wire rack.

6 Wipe the strawberries, hull and slice all but one. Whip the cream with the milk until it holds its shape. Sweeten to taste with a little icing sugar if desired. Put half the cream in a piping bag fitted with a large star nozzle.

7 Reserve eight strawberry slices and fold the remainder into the cream and sandwich the sponge layers together. Pipe eight rosettes of cream on the top layer of sponge and place a strawberry slice on each one. Dust shortbread with icing sugar and arrange at an angle on top of the cream rosettes. Top with the unhulled strawberry cut into three slices.

Strawberry Shortbread Gâteau

WHITE CHOCOLATE GÂTEAU

MAKES ABOUT 16 SLICES

CAKE
75 g (3 oz) butter
6 eggs
175 g (6 oz) caster sugar
150 g (5 oz) plain flour
30 ml (2 level tbsp) cornflour
DARK CHOCOLATE MOUSSE FILLING
175 g (6 oz) plain chocolate
30 ml (2 tbsp) brandy
2 eggs, separated
300 ml (½ pint) double cream
5 ml (1 level tsp) powdered gelatine
DECORATION
275 g (10 oz) white chocolate
300 ml (½ pint) double cream
icing sugar for dusting

COOK'S TIP

A stripping knife is a decorator's tool used for scraping off wallpaper! It has a sharp flexible blade and is ideal for making large chocolate curls. It is worth buying one and keeping it specifically for this purpose. A large sharp knife can be used instead but does not make such large fat curls.

1 For the cake, grease a 23 cm (9 inch) round spring-release tin, line with greaseproof paper and grease the paper.

2 Put the butter into a saucepan and heat gently until melted, then remove from the heat and leave to stand for a few minutes to cool slightly.

3 Put the eggs and sugar in a bowl, place over a saucepan of hot water and whisk until pale and creamy and thick enough to leave a trail on the surface when the whisk is lifted. Remove from the heat and whisk until cool.

4 Sift the flours together into a bowl. Fold half the flour into the egg mixture with a metal spoon. Pour half the cooled butter around the edge of the mixture. Gradually fold in the remaining butter and flour alternately. Fold in very lightly or the butter will sink and result in a heavy cake.

5 Pour into the prepared tin. Bake in the oven at 160°C Circotherm for about 40 minutes, until well risen, firm to the touch and beginning to shrink away from the sides of the tin. Turn out and cool on a wire rack.

6 When the cakes are cold, make the mousse filling. Break the chocolate into a bowl and stand over a pan of simmering water until the chocolate melts. Remove from the heat and stir in the brandy and egg yolks. Whip the cream until it just stands in soft peaks, then fold into the chocolate mixture.

7 In a small bowl, sprinkle the gelatine on to 15 ml (1 tbsp) water. Stand over a pan of simmering water and stir until dissolved. Cool, then stir into the chocolate mixture. Whisk the egg whites until stiff then fold in.

8 Cut the cake in half. Put one piece of sponge back in the tin. Pour the mousse on top. Put the second piece of sponge on top. Leave to set.

9 While the mousse is setting, make the decoration. Melt the white chocolate as in step 6. Spread out thinly on a marble slab or a clean, smooth work surface. Leave until set. When the chocolate is set, push a clean stripping knife (see Cook's Tip) across the chocolate at an angle of about 25° to roll off large fat chocolate curls. Chill until ready for decorating.

10 When the mousse is set, whip the cream until it holds its shape. Ease the cake out of the tin and cover with the cream. Cover with the chocolate curls and dust with icing sugar.

COFFEE PRALINE GÂTEAU

MAKES 8 SLICES

SPONGE
3 large eggs
75 g (3 oz) caster sugar
75 g (3 oz) plain flour
15 ml (1 tbsp) coffee flavouring
PRALINE
25 g (1 oz) caster sugar
25 g (1 oz) blanched almonds
FILLING
300 ml (½ pint) double cream
30 ml (2 tbsp) coffee-flavoured liqueur
icing sugar for dusting

1 Grease a 20.5 cm (8 inch) round cake tin, line the base with greaseproof paper and grease the paper. Dust with caster sugar and flour.

2 To make the sponge, put the eggs and 75 g (3 oz) sugar in a large bowl, place over a saucepan of hot water and whisk until pale and creamy and thick enough to leave a trail on the surface when the whisk is lifted. Remove from the heat and whisk until cool.

3 Sift the flour evenly over the surface of the egg mixture and fold in lightly until no traces of flour remain. Lightly fold in the coffee flavouring.

4 Turn into the prepared tin and bake in the oven at 160°C Circotherm for 20-25 minutes or until the sponge springs back when pressed lightly with a finger and has shrunk away a little from the tin. Turn out on to a wire rack and leave to cool.

5 Meanwhile, make the praline. Oil a baking sheet. Put the caster sugar into a small frying pan with the blanched almonds and heat gently until the sugar dissolves and caramelizes.

6 Pour the praline on to the baking sheet and leave for 10-15 minutes to cool and harden.

7 When cold, grind or crush with the end of a rolling pin in a strong bowl. Whip the cream until it holds its shape then whisk in the liqueur and fold in three-quarters of the praline.

8 Split the sponge in half and sandwich with the cream. Dust the top with icing sugar and decorate with the remaining praline. Refrigerate for 1-2 hours before serving.

Coffee Praline Gâteau

COOK'S TIP

Praline can be made in large quantities and stored in an airtight container for decorating cakes or flavouring mousses and ice creams.

177

BLACK FOREST GÂTEAU

MAKES 10-12 SLICES

CAKE
100 g (4 oz) butter
6 eggs
225 g (8 oz) caster sugar
75 g (3 oz) plain flour
50 g (2 oz) cocoa powder
2.5 ml (½ tsp) vanilla flavouring

FILLING AND DECORATION
two 425 g (15 oz) cans stoned black cherries, drained and syrup reserved
60 ml (4 tbsp) kirsch
600 ml (1 pint) whipping cream
100 g (4 oz) Chocolate Caraque (see page 188)
5 ml (1 level tsp) arrowroot

1 Grease a deep 23 cm (9 inch) round cake tin and line the base with greaseproof paper.

2 Put the butter into a bowl, place over a pan of warm water and beat it until really soft but not melted.

3 Put the eggs and sugar into a large bowl, place over a pan of hot water and whisk until pale and creamy, and thick enough to leave a trail on the surface when the whisk is lifted. Remove from the heat and whisk until cool.

4 Sift the flour and cocoa together, then lightly fold into the mixture with a metal spoon. Fold in the vanilla flavouring and softened butter.

5 Turn the mixture into the prepared tin and tilt the tin to spread the mixture evenly. Bake at 160°C Circotherm for 45-50 minutes until well risen, firm to the touch when pressed and is beginning to shrink away from the sides of tin.

6 Turn out of the tin on to a wire rack, covered with greaseproof paper, and leave to cool for 30 minutes.

7 Cut the cake into three horizontally. Place one layer on a flat plate. Mix together 75 ml (5 tbsp) cherry syrup and the kirsch. Spoon 45 ml (3 tbsp) over the cake layer.

8 Whip the cream until it just holds its shape, then spread a little thinly over the soaked sponge. Reserve a quarter of the cherries for decoration and scatter half the remainder over the cream.

9 Repeat the layers of sponge, cherry syrup, cream and cherries. Top with the third cake round and spoon over the remaining kirsch-flavoured cherry syrup.

10 Spread a thin layer of the remaining cream around the sides of the cake, reserving a third to decorate. Press on the Chocolate Caraque, reserving a few to decorate the top.

11 Spoon the remaining cream into a piping bag, fitted with a large star nozzle and pipe whirls of cream around the edge of the cake. Top each whirl with a chocolate curl.

12 Fill the centre with the reserved cherries. Blend the arrowroot with 45 ml (3 tbsp) cherry syrup, place in a small saucepan, bring to the boil and boil, stirring, for a few minutes until the mixture is clear. Brush the glaze over the top of the cherries.

Opposite: Black Forest Gâteau

If *Dundee Cake* starts to overbrown, cover with several layers of greaseproof paper.

Leave the cake to cool completely then wrap in greaseproof paper and foil and store in an airtight tin for at least 1 week to mature.

Simnel Cake is traditionally served on Easter Sunday. The balls of marzipan represent the 11 faithful disciples.

DUNDEE CAKE

MAKES ABOUT 12 SLICES

100 g (4 oz) currants
100 g (4 oz) seedles raisins
50 g (2 oz) blanched almonds, chopped
100 g (4 oz) chopped mixed peel
275 g (10 oz) plain white flour
225 g (8 oz) butter or margarine
225 g (8 oz) light brown soft sugar
finely grated rind of 1 lemon
4 eggs, beaten
25 g (1 oz) split almonds, to decorate

1 Grease a deep 20.5 cm (8 inch) round cake tin. Line with greased greaseproof paper.
2 Combine the fruit, chopped nuts and mixed peel in a bowl. Sift in a little flour and stir until the fruit is evenly coated.
3 Cream the butter and sugar together until pale and fluffy, then beat in the lemon rind.
4 Add the eggs to the creamed mixture a little at a time, beating well after each addition.
5 Sift the remaining flour over the mixture and fold in lightly with a metal spoon, then fold in the fruit and nut mixture.
6 Turn the mixture into the prepared tin and make a slight hollow in the centre with the back of a metal spoon. Arrange the almonds on top.
7 Bake in the oven at 150°C Circotherm for about 1 hour 50 minutes until a fine warmed skewer inserted in the centre comes out clean. Check after 1½ hours (see Cook's Tips).
8 Cool in the tin for 15 minutes, then turn out on to a wire rack to cool (see Cook's Tips).

SIMNEL CAKE

MAKES ABOUT 20 SLICES

175 g (6 oz) butter or margarine, softened
175 g (6 oz) caster sugar
3 eggs
225 g (8 oz) plain flour
pinch of salt
2.5 ml (½ level tsp) ground cinnamon
2.5 ml (½ level tsp) grated nutmeg
100 g (4 oz) glacé cherries, washed, dried and cut into quarters
50 g (2 oz) chopped mixed peel
250 g (9 oz) currants
100 g (4 oz) sultanas
finely grated rind of 1 lemon
milk, if necessary
Almond Paste (see right) or 450 g (1 lb) bought almond paste
1 egg white, to fix and glaze
ribbon
fresh or crystallized flowers, to decorate

1 Grease an 18 cm (7 inch) round cake tin. Line with greaseproof paper; grease paper.
2 Cream the butter and sugar until pale and fluffy. Gradually beat in the eggs.
3 Sift in the flour, salt and spices and fold into the mixture with a metal spoon. Add all the fruit and the lemon rind, folding together to give a smooth dropping consistency. If a little too firm, add 15-30 ml (1-2 tbsp) milk.
4 Divide the Almond Paste in half. Lightly dust a surface with icing sugar and roll out one half to a 16 cm (6½ inch) circle.

5 Spoon half the cake mixture into the prepared tin. Place the round of Almond Paste on top and cover with the remaining cake mixture. Press down gently with the back of a spoon to level the surface.

6 Tie a double thickness of brown paper round the outside of the tin. Bake in the oven at 140°C Circotherm for about 2¼ hours. When cooked, the cake should be a rich brown colour, and firm to the touch.

7 Cool in the tin for about 1 hour, then turn out. Ease off the greaseproof paper and leave to cool completely on a wire rack.

8 Divide the remaining Almond Paste in two. Roll out one half to a 17 cm (7½ inch) circle and the rest into 11 small balls. Lightly beat the egg white and brush over the top of the cake. Place the circle of Almond Paste on top, crimp the edges, and with a little of the egg white fix the balls around the top edge of the cake.

9 Brush the Almond Paste with the remaining egg white and cook under a hot grill for 1-2 minutes until the paste is well browned. Tie a ribbon around the cake and decorate with fresh or crystallized flowers.

Simnel Cake

ALMOND PASTE

——— MAKES 450 G (1 LB) ———

225 g (8 oz) preserving or granulated sugar
pinch of cream of tartar
175 g (6 oz) ground almonds
1 egg white
50 g (2 oz) icing sugar

1 Put the sugar and 75 ml (5 tbsp) water in a heavy-based saucepan and dissolve over a low heat. When the syrup reaches boiling point, add the cream of tartar and boil to 116°C (240°F).

2 Remove the pan from the heat and stir rapidly until the syrup begins to 'grain'.

3 Stir in the almonds and egg white. Cook for a few minutes over a low heat, stirring.

4 Pour on to an oiled marble slab or wooden chopping board, add icing sugar and work well with a palette knife, lifting the edges of the mixture and turning them into the centre.

5 As soon as the mixture is sufficiently cool, knead it until smooth. Additional icing sugar may be kneaded in if the mixture is to wet. Wrap in cling film until ready to use.

GINGERBREAD SLAB
MAKES 20 SLICES

100 g (4 oz) black treacle
100 g (4 oz) golden syrup
50 g (2 oz) butter or margarine
50 g (2 oz) lard
225 g (8 oz) plain white flour
1.25 ml (¼ level tsp) bicarbonate of soda
5 ml (1 level tsp) mixed spice
5 ml (1 level tsp) ground ginger
100 g (4 oz) dark brown soft sugar
150 ml (¼ pint) milk

1 Grease a deep 18 cm (7 inch) square cake tin. Line with greaseproof paper and then grease the paper.
2 Put the black treacle, golden syrup, butter and lard into a saucepan and heat gently until melted.
3 Sift the flour, bicarbonate of soda and spices into a bowl and stir in the sugar. Make a well in the centre and pour in the milk and treacle mixture. Beat well until smooth and of a thick pouring consistency.
4 Pour into the prepared tin and bake in the oven at 150°C Circotherm for about 1 hour or until a fine warmed skewer inserted in the centre of the cake comes out clean. Cool in the tin for 1 hour, then turn out and cool completely on a wire rack.
5 Wrap in greaseproof paper and foil and store in an airtight tin for 2 days before eating.

ORANGE AND CARAWAY CASTLES
MAKES 10

75 g (3 oz) butter or margarine
50 g (2 oz) caster sugar
120 ml (8 level tbsp) fine shred marmalade
finely grated rind of 1 orange
2 eggs, beaten
125 g (4 oz) self-raising flour
pinch of salt
2.5-5 ml (½-1 level tsp) caraway seeds
125 g (4 oz) toasted flaked almonds, roughly chopped

1 Grease 10 small dariole moulds and stand them on a baking sheet.
2 Cream together the butter and sugar until pale and fluffy. Beat in 30 ml (2 level tbsp) marmalade and the orange rind. Gradually beat in the eggs, then fold in the flour, salt and caraway seeds.
3 Divide the mixture between the prepared dariole moulds and bake in the oven at 150°C Circotherm for 20 minutes or until well risen and firm to the touch. Turn out and cool on a wire rack.
4 Trim the bases of the cakes so that they stand level. Gently heat the remaining marmalade in a saucepan until melted.
5 Spread the chopped toasted almonds out on a large plate. Spear each cake on a skewer, brush the tops and sides with melted marmalade, then roll in the nuts until completely coated.

COOK'S TIP

Gingerbread should always be wrapped tightly in greaseproof paper and foil, then stored in an airtight tin for 2 days before eating. This allows the cake to mature and become moist and stickly.

BOSTON BROWNIES

MAKES ABOUT 16 SMALL
OR 9 LARGE SQUARES

50 g (2 oz) plain chocolate
65 g (2½ oz) butter or margarine, diced
175 g (6 oz) caster sugar
65 g (2½ oz) self-raising flour
1.25 ml (¼ level tsp) salt
2 eggs
2.5 ml (½ tsp) vanilla flavouring
50 g (2 oz) walnuts, roughly chopped

1 Grease a shallow 20.5 cm (8 inch) square cake tin and line with greaseproof paper.
2 Break up the chocolate and put it in a bowl with the butter. Stand the bowl over a saucepan of hot water and heat gently, stirring occasionally, until melted. Add the caster sugar.
3 Sift together the flour and salt into a bowl. Add the chocolate mixture, eggs, vanilla flavouring and walnuts. Mix thoroughly.
4 Pour the mixture into the prepared tin and bake in the oven at 160°C Circotherm for 35-40 minutes until the mixture is risen and just beginning to leave the sides of the cake tin.
5 Cool in the tin, then cut into squares.

CHOCOLATE CHIP COOKIES

MAKES ABOUT 20

75 g (3 oz) butter or margarine
75 g (3 oz) caster sugar
75 g (3 oz) light brown soft sugar
few drops of vanilla flavouring
1 egg
175 g (6 oz) self-raising flour
pinch of salt
50 g (2 oz) walnut pieces, chopped
100 g (4 oz) chocolate chips

1 Grease two baking sheets.
2 Cream together the butter, sugars and vanilla flavouring until pale and fluffy, then gradually beat in the egg.
3 Sift in the flour and salt, then fold in with the nuts and chocolate chips.
4 Drop spoonfuls of the mixture on to the baking sheets and bake in the oven at 160°C Circotherm for 12-15 minutes.
5 Cool on the baking sheets for 1 minute, then transfer to a wire rack to cool completely.

COOK'S TIP

Buy ready-made chocolate chips or polka dots for *Chocolate Chip Cookies*, or make your own by roughly chopping a bar of chocolate.

Left: Boston Brownies

COOK'S TIP

If the chocolate is overheated, it may curdle or thicken instead of melting smoothly. To guard against this, either melt it in a bowl placed over a pan of hot water, as suggested here, or use a double saucepan. If the chocolate does curdle, add a little blended white vegetable fat. Break the fat into small pieces and stir into the chocolate until it reaches the desired consistency.

Opposite: (clockwise from top left) Chocolate Chip Cookies (see page 183); Gingerbread People (see page 186); Cherry Garlands; Florentines

FLORENTINES

MAKES ABOUT 12

| 90 g (3½ oz) butter or margarine |
| 100 g (4 oz) caster sugar |
| 100 g (4 oz) flaked almonds, roughly chopped |
| 25 g (1 oz) sultanas |
| 5 glacé cherries, chopped |
| 25 g (1 oz) chopped mixed peel |
| 15 ml (1 tbsp) single cream |
| 175 g (6 oz) plain chocolate |

1 Line three baking sheets with non-stick paper.
2 Melt the butter in a saucepan over a low heat, add the sugar and boil the mixture for 1 minute.
3 Remove the pan from the heat and add all the remaining ingredients, except the chocolate, stirring well to mix.
4 Drop the mixture in heaped tablespoonfuls on to the prepared sheets, allowing enough room between each for the mixture to spread.
5 Bake in the oven at 160°C Circotherm for 15-20 minutes until golden brown.
6 Remove from the oven and press around the edges of the biscuits with the blade of a knife to neaten the shape. Leave on the baking sheets for 5 minutes until beginning to firm, then lift on to a wire rack to cool for 20 minutes.
7 Break the chocolate into a heatproof bowl and place over a pan of simmering water. Stir until the chocolate has melted, then remove from the heat and leave to cool for 10-15 minutes (see Cook's Tip).

8 Just as the chocolate is beginning to set, spread it over the backs of the biscuits. Draw the prongs of a fork across the chocolate to mark wavy lines and leave to set.

CHERRY GARLANDS

MAKES 32

| 225 g (8 oz) butter or margarine |
| 50 g (2 oz) icing sugar |
| 200 g (7 oz) plain flour |
| 150 g (5 oz) cornflour |
| few drops of vanilla flavouring |
| 50 g (2 oz) glacé cherries, very finely chopped |
| quartered cherries and angelica, to decorate |
| icing sugar for dredging |

1 Grease three baking sheets.
2 Cream the butter and sugar together until pale and fluffy, then beat in the flours, vanilla flavouring and the chopped cherries. Continue beating until very soft.
3 Spoon half of the mixture into a piping bag fitted with a 1 cm (½ inch) star nozzle. Pipe 5 cm (2 inch) rings on to the baking sheets allowing room for spreading. Decorate with quartered cherries and pieces of angelica. Repeat with the remaining mixture.
4 Bake in the oven at 160°C Circotherm for about 20 minutes until pale golden.
5 Allow to firm up slightly on the baking sheets for about 30 seconds before sliding on to a wire rack to cool. Dredge with icing sugar.

GINGERBREAD PEOPLE

— MAKES ABOUT 12 —

350 g (12 oz) plain flour
5 ml (1 level tsp) bicarbonate of soda
10 ml (2 level tsp) ground ginger
100 g (4 oz) butter or margarine
175 g (6 oz) light brown soft sugar
60 ml (4 level tbsp) golden syrup
1 egg
currants, to decorate

1 Grease three baking sheets.

2 Sift the flour, bicarbonate of soda and ginger into a bowl. Rub in the butter until the mixture resembles fine breadcrumbs. Stir in the sugar. Beat the syrup into the egg and stir into the flour mixture.

3 Mix to form a dough and knead until smooth.

4 Divide into two and roll out on a lightly floured surface to about 0.5 cm (¼ inch) thick. Using gingerbread cutters, cut out figures and place them on the baking sheets. Decorate with currants to represent eyes and buttons.

5 Bake in the oven at 160°C Circotherm for 12-15 minutes until golden brown all over. Cool slightly, then transfer to a wire rack to cool.

COOK'S TIP

The finished Gingerbread People can be decorated with glacé icing to give them each a personality of their own.

ALMOND FINGERS

— MAKES 10 —

1 quantity Rich Shortcrust Pastry (see page 190)
45 ml (3 level tbsp) raspberry jam
1 egg white
45 ml (3 level tbsp) ground almonds
50 g (2 oz) caster sugar
few drops of almond flavouring
45 ml (3 level tbsp) flaked almonds

1 Lightly grease a shallow 18 cm (7 inch) square tin.

2 Roll out the pastry to an 18 cm (7 inch) square and use to line the base of the tin. Spread the pastry with the jam, almost to the edges.

3 Whisk the egg white until stiff. Fold in the ground almonds, sugar and flavouring. Spread the mixture over the jam.

4 Sprinkle with flaked almonds and bake in the oven at 160°C Circotherm for about 35 minutes until crisp and golden. Cool in the tin, then cut into 10 fingers and remove with a palette knife.

GLAZED FRUIT TARTS

— MAKES 12 —

1 quantity Pâte Sucrée (see page 190)
150 ml (¼ pint) double cream
50 ml (2 fl oz) single cream
225 g (8 oz) fresh strawberries
60 ml (4 level tbsp) redcurrant jelly, to glaze

1 Roll out the pâte sucrée on a lightly floured working surface and use to line twelve 6.5 cm

(2½ inch) shallow fluted flan tins. Bake blind in the oven at 160°C Circotherm for 10 minutes with paper and beans and then 5 minutes without them. Cool on a wire rack.

2 Whip the creams together until just standing in soft peaks. Spread a layer of cream over the tart bases. Using a sharp knife, slice the strawberries. Arrange on top of the cream in an overlapping circle on each tart.

3 Melt the redcurrant jelly over a very low heat, adding a little water if necessary. Brush over the strawberries to glaze.

VARIATION

Strawberry tarts are always popular, but if preferred, these tarts can be made with a mixture of fruits of your choice instead.

MILLE FEUILLES

— MAKES 6 —

225 g (8 oz) ready prepared puff pastry
100 g (4 oz) raspberry jam
300 ml (½ pint) double cream, whipped
icing sugar for dusting

1 Roll out the pastry on a lightly floured surface into a rectangle measuring 25 x 23 cm (10 x 9 inches) and place on a damp baking sheet. Prick all over with a fork and mark a lattice pattern with the point of a knife.

2 Bake in the oven at 190°C Circotherm for 20-25 minutes until well risen and golden

brown. Transfer to a wire rack and leave for 30 minutes to cool.

3 When cold, trim the pastry edges, cut in half lengthways, and cut each half across into six slices. Spread half with raspberry jam, then cover with the cream.

4 Spread jam on the bases of the remaining pastry pieces and place on top of the first layers.

5 Sift icing sugar over the top.

Mille Feuilles

MAIDS OF HONOUR

— MAKES 12 —

600 ml (1 pint) milk
15 ml (1 tbsp) rennet
125 g (4 oz) ready prepared puff pastry
1 egg, beaten
15 g (½ oz) butter or margarine, melted
50 g (2 oz) caster sugar

1 First make a junket. Gently heat the milk in a saucepan until tepid, then remove from the heat and stir in the rennet. Leave for 1½-2 hours until set.

2 When set, put the junket into a muslin bag and leave to drain overnight. Next day, discard the whey and refrigerate the curd for several hours or until very firm.

3 Grease twelve 6.5 cm (2½ inch) patty tins. On a lightly floured surface, roll out the pastry very thinly and using a 7.5 cm (3 inch) plain cutter, cut out 12 rounds. Line the patty tins with the pastry and prick well.

4 Whisk egg, butter and sugar into the drained curd. Divide the mixture between the pastry cases and bake in the oven at 170°C Circotherm for about 25 minutes until well risen and just firm to the touch. Serve warm.

CHOCOLATE DECORATIONS

Chocolate Caraque
Break 100 g (4 oz) chocolate into small pieces and place in the top of a double saucepan over hot but not boiling water, or in a heatproof bowl standing over a pan of hot water. Pour it in a thin layer on to a marble slab or cold baking tray and leave to set until it no longer sticks to your hand when you touch it. Holding a large knife with both hands, push the blade across the surface of the chocolate to roll pieces off in long curls. Adjust the angle of the blade to get the best curls.

Chocolate Shapes
Make a sheet of chocolate as above, pouring it on to a baking tray lined with silicone paper. Cut into neat triangles or squares with a sharp knife, or stamp out circles with a small round cutter.

Chocolate Curls
Using a potato peeler, pare thin layers from the edge of a block of chocolate.

Chocolate Leaves
Melt 100 g (4 oz) chocolate. Using leaves which have been thoroughly washed and dried, drag the upper surface of each leaf through the chocolate. For small leaves, use a small clean paint brush to brush on the chocolate. Turn the leaves chocolate-side up and place on grease-proof paper to set, then carefully peel off the leaf.

MICROWAVE

Chocolate Decorations
To melt the chocolate in the microwave, break it into small pieces and cook on LOW just until the chocolate is soft and looks glossy on top. Remove from the microwave and stir until melted. Block cooking chocolate heats more slowly – as a guide, 100 g (4 oz) cooking chocolate takes about 4 minutes to melt in the microwave on LOW. The melting times vary according to the material and shape of the container used, so it is advisable to check every minute during melting. Take care not to overcook and do not melt on HIGH or the chocolate may scorch.

SHORTCRUST PASTRY

---

225 g (8 oz) plain flour

pinch of salt

100 g (4 oz) butter or block margarine, chilled and diced

chilled water

---

1 Place the flour and salt in a bowl and add the fat to the flour.

2 Using both hands, rub the fat lightly into the flour until the mixture resembles fine breadcrumbs.

3 Add 45-60 ml (3-4 tbsp) water, sprinkling it evenly over the surface. (Uneven addition may cause blistering when the pastry is cooked.)

4 Stir in with a round-bladed knife until the mixture begins to stick together in large lumps.

5 With one hand, collect the dough mixture together to form a ball.

6 Knead lightly for a few seconds to give a firm, smooth dough. Do not overhandle the dough.

7 To roll out, sprinkle a very little flour on a working surface and the rolling pin (not on the pastry) and roll out the dough evenly in one direction only, turning it occasionally. The usual thickness is 0.3 cm (⅛ inch). Do not pull or stretch the pastry.

8 The pastry can be baked straight away, but it is better if allowed to 'rest' for about 30 minutes in the tin or dish, covered in foil or cling film, in the refrigerator.

Shortcrust Pastry Quantity Guide for Flans

Dish Size	Pastry
Plain or Fluted Flan Ring	Weight indicates the quantity of flour used.
15 cm (6 inch)	100 g (4 oz)
18 cm (7 inch)	150 g (5 oz)
20.5 cm (8 inch)	175 g (6 oz)
23 cm (9 inch)	200 g (7 oz)

Loose-bottomed metal flan tins are shallower than flan rings, china dishes or sandwich tins and require less pastry and filling than indicated in the recipe.

VARIATIONS

Wholemeal Pastry
Follow the recipe and method for Shortcrust Pastry but use plain wholemeal flour instead of white. You may need a little extra water due to the absorbency of wholemeal flour.

Cheese Pastry
Follow the recipe and method for Shortcrust Pastry, but stir in 100 g (4 oz) finely grated Cheddar or other hard cheese and a pinch of mustard powder before adding the water.

COOK'S TIP

Pastry dough can be stored in the refrigerator for 1-2 days before cooking, wrapped in greaseproof paper, cling film or foil, or rolled and shaped ready for filling and cooking at the last minute.

For freezing, wrap unshaped pastry in cling film. To use, thaw at room temperature for 3-4 hours or overnight in the refrigerator. Freeze flan cases cooked or uncooked in foil containers or freezer-proof earthenware or glass dishes. Bake flan cases from frozen, adding about 5 minutes to the normal baking time. Uncooked frozen pastry can be stored for 3-4 months in the freezer and cooked pastry for up to 6 months.

COOK'S TIP

The French, rich, sweet, short pastry *Pâte Sucrée* is the best choice for Continental pâtisserie. It is thin, crisp yet melting in texture and keeps its shape, shrinks very little and does not spread during baking. Although it can be made in a bowl, the classic way to make this pastry is on a flat, cold surface such as marble.

COOK'S TIPS

Always collect the ingredients together before starting to make *Choux Pastry* as all the flour needs to be added quickly as soon as the mixture has come to the boil.

Raw choux paste is too soft and sticky to be rolled out and is, therefore, piped or spooned on to a dampened baking sheet for baking. During baking, the moisture in the dough turns to steam and puffs up the mixture leaving the centre hollow. Thorough cooking is important; if insufficiently cooked, the choux may collapse when taken from the oven and there will be uncooked pastry in the centre to scoop out.

When the cooked choux has cooled and dried out, it can be filled with whipped cream or a savoury filling.

RICH SHORTCRUST PASTRY

100 g (4 oz) plain flour
pinch of salt
50 g (2 oz) butter or margarine, chilled and diced
5 ml (1 tsp) caster sugar
1 egg yolk

1 Mix the flour and salt together in a bowl. Rub the fat into the flour as for Shortcrust Pastry (see page 189), until the mixture resembles fine breadcrumbs. Stir in the sugar.
2 Add the egg yolk and enough water to mix to a firm dough, stirring with a round-bladed knife until the ingredients begin to stick together in large lumps.
3 With one hand, collect the mixture together and knead lightly for a few seconds to give a firm, smooth dough. Roll out as for Shortcrust Pastry.

PÂTE SUCRÉE

100 g (4 oz) plain flour
pinch of salt
50 g (2 oz) caster sugar
50 g (2 oz) butter (at room temperature)
2 egg yolks

1 Sift the flour and salt on to a work surface. Make a well in the centre and add the sugar, butter and yolks.

2 Using the fingertips of one hand, pinch and work the sugar, butter and egg yolks together until well blended.
3 Gradually work in all the flour to bind the mixture together. Knead lightly until smooth.
4 Wrap the pastry in foil or cling film and leave to 'rest' in the refrigerator or a cool place for about 30 minutes, or overnight if possible.

CHOUX PASTRY

65 g (2½ oz) plain or strong plain flour
50 g (2 oz) butter or margarine
2 eggs, lightly beaten

1 Sift the flour on to a plate or piece of paper. Put the butter and 150 ml (¼ pint) water in a saucepan. Heat gently until the butter has melted, then bring to the boil. Remove the pan from the heat. Tip the flour at once into the hot liquid. Beat thoroughly with a wooden spoon.
2 Continue beating the mixture over the heat until smooth and forms a ball in the centre of the pan (take care not to overbeat or the mixture will become fatty). Remove from the heat and leave the mixture to cool for 1-2 minutes.
3 Beat in the eggs, a little at a time, adding only just enough to give a piping consistency.
4 It is important to beat the mixture vigorously at this stage to trap in as much air as possible. A hand held electric mixer is ideal for this purpose. Continue beating until the mixture develops an obvious sheen. Use as required.

INDEX